EDUCATOR'S HANDBOOK of STORIES, QUOTES and HUMOR

M. DALE BAUGHMAN

PRENTICE - HALL, INC.
Englewood Cliffs, N. J.

PRINTED IN THE UNITED STATES OF AMERICA

24071—B & P

DEDICATION

With This Book I Thee Inspire and Amuse

Such is the spirit with which this book is dedicated to the occupants of Baughman's bower, D'Lema, Dala Dee, Dlynn Lea and Brad Dale, each of whom contributed in one way or another, paste, scissors, typewriter to the completed manuscript; and to all my friends and neighbors, especially Jane, Linda and Nancy, who contributed much to the growing accumulation of items which made this compilation possible.

Other Books by M. Dale Baughman

Teacher's Treasury of Stories for Every Occasion
*101 Examples of Creative Teaching in the Junior High
    School*
Pupil Evaluation

CONTENTS

HOW TO USE THIS BOOK

A few years ago, *Time* magazine ran a feature story on Willie Mays. Among other things it said this about him: "Willie plays baseball with a boy's glee, a pro's sureness, and a champion's flair." Really, this is also an apt description of an ace teacher: "a boy's glee, a pro's sureness, and a champion's flair." This book can help you attain these qualities.

Adding Flair and Fanfare to Your Teaching

According to Vern Nickell, former Illinois Superintendent of Public Instruction: "Public schools need teachers burning with the enthusiasm of football coaches. Teachers should induce the lazy and apathetic student to play over his head intellectually just as the grid coach often inspires his boys to play above and beyond the limits of their ability."

Some do. In the words of John Steinbeck describing a former teacher: "She aroused us to shouting, book-waving discussions. We never could stick to . . . the chanted recitation of memorized phyla. Our speculation ranged the world. She breathed curiosity into us so that we brought in facts or truths shielded in our hands like captured butterflies . . . I have had many teachers who told me soon-forgotten facts, but only three who created in me a new thing, a new attitude, a new hunger."

Such testimonials are numerous, yet they describe no more than 10 per cent of our teachers today. To put it boldly there are only two kinds of teachers insofar as compensation is concerned—those who are overpaid and those on whose influence it is impossible to place a cash value. Teachers in the latter class have the keen desire of the artist to communicate and always seem to be highly skilled in the fine art of presenting facts and ideas.

Used judiciously and artistically, the rays of light, the spots of sunshine, and the points to ponder in this book may be a blessing to the teacher who longs to make learning exciting and adventuresome. Though it is not a guarantee, the possibility exists that the provocative nature of much of the material in this book could help convert the kind of teacher who at any salary is overpaid.

Preparing Your Audience

A profound impression on the tender mind is not produced by colorless teachers. Most children, if not all, are rapidly and easily bored by a dull lesson. To produce a profound impression the teacher must have sound knowledge, limitless patience, a wellspring of sympathy for the uninformed mind, and the candle of communication. With these qualities the teacher can put learners in a state of pleased expectancy—a necessary condition for durable learning. The lesson itself should be dramatic in its unfolding. It should and can be both interesting and amusing and at the same time solid and business-like. It should be permeated with variety, jesting, and the use of illustrations and anecdotes. In discussing learning Robert Frost once said, "What is required is sight and insight—then you might add one more; excite."

Using Humor for More Effective Teaching and Speaking

Some stories in this book are so funny that one of the manuscript readers reported his secretary hurt herself when she fell off his lap, laughing. Fortunately, only her dignity was damaged. That may not be an appropriate beginning for this section, but it sure was appropriated! I seldom create a joke but I do repeat the jokes of others, and I do watch people and report the facts. One of my observations can be phrased, "Droll and dreary are seen to quit, when confronted with a ready wit."

There is the story of the high school teacher who had an unruly class but who also possessed a sense of humor. When he came in one morning and found bedlam, he slapped his hand on the desk with a loud plop and lifted his voice, "I demand pandemonium!" Teachers, I ask you only to imagine what happened next in that classroom. What would have been your reaction and your words? It is my conjecture that the demand for pandemonium ended, at least temporarily, the bedlam.

Another teacher exercised both wit and wisdom in dealing with parents when she penned this note: "If you promise not to believe everything your child says happens at school, I'll promise not to believe everything he says happens at home." Humor can and does come from the home occasionally, intentionally or otherwise. One teacher received the following note (as an excuse for tardiness): "Dear Teacher, please excuse John for being late. His uncle died last night and we had a hard time waking him up this morning."

HOW TO USE THIS BOOK

Yes, humor helps you carry your burdens, and you can be humorous in teaching and speaking without telling jokes and long stories. Humor finds outlet in quips, smiles, wordplay, short verse, and couplets. What is humor? It's more than laughing at jokes; it's more than telling funny stories or being witty; it's walking confidently and steadily through life seeing things not in distortion but seeing them as they actually are. Yes, humor helps you see yourself and others in true perspective. Humor is your faithful tranquilizer—it's your safety valve!

> The man who deals in sunshine
> Is the man who gets the crowds;
> He does a lot more business
> Than the man who peddles clouds.

Using Words to Create Moods in Listeners and Learners

The first great human invention was speech—the power to communicate. From that power springs all other powers of man over nature. In education, words are teaching tools, and the teacher who practices the use of words until they create moods and induce imagined experiences is well on the way to becoming a convincing teacher. A good place to start is with the words to be found in this book. Who knows? Soon the teacher may be experimenting with her own selection and combination of words for specific purposes.

The use of words in communicating is more than a pouring out—it is finding the proper emotional wave length for both the speaker and the listener. Use electric words that calm, comfort, jar, soothe, startle, assuage, or assault as the situation demands. Select words that create the action you desire. First, determine your purpose and then judiciously choose words that "carry." Mark Twain once said the difference between the wrong word and the right word is the difference between the lightning bug and lightning!

The right words abound in this book, and your task is to select and place into your message the appropriate rhymes, quips, anecdotes, and illustrations which fit the occasion. I recall members of a certain church congregation commenting in these words about their young and popular minister, "His sermons are packed with 'dynamite' words which seem to be carefully chosen only after dozens of others have been rejected."

To those scholars who are unappreciative of slogans, colorful words, similes, and rhyming couplets which appeal to the emotions, I am compelled to observe that more foolish words are spoken in intended wisdom than are serious words uttered in jest. To those same scholars who avoid like the plague evangelistic urgings in favor of the creative or the intellectual message, I offer this wisdom from Samuel Johnson, "People need to be reminded more than they need to be instructed."

Not only is it important to say the right thing at the right time, but it is far more difficult to leave unsaid the wrong thing at the tempting moment. Some unknown sage became terse in verse:

> I'm careful of the words I say
> To keep them soft and sweet,
> I never know from day to day
> Which ones I'll have to eat.

Adding Sparkle to Your Speeches and Punch to Your Presentations

Perhaps every educational meeting, large or small, should have a keynote address or statement, even if only the fewest words. The person to deliver the address or statement has a major function and he must develop eagerness for it, else he fails. If the speaker meets the first requirement and *develops* eagerness, he is on the way toward justifying his presence; the logical followup is that of *revealing* his eagerness. Usually, he finds that it is effective to include humor in his message. Just a "dash" often helps!

Demosthenes declared that there were three essentials of good oratory: action, action, and action! Little action do we see today behind countless lecterns as educators intone and drone their action-less words from a fixed position. I don't think Demosthenes implied that orators should feel compelled to engage in calisthenics, yet he must have had in mind the sudden use of some appropriate-to-the-occasion action words accompanied perhaps by some type of force-ful gesture. Some speakers can only start a brush fire in the audience-mind; others start it, then feed and fan its flames.

I'm not suggesting that you sing your speech but think on this: Like a good singer, a good speaker has more than one or two notes. There should be mountains and valleys of varying heights and depths. Don't be a Single-toned Sammy or a Plateau Pete! Increase your up and down range, and unlike the droll scholar who decries the evangelistic presentation, you will have listeners and believers.

Some speakers who speak slowly do so because they think it suggests heavy meditation, or some intellectual groping forward to an evasive but portentious idea. Actually, such slow speech (much slower according to research than the thought rate of the listeners) merely suggests and induces slumber. Of course, the speaker can always remark in truth, "I will help you in one way or another; either you will arise strengthened or you will awake refreshed."

Reaching Your Audience

Don't shoot the theme of your message like birdshot, hitting the whole mountainside; use a rifle and send the message with directness! Most audiences are intolerant of vagueness, so put handles on your speeches that they may be more easily carried home.

Someone said, "A little praise now and then is good for the best of men," and few would deny this wisdom. However, many there are who feel that a good speech galls the orthodox and annoys the complacent. Purposeful speech invariably is an endeavor to grasp the listener by the ears and by some manner to some degree influence his behavior. Almost without exception, the goal is one of causing a favorable response.

This little story may give you an idea of what must be done. A sailor has just returned from a whaling voyage and was taken by a friend to hear a famous speaker. After the address the friend asked him how he liked the speech. "Well," said the sailor, "it was shipshape. The masts were high enough, the sails and rigging were all right, but it did not have any harpoons!" He then explained that when a vessel goes on a whaling voyage, the important thing is to get whales. But whales do not come because you have a fine ship —you go after them with harpoons.

It is my contention that harpoons can be used by teachers or speakers, and they can be sharpened and hurled accurately! My best advice is simply regard yourself as one who has something to say, not as one who has to say something.

Your Whole Body Speaks

When you speak to groups, large or small, formally or informally, your aims should be to arouse attention, get a chunk of the listener's mind, and provoke a favorable response. But words alone are insufficient. It takes more than words to communicate ideas. Some feelings and some sensations are most difficult to describe in mere words. A notable example is found in a demonstration where the performer asked his audience to press thumb and forefinger together and then to describe the sensation. No one could! More than words? What, then? Try action, emotion, facial expressions, and sounds.

Everybody's movements, facial expressions, remarks, etc., are the result of their mental pattern. Seldom, if ever, do we deviate from our mental pattern in our remarks, actions, and movements. Nearly everything we do bares our thinking. When we realize this, it is easy to understand what others are thinking, even if they speak not a word.

In accordance with the above concept in communication the following tips for lecturers, speakers, and teachers (for the presentation phases of teaching) are offered:

1. Somehow involve the AUDIENCE in hearing, seeing, feeling, some kind of obvious reacting, not *just* listening.
2. For instant feed-back, look directly at various members of the audience.
3. Usually the most convenient props to use are the most obvious ones; your hands, arms, and fingers. Remember, more than words! Posture, countenance, and muscular tension also communicate!
4. Although you may be well up in front or out in front of your audience, you can still create an impression of being in the middle of their group.
5. Remember that volume, rate and pitch when varied appropriately also contribute to effective communication.

The mere fact that you have read the above tips does not guarantee effective communication behavior on your part. I suggest that you practice. Yes, practice the appropriate gesture, posture, expression, or inflection which fits best the chosen word or words. For example, suppose you were to present this counsel from Edwin Markham, "When you are the anvil, bear; when you are the hammer, strike!" What gesture, what pose, what facial expression would you use to accent the words, "When you are the anvil, bear"? Likewise, what gesture, pose and facial expression would you use to illustrate, "When you are the hammer, strike"? The implication is that practice of such aids to the spoken word is essential if you are to achieve maximum delivery of the message.

Brevity in Speech

An artistic performance is brief and focused! So quit when you're ahead, shut off the word valve when their cup runneth over—that's usually in the first 20 or 30 minutes. Even the old carpenter had some advice for talkers in his admonishment, "Best rule I know for talkin' is the same as the one for measurin'—measure twice and then saw once." It's a fact and Noel Wical was right when he said, "Some speakers confuse the seating capacity of the meeting place with sitting capacity of the audience." I once remarked to Mrs. Baughman that I thought I did quite well during the first 20 minutes of my speeches but after that I didn't seem to know what to do with my hands. With one stroke of expressive genius, she pointed out the solution to my difficulty. Her answer was, "Why don't you try placing them firmly over your mouth?" The very least you can do is be as smart as that washing machine ad which says, "When it spins dry, it shuts itself off automatically."

Help Yourself to Better Speaking

Speech makes up a big part of all we do in education, yet many educators lack the skill to speak in a convincing, persuasive and truly communicative manner. Worst of all, education lacks the coaches to improve skills in oral communication. Swimming and diving are best learned from expert coaches; a champion dash man listens to his coach; no one questions the teaching of surgery in medical schools; but many assume that anyone can make a speech! Only those with a low threshold or tolerance do anything about it —they teach themselves! You can teach yourself and thus become a member of the American Society for the Preservation of the Well-Spoken Message.

If you are unable to apply any or all of the mentioned hints for better verbal communication, just remember—there's one good thing about being a poor speaker; you don't have to worry about having an off night!

Achievement

1. The *Area* of your accomplishment is measured by Ability, Reliability, Energy and Action.

2. You can get almost everything accomplished if you don't care who gets the credit.
—NED HAY, *Personnel Journal*

3. The greatest achievements of mankind have been accomplished by two types of men—those who were smart enough to know it could be done, and those too dumb to know it couldn't.
—*Oakland Tribune*

4. All parents want their children to be in the upper 10 per cent of the class and 90 per cent can't make it.
—*The School Administrator*, AASA

5. Studies of biography show that men who achieve usually have an aim—they sacrifice rest, pleasure and applause for that aim.

6. There's no thrill in easy sailing, when the skies are clear and blue; there's no joy in merely doing things which anyone can do. But there is some satisfaction that is mighty sweet to take, when you reach a destination that you thought you'd never make!
—*Sunshine*

7. If you want a place in the sun, you have to expect some blisters.
—*Rotator*

8.
I'd rather be a Could Be
   If I could not be an Are;
For a Could Be is a May Be,
   With a chance of touching par.
I'd rather be a Has Been
   Than a Might Have Been, by far;
For a Might Have Been has never been,
   But a Has was once an Are.
—*Supervisory News Notes*, Florida State
Department of Education

9. Asked what profit he made, the little newsboy who stood on the corner shouting his papers explained that he bought them for 5¢ from the boy on the next corner and sold them for 5¢ on his own corner. There was no profit—he merely wanted to do some shouting. Aren't many of us like that? We stir around mightily, playing at being busy, shouting about it, but actually accomplishing very little.

—*Scandal Sheet*, Graham, Texas, Rotary Club

10. For many a lad born to rough work and ways,
Strips off his ragged coat and makes men clothe him
with praise.

11. It is more important to know where you are going than to get there quickly; do not mistake activity for achievement.

—MABEL NEWCOMER, *Bulletin, Wisconsin Association of Secondary School Principals*

12. In India they have a proverb which says, "He has not lived in vain who has reared a son, planted a tree, or dug a well."

Most of us go every day drinking from wells we have not dug. Few of us, for instance, have ever paid any great price for our American Citizenship.

—ROY L. SMITH, *Friendly Chat*

Action

13. Now is the time for all good men to come to.

—*The Chap Book*

14. There are two kinds of people; those who want to get things done and those who want to be right.

—ARCHIBALD McLEISH

15. Can you imagine Moses or Jesus having "Brainstorming Sessions" to pound out the "Ten Commandments" or deciding what miracles should be performed?

The fad of group thinking has been carried to ridiculous extremes. In one Illinois *institution* the inmates decide on who shall receive passes and other matters. It is a sad commentary that administrators value the opinions of inmates higher than their own.

—JACK STAEHLE

16. It is better to be idle than busy about nothing.

—ATILIUS

17. Small deeds done are better than great deeds planned.

—PETER MARSHALL

18. If you have a task to do, lad, do it.
Do not dally half a day; get through it.

Do not mix your work with play,
Do not loiter by the way;
Go and do it right away, lad—do it.

19. Father Georges Pire, for all his idealism, is an intensely practical man. "It's better to get one little apple tree well planted," he says, "than a thousand trees in a dream orchard."
—GEORGE KENT, "He Speaks to the Europe of the Heart," *Catholic World*

20. "The time to begin anything is now, so do it today. Perhaps you will say you are not ready, that you must give some additional thought to your proposed undertaking. Well, do it today. Begin now. The things you put off are never done. Someone has wisely observed that we cannot change yesterday, nor begin on tomorrow until it is here. So all that is left for you and for me is to make every today the best that can be. When you can think of yesterday without regret and tomorrow without fear, you will be on the highway to success, because you will be using your todays in the best you know how, and your tomorrows will be rich with promise. Begin now!"
—JOHN H. STOKE

21. When, against one's will, one is high-pressured into making a hurried decision, the best answer is always "No" because "No" is more easily changed to "Yes" than "Yes" is changed to "No."
—CHARLES E. NIELSON, *Forbes*

22. The other day I flew over the Okefenokee Swamp. We were down low and I could see an ugly green film over the water. It looked dirty and unclean—a breeding place for health-destroying creatures. At one time the water in that swamp was sweet and pure, coming from clear springs high in the mountains. But in that low place it had stopped, and having stopped it had stagnated.
So in life, if you stop when you hit low places, your life begins to stagnate.
—CHARLES L. ALLEN, "All Things Are Possible Through Prayer"

23. Heaven never helps the man who will not act.
—*Sophocles*

24. A man who has to be convinced to act before he acts is *not* a man of action. It's as if a tennis player before returning the ball began to question himself as to the physical and moral values of tennis. You must act just as you breathe.

—GEORGES CLEMENCEAU

25. Go-Getter: One who gets in behind you in a revolving door and comes out ahead of you.

—*Breadwinner*

26. To get purposeful action you may need to arouse emotion on the part of the learner. You may convince his intellect that the thing you want him to learn is desirable and will be of benefit to him, but until you awaken in him an urgent hankering to do it, until you persuade him that whatever effort he expands is of little consequence compared with the satisfaction it will bring him, your teaching is lacking a most important ingredient.

—M. DALE BAUGHMAN

27. It is not so much what you believe in that matters, as the way in which you believe it, and proceed to translate that belief into action.

—LIN YUTANG

28. When I was a boy, I'd rather be licked twice than postponed once.

—JOSH BILLINGS

29. Our grand business is not to see what lies dimly at a distance, but to do what lies clearly at hand.

—CARLYLE

30. We cannot do everything at once, but we can do something at once.

—CALVIN COOLIDGE, *Bulletin, Wisconsin Association of Secondary School Principals*

31.   Pluck sweet flowers while you may,
              At eventide or dewy morn.
          Surely there will come a day
              When you must pluck the thorn.

          Do kindly acts at time of need,
              Ere the chance be gone,
          Thus you will implant the seed
              Of deeds yet unknown.

—Author Unknown, *Friendly Chat*

32. Samuel Johnson wrote: "Nothing will ever be attempted if all possible objections must be first overcome."

—The Indiana Teacher

Adolescence

33. A mother, annoyed because her 14-year-old daughter had been calling her boy friend too frequently, took a tip from a former war-time advertisement and posted a sign over the telephone: *Is This Call Necessary?*

Next day there appeared, pencilled on the card, a brief but logical reply: *How Can I Tell till I've Made It?*

—Long Lines

34. Something new is being added to the personality of the seventh grader. He seems wobbly inside and out. He is in the stage of a department store that is being remodeled. For a while it appears that everything is about to be ground into rubble but while the mess, dust and noise seem alarming, they are necessary because improvements are about to be made.

—Fritz Redl, National Institute of Mental Health

35. All any grown-up expects of an adolescent is that he act like an adult and be satisfied to be treated like a child.

—Schools Louisiana

36. Adolescence is a time of rapid changes. Between the ages of 12 and 17, for example, a parent ages as much as 20 years.

—Changing Times

37. Two young teen-age boys were discussing their "chariots." Said one, "I am well pleased with my rag-top (convertible) but I may have too much spaghetti (excess chrome) around the fire-place (grille)."

His companion described his hot-rod in turn, "Well, I've added twin-trumpets (tail pipes) and snowballs (white side-walls) but I've got some more work to do on my binders (brakes)."

—M. Dale Baughman

38. A fellow mentioned that his teenage son was developing a cauliflower ear. Not from boxing—but from using the phone.

39. Adolescents are like modern paintings. You may never like them if you try to understand them.

—M. Dale Baughman

40.
Tho' he zooms past you
　Nose in the air,
Intent on going
　Most anywhere,
With rumbling muffler
　That booms and brays,
And open throttle
　That squawks and neighs,
When your car stalls,
　And you're in trouble,
He'll stop to help you
　On the double.

—Rosa Zagnoni Marinoni, *Chicago Tribune*

41. Infancy and adolescence are perhaps the two most important periods of life; in different ways, they are both times of weaning; the first physical; the second spiritual.

—Oswald Bell, *Girl Scout Leader*

Adult Education

42. A fourth grade boy came home from school one day and announced "Mommie, I'm gonna be a teacher when I get big."

"Fine," said mother, "but what made you decide to want to be a teacher?"

"Well," answered the boy slowly, "with all this adult education coming on I'll probably be in school all the time anyway and I decided that I would rather do the planning and assign the work than plan the doing and work the assignment."

—M. Dale Baughman

43. Adult education is what goes on in a household containing teenage children!

—Laugh Book

Adversity

44. If you encounter no difficulties, the office boy could take your place.

—*Sunshine Magazine*

45. There's no sense in advertising your troubles—there's no market for them.

46. In the presence of trouble, some people grow wings; others buy crutches.

—HAROLD W. RUOPP

47.   All the water in the world
However hard it tried,
Could never, never sink a ship
Unless it got inside.

All the hardships of this world,
Might wear you pretty thin,
But they won't hurt you, one least bit
Unless you let them in.

—Author Unknown

48. "Mishaps are like knives that either serve us or cut us as we grasp them by the blade or by the handle. After all, a smooth sea never made a successful sailor."

—HERMAN MELVILLE

49. Times of great calamity and confusion have ever been productive of the greatest minds. The purest ore is produced from the hottest furnace, and the brightest thunderbolt comes from the darkest storm.

—COLTON

50. Once there lived an old woman who was always so cheerful that everyone wondered at her. "But you must have some clouds in your life," said a visitor.

"Clouds?" she replied, "why of course; if there were no clouds, where would the blessed showers come from?"

—Ave Maria

51. Let the child and the youth be taught that every mistake, every fault, every difficulty, conquered, becomes a stepping stone to better and higher things. It is through such experiences that all who have ever made life worth the living have achieved success.

—ELLEN G. WHITE, Education

52. Among the students at a well known college was a young man on crutches. A homely fellow, he had a talent for friendliness and optimism. He won many scholastic honors and the respect of his classmates. One day a classmate asked the cause of his deformity. When the fellow said briefly, "Infantile paralysis," the friend questioned further. "With a misfortune like that, how can you face the world so confidently?" "Oh," he replied, smiling, "the disease never touched my heart."

—Pentecostal Evangelist

53. The brook would lose its song if we removed the rocks.

Advice

54. Socrates was a Greek philosopher who went around giving good advice. They poisoned him.

55. If you want to launch big ships go where there is deep water.

56. Advice is like snow; the softer it falls the longer it dwells upon, and the deeper it sinks into, the mind.

*—*Coleridge

57. Everyone believes in the golden rule: Give unto others the advice you can't use yourself.

—Personnel Administration

58. There is an old story of an Eastern merchant who was about to send his eldest son forth into the world. "My son," said the merchant, "there are two precepts I would have you keep ever in mind. The first of these is, 'Always keep your word once you have given it.'"

"Yes, father," said the son. "And the second?"
"Never give it."

59. The deadliest word of our generation is "adviser."

—American Mercury

Alumni

60. Describing a high-school reunion: "Another item of interest was the fact that 270 children have been born to the members of the class of '47. Considerable credit is due many unmentioned committee members and individuals."

—Herald Journal, Logan, Utah

61. Blessed are the alumni, for they shall remember their youth ... fortunately, memory has a way of tricking them, erasing many of the unhappy episodes and lending an aura of romance to fond recollections.

—The School Bell

Taking that big step.

Ambition

62. No power in the world can keep a first class man down or a fourth class man up.

—Defender, Defenders of the
Christian Faith, Inc.

63. Some people are satisfied to be average. But do you know what you are when you're average? You are the best of the lousiest and the lousiest of the best. Is that what you want to be?

*—*Gary Gariepy, *Advertiser's Digest*

64. Once the poet Carl Sandburg said, "Before you go to sleep, say to yourself, 'I haven't reached my goal yet, whatever it is, and I'm going to be uncomfortable and in a degree unhappy until I do.'"

—*R & R Magazine*, Research and Review Service of America

65. A person's sights should be as high as his ambitions can raise them, and everyone should try his best to hit his target.

—George E. Ruff, m.d., "Three Secrets of Successful Living," *This Week*

66. "He's daydreaming beyond his talents," said a friend about a mutual acquaintance. The subject of this remark was an overly ambitious young man.

"He would actually go further if he would moderate his ambitions," added my companion.

Paradoxical? However, it's quite true.

Unfortunately, most of us were taught at an early age to "hitch our wagons to a star." This often results in building our hopes beyond our abilities, with the inevitable disappointment. And the higher we fly, the greater the damage when we crash. The wound suffered can cause a sensitive individual to give up a promising career . . .

The rule is simple, but important. Use common sense to keep a check-rein on your daydreams. Moderate your demands on life— and achieve more!

—K. F. Lloyd

67. In the primeval days of America an old Indian Chief was accustomed to test the mettle of his braves by making them run in a single effort as far up the side of the mountain as each could reach without stopping to rest. On an appointed day, four willing braves started on the new adventure before daybreak, to prove their worthiness.

The first returned with a bunch of spruce, indicating the height to which he had attained. The second bore a twig of pine. The third brought an alpine shrub. But it was by the light of the moon that the fourth made his way back. He came, worn and exhausted, his feet torn by the rocks.

"What did you bring, and how high did you ascend?" asked the chief.

"Sire," he replied, "Where I went there was neither spruce nor pine to shelter me from the sun, nor flowers to cheer my path, but only rocks and snow and barren earth. My feet are torn, and I am exhausted. I am late"—and then a wonderful light came into his eyes—"but I saw the sea!"

—Friendly Chat

No, Scott, I said—Add.

Arithmetic

68. *Teacher (patiently):* "If one and one make two, and two and two make four, how much do four and four make?"

Reluctant pupil: "That's not fair, teacher. You answered the easy ones yourself and gave me the hard one."

—The Lookout

69. The teacher in a little backwoods school was at the blackboard explaining arithmetic problems. She was delighted to see her dullest pupil giving slack-jawed attention, which was unusual for him. Her happy thought was that, at last, the gangling lad was beginning to understand.

When she finished, she said to him, "You were so interested, Cicero, that I'm sure you want to ask some questions."

"Yes'm," drawled Cicero, "I got one to ask. Where do them figgers go when you rub 'em off?"

—*Sunshine Magazine*

70. Our daughter, Dala, a second-grader, was practicing some subtraction problems at home. I was asked to pose some problems to be handled without pencil and paper. I began "seven take-away six equals what?" These she could do so I finally slipped in "nine take-away ten equals what?" Without much thought, she replied "one." "Now, think," I urged, and I repeated the problem. This time she said, "You can't do it!"

"That's better," I said and hastened to add that there is an algebraic answer. "But," I went on, "you won't have Algebra until grade nine, probably."

"Oh, don't be too sure," expostulated Dala, "Miss Bennett will probably give it to us; we have everything else!"

—M. DALE BAUGHMAN

71. *Teacher*: "If coal is $25 a ton, how many tons would you get for $100?"

Pupil: "Oh, about 3½ tons."

Teacher: "That isn't right."

Pupil: "I know, but I wish you would convince our coal man."

72. Mother was discussing with the mathematics teacher her child's slow progress in algebra. "It isn't that he refuses to try," she said. "I rather think he just doesn't believe it at all."

—*Weekly News*, New Zealand

73. Miss Oglesby, an elementary school teacher, found that none of her pupils could translate into numerals the two plain words on the blackboard, "One million."

So, she wrote down the numerals 1,000,000 and asked if anyone knew what was represented.

In the center of the class room Johnny jumped to his feet and waved eagerly for recognition.

"Yes, John?" said the teacher, somewhat relieved.

"Miss Oglesby, I know what that is."

"Good, John; I'm glad one knows, at least. Explain to the others the meaning of those symbols on the blackboard."

"Yes, ma'am," said Johnny eagerly. "That's a stick layin' beside six hula hoops!"

—LEN ROBIN, *Quote*

Art

74. The primary and highest function of art is to deliver a message to the soul of man.

—ETHELWYN M. AVERY, "There Is a Plan for the Arts," *New Outlook*

75.
These were beginners, each had come to seek
Expression in a world outside her own,
Exciting world of color and technique,
Of light and shadow, symmetry and tone.

The table held a cabbage, leafy green,
Whose inmost edges sparkled still with dew,
Some looked askance on such a common scene
And thought of still life they would like to do.

Still others penciled outlines hurriedly,
More eager for the color tube and brush,
Then mixing paints they worked determinedly
And with the quiet of cathedral hush.

But only one saw cabbage as a rose
Because she'd taught her heart to understand
That in each common thing some beauty glows,
That loveliness is always near at hand.

And on her finished canvas one could feel
The roughened outer leaves, the inner core,
The cool, sweet drops of dew were all but real
Because her heart had looked for something more.

—VINEY WILDER

76. It is said that Roger Fry once asked a little girl about her method of drawing and obtained this answer: "First I have a think, and then I put a line around it."

—Serge De Gastyne, "Inspiration,"
Music Journal

77. One of our correspondents writes: "The other day I visited a well-known gallery and witnessed the following scene: Two men, one from the Met and the other from the Museum of Modern Art, came to award prizes for sculpture. Some of the pieces were placed on a ledge in front of which stands the desk of the gallery's manager. One of the judges pointed out an object on the shelf and said to his companion that the piece was worthy of an award. He was about to finalize the solemn act of attaching the tag of merit to the object when the gallery's manager turned around and said, 'Sir, that's the electric fan.'"

—*American Artist*

Aspiration

78. Robert Louis Stevenson: "To be what we are and to become what we are capable of becoming, is the only end of life."

79. To travel hopefully toward the end is better than to arrive.

—Robert Louis Stevenson

80. A man may fall and rise again, but a man who is reconciled is truly vanquished.

—Schiller

Athletic Coach

81. Spotted on the desk of a college football coach: "It's remarkable how many people have 20-20 hindsight."

—T. O. White, *Tow Lines*

82. A coach was being congratulated on having a lifetime contract. "I guess it's all right," he said. "But I remember another guy with a lifetime contract. Had a bad year, and the president called him in, pronounced him dead and fired him."

—*Sports Illustrated*

83. The symptoms of laziness and fatigue are almost identical and only a few persons can tell the difference; for instance, coaches.

Crow's Nest

Only a few can tell the difference . . . For instance, coaches.

84. Our coach's five-year-old son frequently attends football practice, and at home, the coach observed his son put water in a coke bottle, take a long drink from it, grab his little football and run, like mad, down the alley. Then he came running back to drink again from the coke bottle. After this procedure had been repeated several times, the coach said, "Son, you're going to drown yourself. Why do you drink that water?" "That's the way football boys do, daddy," was the answer.

—ALICE GRANT, West Frankfort, Illinois

85. *Superintendent*: "No, I can't give you a job. I've had so many applicants for coaching jobs I can't remember their names."

Coach: "Can't you give me a job keeping track of them?"

—*Commerce*

86. A minor sport is one in which the coach earns a paltry remuneration, only slightly more than a full professor, for example.

87. One of the coaches on my staff once assigned an eighth grade English class to write themes on great men. One lad wrote very briefly:

> Paul Revere was a great man. He had a horse. His name was Charlie.

Perhaps only an athletic coach can see the humor here.

—GEORGE SHIVE, Annaway, Illinois

88. And did you hear about the coach who booed the zebras in a circus? Can't stand anything wearing stripes.

89. "Excuse me, sir, I notice you are coaching that football team very well. It must take years of experience to produce a top-flight football coach."

"Oh goodness, I'm really not a football coach. I'm a nuclear physicist. I just do this between wars."

"I see. Do you think every man should be a football coach?"

"No. I think every man should be a nuclear physicist. There is more job security. A football coach can hang for his mistakes. Hanging is old fashioned and messy. But a nuclear physicst makes one mistake and wham!—everyone goes out with him. That's real togetherness."

"With a nuclear physicist as coach, your school must have strict academic requirements."

"Well, we have 39 physics and mathematics majors on our squad. None of them play at the moment. But we have hopes. And they're simply great at counting downs."

"But don't you think coaches should be required to play their most brilliant students? Don't you think it would make a bright light on the horizon of education?"

"Really now. I think that is something every coach should decide for himself."

—BOB COLLINS, *Indianapolis Sunday Star*

90. A football coach, was asked by a fellow coach how he picked a team from a bunch of raw recruits.

"I hate to give away my secrets," he replied, "but I'll tell you. I take them out into the woods. Then, at a given signal I start them running. Those that run around the trees are chosen as guards; those that run into the trees are chosen as tackles."

91. *Things a basketball coach gets tired of hearing:*

"The Board of Education wants to see you."

"Can't you even teach them to shoot free-throws?"

"Well, at least he builds character."

"What did you think about their last-second three point play?"

"You can't win them all."

"My Billy says you make him sit on the bench all the time."

"Okay, fatso, what's your excuse this time?"

"Looks like another building year, eh, coach?"

"Send me in coach."

"How do those state tournament hopes look now, buddy?"

"Your center won't be able to walk on that ankle until at least next May."

"You've got seven men on the court!"

"What you need is a good big man."

"Uh, you forgot your lucky red tie tonight, coach."

"The manager left the basketballs in their locker room."

"The manager is locked in our locker room."

"They're stalling."

"That's five fouls on the big man, coach."

"That's your last time out."

"It's a six-block walk to the dressing room."

"How could you compare them to Pumpkin Center Tech?"

"Why don't you start the cheerleaders this game?"

"Hey, Baldy, how much basketball have you played?"

"What did you tell them at halftime?"

"We forgot the uniforms."

"Three of your starters just went ineligible."

"The driver can't remember where he parked the bus."

"They may only average 5-3, but they're fast."

"Hogwash Hollow just had three seven-foot all-staters transferred from California."

"Who do you think you are? Adolph Rupp?"

"Back to the bean bags."

"Got any extra tickets for the state tournament?"

"Ever hear of defense, coach?"

"Ever hear of offense, coach?"

"Who's got the scorebook?"

"That was their second team."

"They want fifty per cent of the gate."

"He's grooming his three-year-old kid to take over for him . . . next season."

"At least he's a good loser."

—Roger Ebert, Champaign-Urbana News-Gazette

Attitude

92. "Whats the use?" and "Why should I?" are the two most fatal phrases in the English language. They mark the dividing line between success and failure for hundreds of thousands of human beings, according to Chauncey M. Depew, late political figure.

"What's the use?" is the philosophy of the chap who throws up the sponge when the battle has just started. He sits down alongside of the road when he finds the signpost has deceived him—instead of lengthening his stride. He is satisfied with "good enough." He has no goals, no visions. He accepts no challenge.

"Why should I?" is the cry of the work dodger. His aim is to do just enough to "get by." He is a clock-watcher who is afraid he will render more service than he is paid to perform. He is too lazy to think; too selfish to put his shoulder to the wheel in a common cause.

How much more vibrant and dynamic are the phrases, "It can be done!" and "You can count on me!" These phrases sparkle with the spirit of success.

—Sunshine Magazine

93. The greatest discovery of my generation is that human beings can alter their lives by altering their attitudes of mind.

—William James

94. Your attitude may determine your altitude.

95. Attitudes are taught. Attitudes are caught. Attitudes are better taught if caught, and better caught if taught.

—Martin P. Simon, Your Child and You

Baseball

96. Did you hear about the baseball manager who soothingly admonished his prize outfielder?

"Kid," he said, "it's okay if you forget some of those batting tips I gave you. We just traded you."

97. The choir boys of the church were organizing a baseball team, and being short of equipment and money, decided to ask the pastor for assistance. The leading choir boy was authorized to contact the parson. He did, by means of this short note: "We would be glad for any financial aid you could give us. Also, could we please have the use of the bats that the sexton says you have in your belfry?"

—*Sunshine Magazine*

98. In his sand-lot days Yogi Berra was playing one day under a manager who had instructed his players to swing at everything served up by the opposing pitcher unless the situation called for a bunt, in which case he would signal by pulling at his nose. However, he said, if the batter noticed the opposition creeping in on him the bunt signal was off.

During the late innings, Yogi came to bat with none out and runners at first and second. Down two runs, the manager indicated a bunt. Berra promptly smashed the first pitch over the fielder's head, driving in three runs to win the game.

"You were supposed to bunt!" stormed the manager.

"I know," explained Berra. "But I seen that center fielder creepin' in on me."

—JOE GARAGIOLA

99. Johnson & Johnson, the Band-Aid people, have put out a booklet for Little Leaguers entitled *Baseball First-Aid Guide*, which contains useful information for treating such expected ball-field injuries as dislocated fingers and heat exhaustion, but there is one entry which sounds an unexpected note.

"The effect of human bites," the Guide notes laconically, "can be as serious as animal bites."

—*Sports Illustrated*

100. Brown was a cocky ball player. He struck savagely at the first pitch, but it went a foot around the end of his bat. He struck more viciously at the second pitch, but missed it also. He let the third pitch go by for a called strike.

Then he turned to the umpire and said, "Ump, you missed that one a little, didn't you?"

The umpire said, "You missed the first two, didn't you? Why should you care?"

101. Spyros Skouras asked Alfred Hitchcock if he'd seen "The Story of Ruth," and Hitch straightfaced: "No, I never go to baseball pictures."

102. Yogi Berra was extolling the prowess of his teammate, Mickey Mantle. "Mickey," said Berra, "can hit just as good right-handed as he can left-handed. He's naturally amphibious."

—Scholastic Coach

103. "It used to be that when a ball club was falling off at the gate it got some new players. Now it gets a new city."

—Wall Street Journal

104. A radio announcer once asked Leo Durocher, manager of the New York Giants, "Barring the unforeseen, Leo, will your club get the pennant?" Back came Durocher's reply, "There ain't gonna be no unforeseen."

105. "Be sure you're right, then go ahead" is good advice especially for the base runner who has just rounded first.

—M. DALE BAUGHMAN

106. Joe Garagiola, the former big league catcher turned broadcaster, kidding his boyhood pal, Berra, before the game (World Series).

"You amaze me, Yog," said Joe. "You've now become such a world figure that you drew more applause yesterday than either Prime Minister Nehru or Herbert Hoover. Can you explain it?"

"Certainly," said Yogi. "I'm a better hitter."

—ARTHUR DALEY, *N. Y. Times*

107. "What do you call your baseball team?" asked Mrs. Brown of the little boy next door.

"Little Potaters, Ma'am," he replied.

"Why such an odd name?"

"Well, we're awful hard to skin!"

108. The baseball manager who had an ulcer was in his physician's office for a checkup.

"Remember," the doctor said, "don't get excited, don't get mad, and forget about baseball when you're off the field."

Then he added, "By the way, how come you let the pitcher bat yesterday with the tying run on second and two out in the ninth?"

—Chicago Daily News

109. "A baseball fan is a spectator sitting 400 feet from the plate who can see better than an umpire standing five feet away."

—WALTER SLEZAK

110. A few years ago the Yankee star, Mickey Mantle, stumbled in the field and reinjured his bad knee. He was rushed to the hospital and went through a series of x-rays and examinations. One day between tests he sat on the terrace and talked to another patient, an elderly lady who knew nothing about baseball.

"How did you hurt your leg?" she asked.

"Playing ball," was the reply.

"Oh," said the lady, "won't you boys ever grow up?"

—A.M.A. *Journal*

111. Marty Marion was making one of his infrequent appearances at home during his days as White Sox manager and at dinner, as usual, the little ones argued over who was to say grace. A small voice settled it:

"I think Daddy should say it, he's the guest."

—BUD THIES, "Sports Wives," *This Day*

112. "The ball struck Berra on the right temple and knocked him cold. He was taken to Ford Hospital. X-ray pictures of Berra's head showed nothing."

—*New York Herald Tribune*

113. Several evenings after the Russians launched a rocket to the moon, the Indians' pitching coach, Mel Harder, and sportswriter Frank Gibbons were standing on a street corner. Harder looked up at the big moon hanging in the sky.

"It's a lot bigger than home plate," he observed. "How could they possibly miss it?"

—*Scholastic Coach*

114. Apparently Little League baseball in Boonville, Indiana is about like Little League baseball anywhere else. A nine-year-old ballplayer went home and told his father that he had hit a home run.

"You really must have smacked it," said the proud father.

"It wasn't much," the boy replied. "I just hit it and took off running."

"Well," said his dad, "it must have gone over the outfielders head."

"Oh, he wasn't there," the boy said. "He'd gone after a drink of water."

—GRIFF NIBLACK

115. Two peroxide blonds raised quite a fuss at a baseball game. "The bleachers," wrote a cub reporter, "went wild."

—T. O. WHITE, *Champaign-Urbana News Gazette*

116. "I would hafta say that it (the situation) is more improved today than forty years ago. Nowadays when a pitch comes too close to a fella, he walks back with a funny look and says, 'You know, I think that pitcher was throwing at me.' When I come up to the Dodgers, I knew they was throwin' at me!"

—CASEY STENGEL, "How Casey Bats the English Language," by Charles D. Rice, *This Week Magazine*

117. "Always keep your eye on a fly ball. Don't look where you're running—we got ground keepers to see that there's no ditches in this park."

—CASEY STENGEL, "How Casey Bats the English Language," by Charles D. Rice, *This Week Magazine*

118. A dyed-in-the-wool baseball fan was persuaded by friends to go to the horse races. Being a beginner, he picked a 50-1 long shot and put $2 on the nose. Coming into the stretch the long-shot horse was neck and neck with the favorite. As they neared the wire for a photo finish, the baseball man hollered, "Slide, you bum! Slide!"

—*Knight of St. George*

119. One chestnut to be told and retold on baseball's banquet circuit concerns the hayshaker who hit three for three on a particular afternoon . . . but was credited with only two for four when the boxscore appeared in the morning newspaper!

So the hayshaker was waiting when the sports editor showed up at the park for the next afternoon's game. The sports editor caught it good because a woman scorned is a kitten compared to a baseball player who believes himself cheated of a hit. When the storm calmed, the sports editor explained: "Forget it, Joe. That was a typographical error."

"Error, h——l," stormed the hayshaker. "That drive nearly took off the shortstop's head."

—*Philadelphia Enquirer*

Grab more of those rebounds . . . Why, back when I was in school, etc., etc., and . . . Bologna.

Basketball

120. The basketball season is well underway now. Our favorite basketball conference is the Lutheran League, in which St. Martini recently defeated Mt. Olive.

121. The basketball coach really believes in the proverb, "A place for everything and everything in its place," especially the ball in the basket.

M. DALE BAUGHMAN

122. At the end of the basketball season in Harrison County, Benny Brewster, a substitute on the North Central High School team, wrote a composition for his English class on the subject of

"Benchwarming." Benny wrote that as a substitute who sat out most of the games on the bench he found out: "One thing a bench-warmer can brag on is the fact that he can play center, forward and guard; that is, he can lean forward, sit in the center of the bench and guard the water bucket."

123. Does this sound familiar to anyone who's ever coached a basketball team, and lost a game? "Now tomorrow they'll ask us why we didn't press the whole game." It's a quote from a losing coach. Different words maybe, but the same music a thousand times during the season just past.

124. Mahomet went to the mountain, we gather from a story we heard the other day. At any rate, the Fire Department of a Southern Illinois town roared over to the local high school in response to an alarm over a special line from the school gym. Instead of crackling flames, firemen found a red-hot basektball game. Turned out the alarm switch was on a wall close to one of the baskets. A wild shot missed its mark and triggered the alarm.

The principal, shaking his head over the accuracy of his cagers, arranged for a glass door to protect the switch.

—ELMER WOOD

125. Fortunate mentors have 7-foot centers.

—T. O. WHITE, "Tow Lines," *Champaign-Urbana News-Gazette*

126. Any American boy, any Indiana boy, yes, coach, any boy in your school can be a star basketball player when he grows up, up, up!

127. A doctor who was a prominent alumnus was asked to give the boys a pep talk at a rally before the first game of the season. The doctor was most enthusiastic. Throughout the speech he interspersed the following statements: "Give 'em hell, boys! . . . When you get in that game, you want to give 'em H-E-L-L."

The next speaker was a mild-mannered minister. He arose and in a small voice said, "Boys, give them what the doctor ordered."

—*A.M.A. Journal*

128. Harry Combes insists this is true. He asked a prospective basketball player: "If you come to Illinois do you think you could make the first five?"

"I'm not sure," the lad replied, "do you mean long or short shots?"
—T. O. WHITE, *Champaign-Urbana*
News-Gazette

Behavior

129. The enlarged individual has more coastline for harboring incoming craft, laden with criticism or trouble.

130. Strive always to be like a good watch—open face, busy hands, pure gold, well regulated, full of good works.
—*Lee's Bulldog*

131.
Never be annoyed at dawn
By a thing you cannot help
Like rain when you wanted sunshine
Or the neighbor's dogs that yelp
Or the guest you thought was quiet
Who awakened you by a snore
Or the children who rise too early
Or the banging of a door
Never let such things annoy you
Whistle here, a snappy tune,
For the man who is a conqueror
Masters self before the noon.

—C E D

132. There was a very cautious man who never romped or played,
Who never drank or even smoked or kissed a pretty maid.
So when he passed away, his insurance was denied
For since he never lived, they claimed he never died!

133. Be severe with yourself but gentle with others.
—*Sunshine Magazine*

134. The man who wears his pants out before his shoes, makes contact in the wrong places.
—*Johnson County News*, Greenwood, Indiana

135. Maybe the old-time Indians were not so bad after all, as one old chief said: "Indian scalp enemies; white man skin friends."
—*Sunshine Magazine*

136. It's useless to put your best foot forward—and then drag the other.

—REX MOBLEY

137. Cultivate nonchalance, the ability to look like an owl when you have behaved like an ass.

—Phi Delta Kappan

138. At the root of every good life there is the quiet, tenacious respect of the value of the minute.

—Phi Delta Kappan

139. Men usually get somewhere when they develop a brake for the tongue and an accelerator for the brain.

—Sunshine Magazine

140. He had that certain something but I wanted him to have something certain.

141. People count up the faults of those who keep them waiting.

—FRENCH PROVERB

142. It is never the wrong time to do the right thing.

—LUTHERAN DIGEST

143. Blowing out the other fellow's candle won't make yours shine any brighter.

—P-K Sideliner

144. Unless you handle your whims right, you may have the whim-whams.

S.A.Y.

145. No man resolved to make the most of himself can spare time for personal contention. Killing the dog will not cure the bite.

—A. LINCOLN

146. Behavior is a mirror in which everyone shows his image.

—LUTHERAN DIGEST

147. As a rule a man's a fool. When it's hot he wants it cool; when it's cool he wants it hot—always wanting what is not.

—PATER, *Friendly Chat*

148.
I met a stranger in the night
Whose lamp had ceased to shine.
I paused to let him light
His lamp from mine.
A tempest sprang up later on
And shook the world about,
And when the wind was gone
My lamp was out.

But back to me the stranger came—
His lamp was glowing fine.
He held the precious flame
And lighted mine!
—LON WOODRUM, *Sunshine Magazine*

149. Nobody knows about your integrity, your sincerity, your talent or your good will unless you give out samples in action.
—*Weekly Animator*, Alexander Film Co.

150. Some folks don't have many faults, but they sure make the most of those they've got.
—*P-K Sideliner*

151. Jumping at conclusions is not half as good exercise as digging for facts.
—LUTHERAN DIGEST

152. As a rule life is quaint. One says 'tis, the other 'taint. One says don't, the other do—that always leaves it up to you.
—DAUGHTER, *Friendly Chat*

153. If you would prosper, rise early. The sleeping fox catches no poultry.

154. Much as I dislike hypocrisy and much as I advocate the theory of being yourself, I submit it is far better to feign good nature than to be a natural grouch. This is on the theory that the chap who acts as though he were agreeable may some day get the habit!
—GEORGE C. HUBBS, *Lutheran Digest*

155. "When you are good to others, you are best to yourself."
—BEN FRANKLIN

156. A wise man of the Orient once remarked, "There are three kinds of people in all types of organizations—rowboat people, sailboat people, and steamboat people. Rowboat people need to be pushed or shoved along. Sailboat people move when a favorable wind is blowing. Steamboat people move continuously, through calm or storm. They are usually masters of themselves, their surroundings, and their fate."
—DR. CHARLES L. LAPP AND DR. JOHN W. BOWYER,
"Practice Administration Thought-Provokers,"
Oral Hygiene

157. There's always one consolation we can fall back on. If it weren't for the scoundrels that make up a minority of society, how could you measure the goodness of the majority?

—*R & R Magazine*

158. The fellow next door says that if he has a problem, he thinks it out on a river bank. He can sit there all day long with a fish pole in his hand and get things sort of straightened up in his mind. He never catches a fish, but when he comes home, folks speak of him as a "patient fisherman." If he sits in the back yard at home all day thinking things over and putting his mind at ease, people speak of him as "that lazy fellow down the street."

—*Service for Company Publications*

159. It's hard for a fellow to keep a chip on his shoulder if you will allow him to take a bow.

—*Survey Bulletin*

160. What we attend to controls our behavior. What we can get others to attend to controls their behavior.

—HARRY OVERSTREET, *Influencing Human Behavior*

161. Have you ever noticed one odd thing about blunt people? They are the ones who usually come to the point.

162. Are you an active member,
The kind that would be missed.
Or are you just contented
That your name is on the list?
Do you attend the meeting,
And mingle with the flock,
Or do you stay at home
And criticize and knock?
Do you take an active part
To help the work along,
Or are you satisfied
To be the kind that just belongs?
Do you do your job well
And without a kick,
Or do you leave the work to just a few
And talk about the clique?
There's quite a program scheduled,
That I'm sure you've heard about,

And 'twill be appreciated, too,
If you will come and help out.
Think this over, member,
You know right from wrong,
Are you an active member,
Or do you just belong?

—*The KSFTA Bi-monthly News*

Books

163. It was Junior's birthday and the mailman brought him a book as a present from Aunt Alice. "What is it?" he asked gloomily. "That's what they call a book, dear," his mother explained. "It's what they make a movie out of for television."

—*American Mercury*

164. Libraries are holding their own against all competitors: TV, automobiles and lawnmowers . . . . TV will never replace a book; surveys show that it actually stimulates children's interest in non-fiction reading. "I wasn't going to take books today, but I think I'd better," a (Canadian) boy told his librarian. "I might get lonesome for them over the holidays." For all those like him, a Massachusetts children's library displays this inscription: "Books are keys to wisdom's treasure; Books are gates to lands of pleasure; Books are paths that upward lead; Books are friends. Come, let us read."

—"Books are Friends," *Imperial Oil Review*

165. To produce a mighty book, you must choose a mighty theme. No great and enduring volume can ever be written on the flea, though many there be that have tried it.

—Herman Melville

166. A small boy paying a 2-cent fine for an overdue book he had returned to the library, looked thoughtfully at the librarian and asked: "Can you make a living out of this?"

—*Capper's Weekly*

167. The love of books is an infectious sort of thing. Children catch it, they don't learn it.

—Walter B. Barbe, *Education*

168. Books are the gun powder of the mind.

169. J. Stevens Stock, a researcher whose job is to try to predict the sales of paperback books in advance of publication, relates an interesting experience in connection with one of their tests: "We asked a group of people to list their favorite books. They came up with the usual responses—Shakespeare, the Bible, and so on. Then, at the end of the interview we handed each a list of titles, offering a free book for their trouble. The most popular pick was *Murder of a Burlesque Queen.* Just goes to show the biggest trap you can fall into is believing what people tell you they want!"

170. The child attending school today in the United States has 20 per cent fewer textbooks than the child of ten years ago, claims the American Textbook Publishers Institute. . . .

—Education Digest

171. Books have led some to learning, and others to madness when they swallow more than they can digest.

*—*Petrarch, *Saturday Review*

172. For several years two men had played chess regularly together. They were quite evenly matched and there was keen rivalry between them. Then, one man's game improved so much he started beating his rival nearly every game they played. The other man, after much thought, finally came up with an idea. He went to a bookstore, picked up a 4-volume set on *How to Play Chess.* He sent the books to his friend as a gift. It wasn't long before they were evenly matched again!

*—*Dan Bennett

173. Who without books essays to learn
Draws water in a leaky urn.

*—*R. D. Emerson, *Saturday Review*

174. Many of the finer things are to be found in books if we profit by the opinions of learned people. The following expresses the estimate of a few writers as to the value of books:

Channing said: "God be thanked for books. They are the voices of the distant and the dead, and make us heir of the spiritual life of the past ages. In the best books, great men talk to us, give us our most precious thoughts, and pour their souls into ours."

Carlyle said: "All that mankind has done, thought, or been is lying as in magic preservation in the pages of books. They are the chosen possession of men."

Emerson said: "Give me a book, health, and a summer day, and I will make the pomp of kings look ridiculous."

—Sunshine Magazine

175. A bookseller had a statement for a book curtly returned to him with an accompanying note which read:

"Dear Sir: I didn't order this book. If I did, you didn't send it. If you sent it, I didn't get it; if I got it, I paid for it. If I didn't, I won't."

176.   They borrow books they will not buy,
They have no ethics or religions.
I wish some kind of Burbankian guy
Could cross my books with homing pigeons.

—CAROLYN WELLS, Saturday Review

177. "How dare you recommend such a vile book for my daughter to read," cried an enraged parent to the English teacher. The teacher, completely baffled, asked for further elucidation.

"Why," said the mother indignantly, "she tells me you recommended a book called *The Vices of the Virgins!*"

"Oh," the teacher breathed a sigh of relief, "There has been a slight misunderstanding. The book I suggested was *Devices for Diversions.*"

—M. M. MYERS, Los Angeles School Journal

178. Bennett Cerf points out, somewhat ironically, that while there are 18,000 blacksmiths still going strong in the U.S., this nation despite a boom in the number of books published, supports only 7,400 bookstores.

—Quote

179.   When I am dead
I hope it may be said
His sins were scarlet
But his books were read.

—HILAIRE BELLOC, Quote

180.   The books which tend
To have a sad end
Are those I lend
To a so-called friend.

—SIDNEY BRODY, Quote

Camping

181. *Camp Greenlake-in-the-Pines*
Administration Office

Attention, all Senior Counselors! Many new campers have been with us this year, and some were never away from their parents before. As you know, most boys are rather uncommunicative in their letters home; thus parents are always anxious to know how their youngsters really adjusted to camp life. (However, they want facts, not trivial details.) In view of this, all Counselors must exercise great discretion when writing parents our customary end-of-season reports. We particularly urge you to use the following time-tested guide in composing your reports:

If . . .	Write . . .
The boy wouldn't go near the water.	Although swimming was not Bobby's favorite sport. . .
He was a miserable eater.	He never made a glutton of himself at the table.
He couldn't get along with his tent-mates.	He made a constant effort to find new friends.
He was a bully.	Bobby took pride in demonstrating his wrestling skills to younger boys.
He cheated in games.	He seems to have a strongly developed will-to-win.
His tent was always messy.	Of course, boys of his age aren't always as neat as they could be.
He put a garter snake in another boy's bed.	Bobby took an active interest in our wildlife.
He always got lost on hikes.	His sense of direction is quite unusual.
He smashed another boy's watch to see what was inside.	He's intensely curious about machinery.

—WILLIAM GARVIN

182. It now takes 10 times the gear for a cookout that great-great grandpappy needed to conquer the wilderness. Ah! The march of progress.

—*Cincinnati Enquirer*

183. At the youth camp the rich man's son was trying to get a large check cashed. The postmaster explained, "I'm sorry but I can't cash the check without someone to identify you. Don't you have a friend here?" "Not me," replied the crestfallen boy. "I'm the camp bugler."

184. Already he has won a fight
Who knows his cause is just and right.

185. A pig swallowed a stick of dynamite, rubbed against a building and caused an explosion that razed four city blocks. "It sure was upsetting," said the pig's owner. "For a couple of days we had a mighty sick pig on our hands."

—Barbara Oliver, *Martinsville, Indiana*

186. A pig ate his fill of acorns under an oak tree and then started to root around the tree. A crow remarked, "You should not do this. If you lay bare the roots, the tree will wither and die." "Let it die," replied the pig. "Who cares as long as there are acorns?"

—Russian Fable

Chairman

187. The hardest thing to stop is a temporary chairman.

—Kin Hubbard

188. According to Nan Hampton, a chairman of a meeting is like the minor official at a bullfight whose main function is to open and close the gates to let the bull in and out.

Challenge

189. When a man is determined what can stop him? Cripple him and you have a Sir Walter Scott; put him in a prison cell and you have John Bunyan; bury him in the snows of Valley Forge and you have a George Washington. Have him born in abject poverty and you have a Lincoln; load him with bitter racial prejudice and you have a Disraeli; afflict him with asthma until as a boy he lies choking in his father's arms and you have a Theodore Roosevelt; stab him with rheumatic pains until for years he cannot sleep without an opiate and you have a Steinmetz; put him in a grease pit of a locomotive roundhouse and you have a Walter Chrysler; make him a second fiddle in an obscure South American orchestra and you have a Toscanini.

—PAUL SPEIKER

190. Challenge is powerful as an attention-arousing technique, but it must be fair. Any power to influence is undergirded by a skill in inducing participation by the other person.

191. You have all seen athletes at times "play over their heads." Why? Because of the challenge and its acceptance.

It is men who have counted struggle as a blessing who get the big rewards of life. As Emerson said, "God keeps an honest account with men."

The hard surgical cases, where life hangs on a heartbeat, do not go to the dilettante surgeon. The tough engineering problem, like building a bridge across a mighty river, does not go to the engineer who has always looked for the easy jobs. And the same for lawyers, and top executives in business.

You will remember the poem of the frontier:
I dream no dream of a nursemaid state
That spoons me out my food.
No, the stout heart sings in its strife with fate,
For the toil and the sweat are good.
—SAMUEL B. PETTINGILL, *The Freeman*

192. Clarence, little Clarence, had to have iodine put on an abrasion for the first time. "Do you know how I can tell how old you are when I put iodine on this bruise?"

"How?"

"It will tickle you a little. Might even hurt some. If you scream and kick, I shall know you are a baby only two years old. If you cry and fuss, you are just four years old. But if you merely say, "Ouch!" and laugh and dance the iodine dance that goes something like this (making appropriate gestures, ridiculous enough so that he laughed) you might be as old as SIX!"

Clarence was four.

"I'll bet you're only two."

Tense moments. Then—Ouch! Ouch! OUCH! and hilarious laughter and dancing through tears.

"So big? So soon? How did you do it?"

"O—I just grewed up."

—ANNA G. NOYES

Character

193. Don't envy the lucky fellow whose path is smoothed for him. Pity him. Some day he will seek your favor. Success is the product of *character*. The development of your character is in your own hands, and poverty plus honest ambition is the best environment for character-building.

—*Du Pont Magazine*

194. The measure of a man's real character is what he would do, if he knew he would never be found out.

—*Macaulay*

195. "Character is a by-product; it is produced in the great manufacture of daily duty."

—WOODROW WILSON, *Friendly Chat*
—BAYARD TAYLOR

196. I was interested to hear a major exec point out that the criteria he uses for selecting employes run in this order: character, intelligence, experience. "A really bright exec picks up experience very quickly," he told me. "But the man we need and want most, in important places, is a man with character sufficient to resist many kinds of pressures when the going gets rough. We find, then, that character is the most important ingredient of all, particularly if the man is to be responsible for policy making. An exec can buy brains and can buy experience, but character is something he must supply himself."

—*Fortune*

197. Be genuine and sincere; remember the words of the little rhyme: "Don't be veneer stuck on with glue, be solid mahogany all the way through."

—*Briefs*

198. When it comes to judging men, either for employment or for advancement, most execs have their own list of favorable or danger signals to watch for. These are outside the traits personnel experts measure and approve. We overheard one: "I'll tell you one thing I've discovered, and sad experience over the years has proved it: never trust a man who can dish out punishment—but not take it. These fellows are often very bright, and very likeable when the going is smooth and easy. But in a pinch, when pressure is on—look out. They'll turn on you every time."

—*Management Briefs*

Children

199.   What shall you give to one small boy?
A glamorous game, a tinseled toy,
A barlow knife, a puzzle pack,
A train that runs on curving track?
A picture book, a real live pet. . .
No, there's plenty of time for such things yet.
Give him a DAY for his very own—
Just one small boy and his dad alone;
A walk in the woods, a romp in the park,
A fishing trip from dawn to dark,
Give the gift that only you can—
The companionship of his Old Man.
Games are outgrown, and toys decay—
But he'll never forget if you "Give him a day."

—*Anon.*

200. It was Washington's birthday. Johnny called over to his neighbor, Danny, "Say, aren't you going to put up your flag today?"

"Naw," answered Danny. "I don't even put the flag up for my own birthday!"

201. A mother's mission in life is not to be a leaning post but to make leaning unnecessary.

—*Bobs and Bubbles*

202. The mother was deeply concerned about her daughter's new boy friend. "Remember, dear," she said, "get to know him before you become serious. Be sure he's considerate, for example."

"Oh, I already know he's considerate," the young girl replied. "Just the other day he told me that he put his shirt on a horse that was scratched."

Cuneo Topics

203. A mother listening to the evening prayers of her sleepy little daughter was astonished and amazed to hear the following:

"Now I lay me down to sleep,
I pray the Lord my soul to keep.
When he hollers let him go,
Eenie, meenie, miny, mo."
—*Balance Sheet*

204. My three children are at the perfect age—too old to cry at night and too young to borrow my car.
—Walter Slezak

205. Many a child has grown up to be fairly level-headed because his parents couldn't find the guidance book they were looking for.
—Raymond Duncan, quoted in *Townsend National Weekly*

206. Johnny, who had acquired the habit of using profane language quite extensively, was warned by his mother never to say such words again, or she would pack his clothes and turn him out.

Johnny promised his mother that he wouldn't, but it was not very long until she heard him swear. She immediately packed his clothes and put him out of the house.

The boy stood on the steps for approximately an hour, his mother watching him from the window, and finally she opened the door and asked him why he did not leave.

"I was wondering," he replied, "where the hell I would go."
—*Oral Hygiene*

207. It makes sense that the pediatrician injects penicillin in junior's bottom when he has a sore throat. His mommy kisses him on the neck to heal a little toe that has been stumped.
—Mrs. Dale Baughman

208. A man was warning the little boy next door about being careful crossing the streets.

"Oh, don't worry," the youngster assured him. "I always wait for the empty space to come by."
—*The Lookout*

209. Five-year-old Carol misbehaved at church. Her punishment was to eat dinner alone at a small table in the corner of the dining room. When her father finished giving thanks for the food, her small echo came from the corner. "And thank you, dear Lord, for preparing a table before me in the presence of my enemies. Amen."

—The Lookout

210. *Directions on a Nursing Bottle:* When the baby is done drinking it should be unscrewed and laid in a cool place. If the baby does not thrive on fresh milk it should be boiled.

—Typographic

211. One blistering hot day when they had guests for dinner, a mother asked her 4-year-old son to say the blessing. "But, mother, I don't know what to say," he protested.

"Oh, just say what you've heard me say," she told him.

Obediently he bowed his little head and said, "Oh, Lord, why did I invite those people here on a hot day like this?"

—Automotive Service Digest

212. "There, there, little man," said the kindly woman to the boy beside her in the surf, "you mustn't be afraid—why don't you just splash right in and swim?"

"I would," was the timid reply, "but you're standing on my flippers."

—Quote

213. If children did not ask questions, they would never learn how little adults know.

214. My wife and I were engrossed in the Ed Sullivan Show one Sunday evening. Meanwhile in playing around the TV set our 2-year-old son Brad accidentally bumped it. Since the set was on a swivel base, the screen rotated around and away from our vision.

With some irritation and impatience I commanded, "Brad, turn the TV around." He did, but not far enough. "More, Brad, turn it more," I implored. He did but this time, too far. Finally in desperation, I said, "Come on, Brad, turn it so that we can see it. Use your head." You guessed it; sure enough, he leaned over, placed his head against the side of the set and pushed it into its exact original position.

—M. Dale Baughman

215. A picture window will bring the outdoors into a living room, but a little boy's two little feet will bring in more of it.

216. The childhood shows the man as morning shows the day.

—John Milton, Paradise Regained

217. "I want to buy that book in the window called *How to Captivate Men*," said the little girl to the sales clerk.

The man looks dubiously at the child.

"That's not the sort of book for you," he said, "What do you want it for?"

"I want to give it to my daddy for a Christmas present."

"But surely there are hundreds of books he would rather have?"

"No, I know he would like that one. You see, he's a policeman."

218. Life is full of puzzles for children of the modern age. Albert Edward Wiggam tells of a ten-year-old boy who, seeing a horse and buggy ambling down the street, asked his father, "Dad, when you want to make a horse go slower, how do you put him in low?"
—*The Lookout*

219. She doesn't wink, she doesn't flirt,
She spreads no gossip, tells no dirt,
She has no "line," she plays no tricks,
But give her time—she's only six.

220. Why is it that our own kids commit no errors, while neighbors' kids are holy terrors?

221. A mountain in Nevada jumped four inches when an atomic blast was set off inside it. This is comparable to the effect of a Cub den meeting in the basement of a nine-room house.
—Senator Soaper

222. In Berchtesgaden, Germany, last March I saw and heard many inspiring and sobering sights (the latter associated with the devastation and diabolical cleverness of the Nazis). But I was reassured when I heard a father tell what a teenager has asked him one bright morning. "Dad (mein papa), what is a hydramatic polecat?" "I give up." "A hydramatic polecat is a shiftless skunk."
—Dr. David A. MacLennan, *Church Management*

223. The young son of a man whose speech was punctuated with proverbs was playing near the barn at the foot of a hill.

A loose stone rolled down the hillside, struck the barn knocking off a loose board. The lad first surveyed the damage and then the stone, adding this observation, "Sure enough, no moss."

224. A small boy's overalls are a kind of calendar of the seasons. January, a Brazil nut; February, a valentine; March, a marble; April, a piece of kite string; May, a piece of paper with a few lines of a school piece to be memorized; June, a fish hook; July, a fire-cracker; August, a plum pit; September, a bright red maple leaf; October, a pheasant feather; November, the stub of a jack-o-lantern candle; December, a rabbit's foot.

—FRAWLEY HYNES, *Columbia*

225. The Blakes' boy, Charles, turned out to be a splendid young fellow, and his dad explains why: "When he was little, he'd always have a tantrum when we refused him something, so we'd let him have it—the tantrum, that is."

226. Every couple knows how to raise the neighbor's children, so why not have all families swap children?

227. A 5-year-old rehearsing at home for the school Christmas program sang:

"Hark, the herald angels sing
Glory to the new-born king!
Peace on earth and mercy mild,
God and sitters reconciled."

—Delta Kappa Gamma Bulletin

228. Apt simile: As excited as a boy with a bumble bee in his space helmet.

—T. O. WHITE, *Champaign-Urbana News Gazette*

229. *Little boy:* "Was George Washington as honest as they say he was?"
Father: "Yes, of course."
Little boy: "Then why do they close the banks on his birthday?"

—The Lookout

230. *Father:* "Why are you always at the bottom of your class?"
Dennis: "It doesn't make any difference. They teach the same thing at both ends."

231.   He'll make his mark, my neighbor said,
Referring to her little son,
I'd judge the lad was way ahead
With handiwork he has begun.
From gouging chairs to smashing glass
One truth emerges grim and stark,
This lad can't wait for time to pass
He has already made his mark!

—VINEY WILDER

232. Little Mary was visiting her grandmother in the country. Walking in the garden, Mary chanced to see a peacock, a bird that she had never seen before.

After gazing in silent admiration, she ran into the house and cried out: "Oh, Granny, come and see! One of your chickens is in bloom!"
—The Lookout

233. "Billy, get your little brother's hat out of that mud puddle."
"I can't ma, he's got it strapped too tight under his chin."
—Pelican

234. I was reading a letter from relatives as four-year-old Brad stood by in silence. When I was about half way through, he could contain his curiosity and patience no longer.

"Dad," he entreated, "why don't you read with your mouth?"
—M. DALE BAUGHMAN

235. *Mother:* "Bobby, last night there were two pieces of cake in the pantry and now there is only one. How do you explain that?"
Bobby: "I guess I didn't see the other piece."

236. A fourth grader asking for books about Jim Bowie, explained: "You know . . . that man that died in the alimony."
—Library Journal

237. In Indianapolis there was the little boy who asked his mother if he could start shaving. He said he had watched his daddy and knew the words.
—GRIFF NIBLACK

238. A small boy with a penny tightly clutched in his hot little hand entered the toy shop and drove the proprietor to distraction asking to see this and that and everything without ever making up his mind.

"Look here, my boy," said the storekeeper finally, "what do you want to buy for a penny—the whole world with a fence around it?"

The boy thought for a moment and then replied: "Let's see it."

239. Tots are so precocious today they use their parents' mental blocks for toys.
—American Mercury

240. One boy said his father gave him a penny and a pat on the head every day. On his fourteenth birthday he had $47.45 and a flat head.

241. When she was five years old, Dlynn Lea knew what toilet water was and where it came from. Her mother and older sister, Dala, had taught her that. But two-year-old Brad didn't know about toilet water, or at least we thought he didn't.

As Dlynn displayed and sprayed her potion of scented and colored toilet water, Brad was conspicuously quiet and absent. Suddenly he entered the scene with a small bottle half-filled with liquid from a questionable source. Demanding to know from whence it came, his mother trailed him to the bathroom where he pointed to the lavatory and explained, "Mine's real toilet water, Mommy."

—M. DALE BAUGHMAN

242. One nice thing about kids is that they don't keep telling you boring stories about the clever things their parents said.

—LYDA FAIRBANKS

243. A Milwaukee lady was prodding her three-year-old nephew to show a friend of hers how smart he was.

"Tell the lady how old you are," she said.

"I can't," the youngster retorted. "I've got my mittens on."

—DOYLE K. GETTER, *Milwaukee Journal*

244. Children are a great comfort in your old age . . . they help you get there faster too.

—*RIB,* Beeville, Texas

245. First-grader Melanie was engaged to marry the young gentleman next door, but the engagement was broken abruptly.

"Why aren't you going to marry Danny?" asked Melanie's mother.

"Well," the child said loftily, "he just isn't ready for marriage yet." And then she added as an afterthought, "Besides that, he scribbled in my coloring book."

Wall Street Journal

246. Our seven-year-old daughter Dala Dee wanted to be popular with her age-mates. One proof of popularity seemed to be the frequency with which the second-grade boys chased her on the playground. On one occasion the chaser became a little rough after the "catch." That night at home Dala complained. I asked why the boy had chased her in the first place. "Well," she explained, "because I pushed him." "And why did you push him?" I inquired. "So he'd chase me," she admitted.

—M. DALE BAUGHMAN

247. *Sam:* "My daddy has a sword of Washington and a hat of Lincoln."

Bill: "My father has an Adam's apple."

248. My six-year-old daughter, Dlynn Lea, was attending a PTA meeting with us. Listening attentively to the words of the presiding official, she suddenly tensed and became obviously apprehensive. When I asked for an explanation, she reminded me that the speaker had said, "Let's get a second to the motion and then the floor will be thrown open."

—M. Dale Baughman

249. Our miniature dachshund, pet for our daughters aged 10 and 7 and 4-year-old son, disappeared on Christmas day.

Three days later we discovered that he had been delivered to an animal shelter. While driving there with three children to claim him, I suddenly asked, "Suppose the man makes you describe him. How will you do it?"

The seven-year-old answered first, "Well, his nose is cold, for one thing."

—M. Dale Baughman

250. One mile of superhighway looks much like another, and with the restaurant chains using the same floor plan in each establishment, it is hard to remember just where you are. But a family that had breakfast, lunch and dinner in three such turnpike restaurants didn't realize how confused one member was getting. As they walked into the restaurant for dinner—some 500 miles from the one where they had breakfasted—their four-year-old exclaimed in bewilderment, "We're been traveling all day, and here we are again!"

—Dorothy DeCamp, Oak Ridge, Tenn.

251. Six-year-old Andrea Halverson of Elm Grove, Wisconsin, went fishing with her dad. She came home proudly holding aloft her catch of two.

"This one is a perch," she told her mother, "and this other one is a loud mouth bass."

—Doyle K. Getter, *Milwaukee Journal*

252. Our evening newspaper is usually tossed, rolled and bound with a rubber band, from a fast moving bicycle in the general direction of the front door.

Our three-year-old son had been bringing it to my favorite chair only to throw it on the floor beside me. This went on and on, until I finally demanded to know why (I should have guessed why) he threw the paper instead of handing it to me.

"Why, daddy," he explained, "that's the way the paper boy does it." Of course.

—M. Dale Baughman

252. "So the teacher kept you in after school," said the angry father. "What happened?"

"Nothing, Dad, she just wasn't my type."

—*Laugh Book*

254. A four-year-old was invited to a birthday party. When the question of a gift arose, he said he wanted to take his friend a book.

"What kind of book?" his mother asked.

"One like Daddy reads," he replied. "You know, with a lady on the cover with all her clothes blowed off."

—*Laugh Book*

255. I was trying to impress my eight-year-old daughter Dala with the importance of desire and perseverance. I quoted to her this thought: "If you don't get what you want, it is a sign either that you did not seriously want it, or that you tried to bargain over the price." "For example," I went on, "let's suppose you want to become a good dancer." Dala picked up the moral quickly, "I get it, Daddy," she exclaimed, "if I really want to be a good dancer, I must work hard." That's right," I answered, "or at least that's what I think Rudyard Kipling meant." "Oh, did he say that about getting what you want? I wonder if he got everything he wanted!"

—M. Dale Baughman

256. Ardent Little Leaguer Jimmie Lipski, nine years old, looked up from a period of deep concentration and said: "I've been thinking, Mommy. What am I going to do when I grow up? . . . I mean, during the off season."

—Mark Beltaire, *Laugh Book*

257. Little Johnnie had been raised in a small town by strict parents. His only recreation was the weekly prayer meeting.

The day his aunt took him to the circus for the first time he came home all excited and ran to his mother saying, "Mother, if you went to the circus just once you'd never go to a prayer meeting again in your whole life."

—Anna Herbert, *Laugh Book*

258. Our four-year-old son Brad was proudly carrying an old dollar pocket watch of mine. A neighbor lady, observing him playing with the watch, asked, "Does it tell time?" Little Brad, looking at the neighbor lady in disgust, answered, "Nope, you gotta look at it."

—M. DALE BAUGHMAN

259. The psychiatrist was examining Willie, who had been giving his parents much concern.

"What do you like to do best, Willie?"

"I like to shoot birds."

"And what do you like to do next best?" asked the psychiatrist.

"Well, I like to make sling shots to shoot birds with."

"Then, what do you like to do next best?"

"I like to take little girls' bloomers off."

Ah, thought the psychiatrist, now I'm getting somewhere. "And what do you like to do then?"

"Take the elatsic out of their bloomers to make more sling shots to shoot more birds with."

—*Laugh Book*

260. I was preparing to leave on a four-day trip and a pocketful of change was scattered on the dresser. Son Brad, aged four, looked over the pile and started to help himself. My wife noticed his intentions and admonished, "No! No! Brad, Daddy will need every penny of that." Brad hesitated for only a moment and then picked up the dimes, nickels and quarters.

—M. DALE BAUGHMAN

261. *Embarrassing Moment:* When the six-year-old son of the family comes into the kitchen, looks his mother over carefully and then shouts loudly to his father, who is hiding behind a newspaper in the living room, "But, Daddy, I don't see that chip you said she had on her shoulder."

262. Riding up a scenic canyon road out of Missoula, Montana, with Professor Aaron Harper of the University of Montana, and son Jimmy Harper, I couldn't contain my feelings any longer and exclaimed, "What interesting terrain!" Young Jimmy asked in wonderment, "Where's a train?"

—M. DALE BAUGHMAN

263. A brilliant child is one who asks the guests questions they can answer.

—O. A. BATTISTA

264. My daughter and my two small grandaughters had been visiting me for a week. Everyone had helped put the dishes away. One morning a small pitcher I wished to use for breakfast was missing. I opened one cupboard door after another looking for it.

Little Lucile watched me and finally she said, "Grandmother, shouldn't you have a place for your things and keep them there?"

—RUTH M. BENSON, *Christian Science Monitor*

265. Adults are constantly saying one day when you grow up and get big you can do so and so; well, the tables were turned one evening at our home. My husband had just applied the ruler to our four-and-a-half-year-old son for some mischievous act. Brad accepted the punishment, we thought, but in a short time he said, "Daddy, one of these days when you get to be a little boy again I'm gonna spank you real hard with the ruler when you're bad."

—MRS. M. D. BAUGHMAN

266. I, for one . . . am convinced children want to know the answers. Living in an area where there are few or no sheep at all . . . our two-year-old son Greg, was amazed when he saw a pasture full of them on a trip to Illinois. He didn't know what they were but since he thought they were a kindly looking crowd he screamed, "Mommie, look at all those *prune faces.*" This is his Daddy's pet name for little Greg, because of all the funny faces he makes.

—DONNA RHOADES, Bloomington, Indiana

267. My mother, lives on her small farm all by herself, where she settled as a bride some 70 odd years ago. As her children have left their home nest to establish their own homes, Mother's love, care, and enthusiasm for her beautiful roses and other flowers has increased.

One of her many loving neighbors sent her seven-year-old Susie up the road with a heaping basket of bright, freshly-picked strawberries for Mother. Susie is quite shy, and after a rather brief visit modestly started her leave-taking, so Mother gave her cookies and some lovely roses to take with her.

When Susie reached home she was very pensive, and said to her Mother. "She is such a nice lady and raises such beautiful flowers—she must be Mother Nature."

—MRS. ARCH LUDE, Worthington, Ohio, *Christian Science Monitor*

Children—Parents

268. Parents wonder why the streams are bitter when they themselves have poisoned the fountain.

—Forbes

269. I came home with my first "Homburg" hat the other day. I had it made by a Champaign hatter. *I* liked it and my wife thought it looked good on me. While in the mirror I surveyed the image, three-year-old Brad piped up, "Dad, it looks like a magician's hat." No sooner had he finished than my third-grade daughter added, "They sure wasted lots of material in that big hump."

—M. DALE BAUGHMAN

270. Little Wanda was lying on her back on the nursery floor, singing a happy song. The next time her mother looked in on her, Wanda was lying on her stomach, shrilling a tune.

"Playing a game, dear?" mother asked.

"Yes," Wanda replied, "I'm pretending I'm a phonograph record, and I've just turned myself over."

—Sunshine Magazine

271. Johnny hurried to get the evening paper. Tomorrow was picnic day, and he wanted to know what the weather forecast was.

"Well, Johnny, what do they predict?" his mother asked.

"They haven't decided yet," said Johnny gloomily.

"Haven't decided?"

"No," said Johnny, "It says, 'Unsettled.'"

—Sunshine Magazine

272. Parents spend the first part of a child's life getting him to walk and talk, and the rest of his childhood getting him to sit down and shut up.

—Automotive Service Digest

273. It is said that we spend more on wild life than we do on child life in this country. Parents will find this a puzzling distinction.

274. *Lady:* "Are you a good little boy?"

Little Boy: "No, ma'm, I'm the kind of child my mother won't let me play with."

—Sunshine Magazine

275. My wife caught our four-year-old daughter, Lindy, hurrying down the hall with the pepper shaker. When a full confession had been extracted, it was discovered that she had found a "pet" fly and she wanted to see if it could sneeze.

—M. DALE BAUGHMAN

276. *Father to teen-age son:* "Mind if I use the car myself tonight? I'm taking your mother out and I want to impress her."

277. Three women went to a psychiatrist with their young daughters. The psychiatrist examined the first woman and said, "Madame, you have a deep subconscious urge for money and so you named your daughter Penny."

The second lady, a fat woman, went in and the psychiatrist said, "Madame, you have a deep subconscious urge for sweets and so you named your little girl Candy."

The third woman, hearing this, took her little girl by the hand and said, "Come Schenley dear, we're leaving."

—Information

278. A six-year-old youngster had listened to friends of his parents discuss their ailments and those of others. One of them summed up the situation, saying, "everything just seems to be going to pieces."

That night the lad remembered when he said his prayer.

"God, bless daddy and mamma," he said, "and all those other people who are falling apart."

—News-Gazette

279. Mrs. Jones was very proud of her son, who showed promise as an athlete.

"Yes, he must be a very fast runner," she explained proudly to a neighbor. "Look at this newspaper report. It says he fairly burned up the track."

"And it's quite true," she added, confidently. "I went to see the track this morning and it's nothing but cinders."

—The Lookout

280. The trouble with your children is that when they're not being a lump in your throat, they're being a pain in your neck.

281. One little man said to his father, "I'd like to be like Superman—rich, strong and handsome, but if I can't, I'd like to be like you."

282. The mother of 8 children under 11 tells of the time she was extremely unhappy with her brood. "This morning the children were so noisy that I threatened 'The first person in this house who screams is going to get his mouth soaped.' And you know, I can still taste the stuff!"

—Lion

283. *Mother:* "When that naughty boy threw stones at you, why didn't you come and tell me instead of throwing stones back at him?"

Practical-minded youngster: "What good would that do? You couldn't hit the side of a barn!"

—The Lookout

284. Little Nellie, a six-year-old, complained, "Mother, I've got a stomach ache."

"That's because your stomach is empty," Mother replied. "You would feel better if you had something in it."

That afternoon the minister called, and in the course of conversation remarked that he had been suffering all day with a severe headache.

Little Nellie was alert. "That's because its empty," she said. "You'd feel better if you had something in it."

—Wall Street Journal

285. How fortunate indeed you have become
For my young son is now gracing your presence.
Naturally I'd like to facilitate your efforts.
And so I'll tell you a bit about this *unusual* young man.
You with your magnificent perception have
Undoubtedly realized his capabilities.
Unusual? Of course he's unusual—he's my son.

I realize that you have all those other *average*
Children to deal with
And my son is—as you would expect—well above average.
Your intelligence and achievement tests didn't exactly indicate
      this
But—I'm sure you'll agree that such tests are
Still a long way from being perfected.
And then, too—such tests probably don't forsee
The possibility of an above average boy such as mine.
Above average? Of course he's above average—he's my son.

You should know however—that he is
Unusual as well as above average—he is a

Very sensitive child.
Naturally—you must devote *some* of your time to
Those other children.
But you'll understand him more readily if you're aware
Of his sensitivity.
Of course *talented* people are usually sensitive.
Talented? Of course he's talented—he's my son.

You know—it suddenly occurs to me that all
Parents are a collection of such people as I.
Therefore—every morning you must face an
Entire class of *unusual, above average, abnormally*
Sensitive and *talented* children!
You are indeed fortunate—but this raises a
Question:
How do you manage to contend with us unusual
Above average, sensitive and talented parents?
May God bless your patience!
—J. R. Evans, *Cook County Education Digest*

286. A six-year-old boy, separated from his mother in a super-market, began to call frantically for "Martha! Martha! Martha!"

That was his mother's name and she came running to him quickly. "But, honey," she admonished, "you shouldn't call me Martha. I'm 'Mother' to you.'

"Yes, I know," he answered, "but this store is full of mothers."

287. Yes sir, I took my boy-a-fishin'. Sure, his mother told me to, but besides, I kind of done it 'cause it seemed the thing to do.

It's a heap more fun a-fishin' when I'm out there with my son, 'cause we really get acquainted through a little fishin' fun.

When my creel of life is empty, and my life's line sort of worn, I shall always keep rememberin' that first early summer morn when I took my boy a-fishin', and I really learned the joy that comes to every father when he really knows his boy.

—*Smiles*

288. "When my son came bounding into the house carrying a football he had won in a box-top contest, I was amazed. The rules had stated that prizes would be awarded to the youngsters who wrote the best sentences on why they liked the product. The judges must have had a sense of humor because my prodigy's contribution

was: "I like your cereal because it doesn't snap, crackle, or pop—
it just lays there quietly and sogs."

—*Smiles*

289. The worst eternal triangle known: teen-ager, parent and
telephone.

—LAVONNE MATHISON, *The Christian Home*

290. "I can't figure it out," said the small boy trying to get his
father to help him with his arithmetic. "If a carpenter was paid
three dollars a day, how much did he earn in four days?"

"No wonder you can't figure it out," replied his father. "That's
not arithmetic—that's ancient history!"

—SELMA HAGG in Prentice, Wisconsin *News*

291. Our third grader, Dala Dee, hastened home the other day
to tell her mother how her romance was going.

"Richard spoke to me," she announced proudly.

"And what did he say?" asked her mother.

"I grabbed his cap and he said 'that's all, sister.'"

—M. DALE BAUGHMAN

292. A couple of Little Leaguers were asked how the big game
had gone. "Oh, it was a very good game until the third inning,"
one replied. "Then they had to call it because the parents were
rioting all over the field."

—Almanac in *Minneapolis Tribune*

293.

Don't let me push them
Day after day;
Life's game is played
In a leisurely way.

Don't let me bind them
To pinafore strings;
They must be free to
Try out their wings.

Don't let me hinder
What they should do;
Some secret talent
I might subdue.

Don't let me make them

What they should be;
Just let me live it
For them to see.

—RUTH KENT, *Sunshine Magazine*

294. "After a difficult day with the children," a young mother says, "I like to take the car and go for a drive; I like to have something in my hands I can control."

—LAWRENCE P. FITZGERALD, *The Link*

295. *Mother:* "And what did you learn in school today, dear?"
Elsie: "Oh, mother, I don't have to educate you all over again, do I?"

—*Boston Transcript*

296. A young woman who had three small children received a gift of a play pen from her uncle and aunt. They were flabbergasted when they received this note from their niece:

"Thank you so much for the pen. It is a perfect Godsend. I sit in it every afternoon and read, and the children can't get near me."

297. *Little boy to his father:* "I'm glad you are my Daddy and that we have the same germs, so that I can kiss you."

298. A child sometimes is a composite of Mom and Dad. However, often the girls take after their fathers—and after that, they take after other fellows.

299. *Mother:* "Johnny, I wish you'd stop reaching for things. Don't you have a tongue?"
Johnny: "Yes, Mother, but my arm is longer."

300.   I spanked a little boy last night
I thought I was doing right;
I thought that I was punishing
A little boy for some wrong thing.
Today I bought a ball and kite
For that same boy I spanked last night
Bought marbles, tops and everything
To counteract the punishing.
You see through tears this little lad
Tried hard to smile and then said, "Dad,
Will spanking make me good like you?"
I think you would have bought those things, too.

—*Author Unknown*

301. "Son, why aren't you as bright as Mrs. Jones' boy Billy? He never gets failing marks, does he?"

"No, but then he has a certain advantage. He has intelligent parents."

302. "Parents are only human," said a fifteen-year-old panelist on a youth forum. "They can't be right all the time any more than we can."

—National Parent-Teacher

303. At the carnival a little girl kept asking her mother for money. Finally, in exasperation mother explained, "I don't have any money to spare!" The child shot back, "I don't want to spare it, I want to spend it."

304. Eight-year-old Dala was getting to do far too many things to suit Dlynn who is only four. For the fourth time in two days Dlynn was told that she was just not big enough and old enough to be allowed to engage in some of the activities available to her older sister. In utter dismay Dlynn complained, "It's not fair, mommy! How did Dala get such a head start on me?"

—M. DALE BAUGHMAN

305. A young mother paying a visit to her doctor, made no attempt to restrain her five-year-old son, who was ransacking an adjoining treatment room. But finally an extra-loud clatter of bottles did prompt her to say, "I hope, doctor, you don't mind Billy being in your examining room."

"No," said the doctor calmly. "He'll be quiet in a moment when he gets to the poisons."

—Scarboro Missions

306. The small daughter watched her mother soberly while she marked her ballot at the polls, then remarked, "You voted for the man you loves best, didn't you, Mother?"

"Gracious, child!" exclaimed the mother, "why ask that?"

"You put a kiss by his name."

—Sunshine Magazine

307. The father of six old maid daughters was overheard praying: "Dear Lord, I am not asking anything for myself, but please give six eligible young men six deductible wives."

—Back Bay Breeze

308. *Little Mary:* "I don't think Mamma knows much about bringing up children."

Father: "Why, Mary, what makes you say that?"

Mary: "Well, she makes me go to bed when I'm wide awake and she makes me get up when I'm sleepy."

—The Lookout

309. One snowy morning prior to his father's departure: "Mommy, can Freddie and I go out and listen to Daddy put on the tire chains?"

—Philnews

310. Asked a small boy, looking up from the evening paper, "Dad, do political plums grow from seeds?"

"No," replied his father, "they result from clever grafting."

—American Mercury

311. *Mother:* "Did you push your little sister down the stairs?"

Bobby: "I only pushed her down one step. She fell the rest of the way."

312. *Father (to thoughtful son):* "A penny for your thoughts, Jimmy."

Jimmy: "To tell the truth, Pop, I was thinking of a quarter."

313. A teacher was telling of the hardships of the Pilgrims. One first-grader raised her hand and said, "I wish my mommy had been there. She always knows just what to do."

—The Lookout

314. "Did Edison make the first talking machine, Papa?"

"No, son, God made the first one, but Edison made the first one that could be shut off."

315. *Mother of small boy to child psychiatrist:* "Well, I don't know whether or not he feels insecure, but everybody else in the neighborhood certainly does!"

—Tracks

316. "Did you miss any of these?" asked Johnny's father after reading over a list of five questions which his son had been called upon to answer in school that day.

"Only the first two and the last three," said Johnny.

317. "Mommy," said the 4-year-old, "why did you marry Daddy?"

"So!" exclaimed her mother. "Even you are puzzled!"

—Nuggets

318. Mary Anne, who had been learning to sing Christmas carols in kindergarten, often sang herself to sleep. And one night, this is what her family heard her sing: "While shepherds washed their socks by night."

—MARGARET HORNER, *Washington, D.C.*
NEA Journal

319. My son had been having trouble with his grammar studies in school. For several weeks we worked at night on the three degrees of adjectives and adverbs. After patiently emphasizing that the comparative degree was stronger and that the superlative was strongest, I dictated a list of words to compare, which included the adjective "high."

On his tablet I was amazed to find: "Positive degree—Hi. Comparative degree—Hello. Superlative degree—How do you do?"

—ERNEST BLEVINS, *Your Life*

320. His homework's done to radio,
TV, and records' riot ...
I wonder that his thoughts can flow
In school, where it's so quiet!

—MARIE DAERR

321. Mother was telling her small son about the good times she had when she was a little girl—riding a pony, sliding down a haystack, and wading in a brook.

"Mother," he said at last, with a sigh, "I wish I'd met you earlier!"

322. Nephew Buddy Smith adamantly refused a nicely browned slice of toast with the comment, "I don't want dirty bread, I want clean bread."

—M. DALE BAUGHMAN

323. No parent should spend all his time in the garden of a child's life digging up weeds; there is always the danger of scratching out flowers not yet above the ground.

324. A report from a scientific conference is headlined "Daily Noise Level Reaching Danger Point." Exactly what we told the kids last night while trying to read the evening paper.

—*Changing Times*

325. One parent we know thinks it only fair to apply a withholding tax to the youngster's allowance just so the younger generation can get gradually accustomed to a procedure to which adults are now hardened.

—Christian Science Monitor

326. A mother's heart leaped up when she heard her non-intellectual son whistling Mendelssohn's "Spring Song" as he did his nightly minimum of homework. "Where," she asked eagerly, "did you learn that music?"

"Oh, that? That," replied the lad, "is what they play on TV when somebody gets bopped on the head."

—Mrs. Dean Binder, Catholic Digest

327. "My, what a sweet-looking little fellow," cooed the lady artist; "would you like me to paint you?"

"I guess I wouldn't mind," the youngster replied, "but I don't think my ma would like it cause she'd have to get it off."

—Sunshine Magazine

328. Mother heard a big noise on the back porch where the small boy was playing.

"What are you doing out there?" she asked.

"Nothing," came the reply.

"What are you doing it with?" she continued.

"With the hammer," was the answer.

—Clinton County News

329. A young father reached the ultimate the other night when he overheard himself yelling up the stairs: "O.K. This is the last time I'm going to tell you kids for the last time!"

—Bill Vaughan, NANA

330. After a hard day at the office, a man went home to his wife and cute little three-year old daughter.

"Have you a kiss for Daddy?" he asked.

"No."

"I'm ashamed of you! Your Daddy works hard all day to bring home some money, and you behave like that. Come on now, where's the kiss?"

Looking him right in the eye, the three-year-old said, "Where's the money?"

331. Harry, a bright youngster, was told by his mother that she would give him ten cents for every dozen pins he rescued from the floor, thus preventing her one-year-old babe, who was just beginning to crawl, from finding them.

"What will you do with the money when you earn it, Harry?" he was asked by a neighbor.

"With the first ten cents," said Harry promptly, "I'll buy a paper of pins and scatter them all over the house!"

—*Sunshine Magazine*

332. After his return from church one Sunday a small boy said, "You know what, Mommie? I'm going to be a minister when I grow up."

"That's fine," said his mother. "But what made you decide you want to be a preacher?"

"Well," said the boy pensively, "I'll have to go to church on Sunday anyway, and I think it would be more fun to stand up and yell than to sit still and listen.'

—*Sunshine Magazine*

333. A small boy asked his father the meaning of the word "transatlantic" and was told that it meant "across the Atlantic."

"Well, does 'trans' always mean across?" asked the boy.

"Yes," replied Father, sharply.

"Then," said the small boy meekly, "I suppose 'transparent' means a cross parent."

334. A young English lad, tired of being reminded by his father of his poor grades, put this ad in a Lancashire newspaper: "Will anyone who went to school with my father in 1923 please tell me what kind of scholar he was?"

—*Indiana Teacher*

335. It's a story told by Ford Wilson of Zion. During one of the first services in the sanctuary of the new Bonnie Brook Baptist church in Waukegan, a collection was taken for "aisle runners" to carpet the church aisles.

Upon arrival home afterward, an 11-year-old son of one of the ushers queried, "Mom, how much money did Dad get in the collection?"

The astonished mother answered, "Why, your father got none of the money—it was for aisle runners!"

"But isn't Dad an aisle runner?" asked the boy.

—*Chicago Tribune*

336. "Every parent knows that children can instantly sense the different emotional overtones between 'I have to play with you' and 'I want to play with you,'" psychiatrist Lena Levine told me.

"If a father spends only two hours a week with his children, but gives fully of his love and interest during that time it is better than twenty hours grudgingly yielded."

—NORMAN M. LOBSENZ, "The Growing Pressure of Young Fathers," *Redbook*

College

337. Ad in the *Washington Post and Times Herald*: "Officer, Army (retired), who worked way through college washing dishes, finds it necessary to work daughter's way through college and wishes to try some other field."

338. Asked Frank Meadows how his boy's getting along at the state university, where he's a freshman in business administration. "Fine, I guess," Frank replied. "He's quit asking me for money. Now he just bills me."

339. I find that the three major administrative problems on a campus are sex for the students, athletics for the alumni, and parking for the faculty.

—CLARK KERR, University of California
Education Digest

340. *Sally:* "So you graduated from barber college. What was your college yell?"

Jim: "Cut his lip; cut his jaw; leave his face Raw! Raw! Raw!"

—*The Lookout*

341. Big organizations are holding out their richest rewards— their best jobs—to the college trained. The little group that Vance Packard calls the diploma elite. It will pay you well to crowd into that group.

342. From a Northwestern University release: "There will be a meeting today of all students interested in playing golf, tennis, badminton and field hockey in room 124 in McGraw Hall."

Must get awfully crowded at times.

—T. O. WHITE

343. Ed Graham, advertising genius, went to Dartmouth with a writing career in mind. He flunked his first freshman theme but sent it to *Saturday Evening Post* who bought it for $50.

This brought him some fame on campus; his next theme brought an A from his professor with this note, "Sorry I can't give you $50."

It's your shot, but . . . Three?

344. Recently, the U. S. Office of Education declared colleges could handle an additional 60,000 live-in students or 250,000 day students if they used space efficiently. Some use only 35% of capacity. While no one expects every desk to be filled all the time, experts believe 60% of capacity is not unreasonable. Temple University has topped 80% without apparent loss of education quality. Traditionally, colleges run at half-speed in the afternoons and on Saturdays. Dr. Harold Stoke, president of Queens College, commented recently: "I know many campuses where a gunshot in the middle of the afternoon would not only hit no one; there would scarcely be anyone about to hear it."

—ED KIESTER, *Parade*

345. A man wouldn't choose a home by moonlight but he often lets his son choose a college with no more illumination than that.

346. Salesman stranded in my home town asked if there was a movie; no, no pool room or bowling alley.

"What form of amusement do you have here?"
"There is a freshman home from the university."

347. Laurence Lafore is a professor at Swarthmore College. He prohibits his students to use any of the following words in their papers: area (except in a geographical sense), concept, correlate, data, dichotomy, effectuate, factor, feel (for believe), framework (except in buildings), frame of reference, in terms of, level, meaningful, norm, orientate, pragmatic, program, schema, structure (as a verb), and oriented, preceded by any word.

348. With the growing avalanche of college applications, this joke, purportedly based on a true incident, gets dusted off.

An honest father wrote to the dean at a women's college, objectively appraising his daughter's qualifications. "While she is not an outstanding leader," he admitted, "she does follow well."

Back came the dean's reply: "We have already admitted 267 leaders to this year's freshman class and desperately need your daughter since she is the only follower."

—*Changing Times*

349. While I was a student at Washington and Jefferson, I went into the room of a classmate one day, and there, above his desk, was tacked a simple, hand-lettered sign: 'I am third.' I said to him, 'Bill, I know you play baseball, but I don't understand what you mean by that sign.' But Bill wouldn't tell me what he meant. All through college that sign stayed above his desk, and he never told me why. Then, just before he was graduated, I asked him again, and this is what he said:

"When I left home, my mother told me always to remember that God is first, others are second, and I am third. I was afraid I wouldn't remember, so I made that little sign and tacked it up.' I am sure Bill was the only one in college to whom that sign did apply—he always followed its teachings."

—Captain Maurice M. Witherspoon
Sunshine Magazine

350. College never hurt a man—unless, of course, he happened to be the student's father....

—*Laugh Book*

351. Over in the Registrar's office they were busy compiling statistics about student religious preferences. They found the usual number of Methodists, Lutherans, Catholics, etc., listed under "Church Preference." But a neatly lettered card filled in by an architecture major really stopped them. His Church Preference was "Gothic."

—Pelican

352. A sign on the cigaret machine in Detroit's Wayne University Student Center lobby reads: "Freshmen are forbidden to buy thinking men's cigarets before they have taken mid-semester exams."

—Laugh Book

353. "May I give you one piece of advice, Sir?" asked Pres. Robert E. Lee of a Washington College faculty member who tended to be harsh with struggling students and hasty in giving them low or failing grades. "Well, Sir," he said, "always observe the stage driver's rule: Take care of the poor horses."

—CLARENCE EDWIN FLYNN, "Survival in Learning," *American Mercury*

354. Once, before a college audience, Bill Tuttle arose to extol the virtues of higher education. "As you may know, I went to Bradley," began Tuttle, "and I've always been grateful for the opportunity. They learnt me a lot there." When the uproar had died down, Bed (Leavitt Leo) Daley (baseball player) arose. "I didn't go to college," he said, "and after listening to Bill Tuttle, I'm glad that's one thing I missed."

—Excerpts from the article, "The Pork Chop All-Star," as printed by permission of *Sports Illustrated*

355. A stranger mistook an insane asylum for a college. Realizing his mistake, he said to a guard: "I suppose after all there isn't much difference between them."

"Oh, yes, there is," replied the guard. "In this place, you've got to show improvement before you can get out."

—Laugh Book

356. College reunions may be pretty much the same but the 50th reunion of a class may be different. That's when men and women are housed in the same dormitory.

357. Undismayed by her college marks one lass wrote in the blank space on the college application form calling for her class standing, "Top ¾."

358. "It is (the student's) privilege, I might say his duty, to walk out when a lecturer walks in and says in word or manner, 'Well, what can I bore you with today?'"

—Guy Stanton Ford, *Emory University Quarterly*

359. Bill Brown's daughter Betsy is going happily back for her junior year in college, with her student husband and a layette. "I can't figure how they'll support a baby," Bill groused last night. "I made careful study of the kids' income and expenses together last year, and my chart on them proves conclusively that they starved to death about Christmas."

—*Better Homes and Gardens*

360. Did you hear about the newly rich mother who upon looking up the best schools in the East for her daughters declared she wanted them to be well macadamized?

361. The Ozark mountain daughter was sent away for the first time to a fancy Eastern college. After a few months she wrote her mother: "Mother, I made the pep squad and I need $5 for pep pants." In a short time her mother's letter arrived and said: "Here is the $5 for your pep pants, and another $5. Please send your father a pair."

—Frances Benson

362. *Graduate*: "Professor, I have made some money and I want to do something for my old college. I don't remember what studies I excelled in."

Professor: "In my classes you slept most of the time."

Graduate: "Fine! I'll build a dormitory."

—*The Lookout*

363. One father had heard this spot announcement on TV, "When your child is ready for college, will college be ready for him?" so many times that he became concerned about the academic seriousness of his seven-year-old son who he hopes will go to college some day. He told his son how important it is to study in the second grade and get ready for college.

Several days later the mother overheard this conversation between her son and his neighbor playmate: "My daddy says I must study hard in school and get a good education so I can go to college. He didn't go to college and he has an awful time paying his bills."

"Oh, heck," said his playmate disdainfully, "don't pay any attention to that. My daddy went to college and he has a hard time paying his bills, too!"

—MARIE FRASER, *Indiana Teacher*

364. The Denver Extension Center of the University of Colorado offers a course in a neglected subject—"Common Sense."

365.   College English as it were,
Has qualified me very well
Ten munce ago I couldn't spel,
Now I am an editer.

—EVERETT J. LANDERS
Newark, New Jersey News

366. Two college presidents were comparing experiences. "When I retire," declared one, "I would like to be superintendent of an orphan asylum. Then I wouldn't get letters from parents."

"That's not a bad ambition," replied the other, "but when I retire I want to be a warden of a penitentiary—the alumni never willingly come back to visit."

—*Wisconsin Journal of Education*

367. A young man who had just received his degree from college rushed out and exclaimed, "Here I am, World—I have my A.B.!"

The World replied, "Sit down, son, and I'll teach you the rest of the alphabet."

368. A college education is supposed to fit you for a position— not entitle you to one.

College Professor

369. The child of an English professor rushed into the room, reports NBC-TV's Johnny Carson, shouting, "Daddy, the baby has fell out of the window." The professor replied: " 'Fallen,' you mean. Quick, run for the doctor."

—T. O. WHITE

370. A group of professional men had gathered in the lobby of a hotel where a banquet was being given, and they proceeded to make themselves known to each other.

"My name is Rodale," said one, extending his hand. "I'm a painter, work in water colors, chiefly."

"I'm particularly happy to know you," replied the other. "I'm an artist, too. I work in bronze."

"Now, isn't that a coincidence?" chimed in a third. "I happen to be a sculptor, I work in marble."

Then a quiet fellow, bespectacled and with a short beard, who had been inclined to keep apart, stepped up and extended his hand. "Glad to make the acquaintance of you gentlemen," he said, "for I have a common interest with you. I work in ivory. I'm a college professor."

—*The Bronze*

371. Advice to new college faculty member: "You're likely to be nervous at first, but don't let it upset you. I, too, was frustrated, bewildered, and subdued. It works like this, so don't worry: The first year you're on the staff, you will ask yourself 'what am I doing here?' After a while you will have another question, 'what are the rest of 'em doing here?' "

372.
Now here, it seems, we have a prof
Who is a bit inclined to scoff,
A man of erudition vast
Who's also an iconoclast.

He says, while peering through his glasses,
That students ought to cut more classes,
He seems in earnest, sounds devoted,
And knows darned well that he'll be quoted.

Yes, Students, if they would succeed,
Should simply get a book and read,
Not waste their time, or think they're working,
With lectures long and dull and irking.

Professor, you are quite a card,
Held high in popular regard.
We'll think of you, with some enjoyment,
When you are looking for employment.

—*Quote*

373. It should be the chief aim of a university professor to exhibit himself in his own true character—that is, an ignorant man thinking, actively utilizing his small share of knowledge.

—ALFRED NORTH WHITEHEAD

374. A theory is better than money in the bank. You can't get ahead in this profession unless you publish a theory—any theory.
—ANDREW HALPIN, *Administrative Theory in Education*

375. The professor returned to his classroom after grading all the latest examination papers. He requested that the students sit down.

"If you all stood up now, it is conceivable that you might form a circle—in which case I could be arrested for maintaining a dope ring."
—*Santa Fe Magazine*

376. *Dinner guest:* "Will you pass the nuts, professor?"
Absent-minded professor: "I suppose so, but they should flunk."
—*The Lookout*

377. "So you use three pairs of glasses, Professor?"
"Yes, one pair for long sight, one pair for short sight, and the third to look for the other two."
—*The Lookout*

378. The professor at a small college was trying to obtain a raise but the local farmers on the committee were solidly against it. They couldn't understand why the college should pay him more for just talking a few hours a week.

Then, a faculty representative spoke forth, "Gentlemen, a college professor is a little like a bull. It's not the amount of time he spends. It's the importance of what he does!"
—*Inspiration*

379. A professor of law once advised his students: "When you're fighting a case, if you have the facts on your side, hammer them into the jury. If you have the law on your side, hammer it into the judge."

"But, sir, what if you have neither the facts nor the law?" inquired one student.

"Then," answered the professor, "hammer the table!"

380. In today's economy more than one college professor has one big financial problem—running out of money before running out of month.
—T. O. WHITE

381. *News Item*—The dean of women at an Eastern college told the student body "the president and I have decided to stop necking on the campus." (And it's about time, too.)

382. *Professor of English to a sophomore student:* "Your vocabulary is mean and impoverished, but entirely adequate to express your thoughts."

—*Kreolite News*

383. The professor approached the men's hat area of a bargain basement in Chicago. There were three tables of unboxed sub-perfect pieces of headgear in complete disarray. A variety of would-be customers were putting on, taking off the bargain priced hats.

Finally, the professor's eye fell on a few he decided to try on for size. First at one table, then the other, he tried hats which were too small. All at once the ludicrous thought occurred to him, "What if I left my own hat on a table and someone buys it." Frantically, he tried to recall where he had placed it. When he finally remembered the depositary, sure enough, there it was being tried on along with the others. He retrieved it before it was sold. I know, because I was the professor.

If only I had bought my own hat I could have then been called an absolutely absent-minded professor.

—M. Dale Baughman

384. A pretty girl after applying for a secretary's position was asked by the professor what her special strengths had been in previous positions. She quickly and confidently announced, "I had a story published by *True Confessions* and I won some puzzle contests."

"You must be very proud," the professor complimented, "but I'm looking for a girl who will use her brain power during office hours."

"This *was* during office hours," triumphantly explained the applicant.

385. A young profesor of economics at the University of Illinois met his class in Labor Management for the first time in September. Observing an unusually large number of young ladies in the class, he remarked without thinking, "It's nice to see so many young women in Labor."

—M. Dale Baughman

386. Policeman (to bespectacled fat professor who has witnessed smash): "You say you saw the accident, sir. What was the number of the car that knocked this man down?"

Professor Matteossian: "I'm afraid I've forgotten it. But I remember noticing that if it were multipled by itself, the cube root of the product would be equal to the sum of the digits reversed."

—*Pathfinder*

387. The chemistry professor was giving a demonstration of the properties of various acids. "Now, I am going to drop this silver dollar into this glass of acid. Will it disolve?"

A student in the rear promptly answered, "No, sir."

"No?" queried the professor with a glint in his eye. "Perhaps the young man will explain to the class why the silver dollar won't dissolve."

The young student arose to his full length, and said, "Because if it would, the professor would not have dropped it in."

—*Rotary News*, Oak Hill, West Virginia

388. The professor's car broke down and he drove into the local garage for repairs. "I hope you'll charge a fair price," he said to the garage owner. "I'm just a poor college professor." "I know," was the answer. "I've heard you lecture."

389. *Definition of an associate dean:* the only man in the college who will associate with the Dean.

390. *Professor:* "Too bad. One of my pupils to whom I have given two courses of instruction in the cultivation of the memory has forgotten to pay me, and, worst of it is, I can't think of his name."

391. *Dean:* "Why do you ask for a raise?"

Assistant Professor: "Well, sir, I wouldn't ask for a raise, but somehow my kids found out that other families eat three times a day."

392. Summoned to the accounting office, the returned, traveling college professor was confronted by the comptroller: "This expense account amazes us. How do you manage to spend $14 a day for food for yourself?"

"I manage," came the reply, "by skipping breakfast."

College Student

393. *Chemistry Professor:* "What can you tell about nitrates?"

Student: "Well—er—they're a lot cheaper than day rates."

The ball players can't get much taller—the faucets are as high as they can go.

394. Many college students who demand a front seat in the bus try to even things up by taking a back seat in the classroom.

395. A carpenter's son was filling out applications for college admission. When he came to the line "length of residence in home town" he answered "about 40 feet."

396. Overheard on a New York Central train, college girl to middle-aged man: "Oh, some discussion groups are all right, but, honestly, how can you discuss history?"

397. *Professor:* "Jones, can you tell me who built the Sphinx?"
Student: "I-I-I did know, sir, but I've forgotten."
Professor: "Great guns, what a calamity! The only man living who knows, and he has forgotten!"

398. Nothing irks the hard-pressed college students more than shaking out an envelope from home and finding nothing in it but news and love.

399. A young college student wrote home to his family:
"Dear Mom and Dad: I haven't heard from you in nearly a month. Please send a check so I'll know you're all right."
—Rotary Realist, LaSalle, Illinois

400. *Joe:* "That college turns out some great men."
Bill: "When did you graduate?"
Joe: "I didn't graduate. I was turned out."
—The Lookout

401. *Mother of boy at Rice University:* "My son's letters always send me to the dictionary."
Mother of boy at University of Houston: "My son's letters always send me to the bank."
—Laugh Book

402. *Eavesdropping Around the Campus:* In the coffee shop—
"Let's cut philosophy class today." "Can't. I need sleep."

403. "Your school is not a seminary, it's a match factory," said the smart young college man to the girl student.
"You're right," said the girl. "We furnish the heads and get the sticks from the men's colleges."
—The Continent (Chicago)

404. From an alumnus' report on an interview with a girl applicant: "She is at present very much of a young lady. However, she might adapt herself to our college community very well."

405. *Friend:* "You look all broken up. What's the matter?"
College student: "I wrote home for money for a study lamp."
Friend: "So what?"
College student: "They sent the lamp."
—Laugh Book

406. A college boy sent a telegram home saying "Mom! Have failed everything . . . prepare Pop."
The reply came the next day, "Pop prepared . . . prepare yourself."

407. *Music Professor:* "What do you think of Kreisler?"
Student: "Great! Splendid! Swell pickup, a lot of pep, and twenty miles on a gallon!"

408. When a student at Hailebury College was asked to specify where elephants are found, he replied, "Owing to their enormous size, they rarely are lost."

409. And there was the girl graduate who sighed, "Four years in college, and whom has it got me?"

—*Inspiration*

410. A coed, looking over the rack of assorted greeting cards, finally found one with plenty of sentiment. The message was, "To the only one I ever loved."
She approached the clerk and announced, "I'll take ten of them."

411. At a northern Minnesota college a strapping, healthy looking girl appeared to register for a course in English.
The recording clerk asked, "Have you a hobby?" The girl replied, "No, Ay ban single."

Commencement

412. The year that I was one of two teachers in a two-teacher rural Alabama school we planned a real commencement program for our eighth graders, with stage, speaker and all the decorations. The county superintendent delivered the address and I nodded to the pianist to start the recessional. She hesitated, looked at me in wonderment and started to play only after I had nodded my head vigorously the third time. They all marched out beautifully and I stood there full of pride when all at once I felt a tug at my coat. There was the runtiest eighth grader of all and he was still sitting there. He had not marched out with the rest. In a bewildered tone, he asked, "Ain't we gonna' get our diplomers, Mr. Hadley?"
In the excitement, of supervising my first graduation exercises, I forgot to distribute the diplomas. The pupils marched back in, received their diplomas and all was well.

—WILLIAM HADLEY, Superintendent of
Glen Ellyn Schools, Illinois

413. Just before graduation exercises were to get under way a commencement speaker sat down on a newly painted bench just before he was to speak. He turned disaster into triumph, however, by opening his remarks with "I had hoped to bring you an unvarnished tale this day, but fate decreed otherwise."

Graduating class, the main thing is thoroughness . . . Never leave a job unfinished.

Committee

414. One of the most cogent reasons yet enumerated for regular attendance at committee meetings comes from a young matron of our acquaintance, who was asked to serve on a School Library Committee. She agreed to do so, but explained that she would be unable to attend the initial meeting. The next letter she received from the group began, "Dear Chairman..."

415. "And now," the chairman said, "I would like to notify the members of the volunteer committee of their appointment."

—Food Marketing in New England

416. Committee work is like a soft chair—easy to get into but hard to get out of.

—KENNETH J. SHIVLEY

Communication

417. You and I broadcast every day, not knowing how many receivers we reach.

418. Communication is a process of sharing experience till it becomes a common possession. It modifies the disposition of both parties who partake in it.

—JOHN DEWEY

419. As one enlarges his capacity to make himself understood, he opens to that extent his opportunities for usefulness.

It is an ability without which it is difficult to succeed.

—OWEN D. YOUNG

420. When persons get out of communication with others, when they cannot freely communicate, they develop prejudices, suffer ill-health, run away and hide, or want to hit somebody. Their experiences enslave them instead of setting them free. It is interesting that therapy for the mentally ill is designed to help them learn new ways of freely associating with others. A well person can put himself in the other fellow's shoes. He can, in short, communicate with him.

—EDGAR DALE, *The News Letter*

421. Effective communication with the consumer of research remains a difficult problem, as Mr. Clymer indicates. Researchers develop special interests and tend to become language-bound. Fortunately, the situation in education is not quite so difficult as that reported by F. F. Colton in an article for the September, 1949, *Scientific Monthly* titled "Some of My Best Friends are Scientists." Mr. Colton wrote:

"A New York plumber of foreign extraction with a limited command of English wrote the National Bureau of Standards and said he found that hydrochloric acid quickly opened drainage pipes when they got clogged and asked if it was a good thing to use.

A Bureau scientist replied:

"The efficacy of hydrochloric acid is indisputable, but the corrosive residue is incompatible with metallic permanence."

The plumber wrote back thanking the Bureau for telling him the method was all right. The scientist was a little disturbed and showed the correspondence to his boss, another scientist. The latter wrote the plumber:

"We cannot assume responsibility for the production of toxic and noxious residue with hydrochloric acid and suggest you use an alternative procedure."

The plumber wrote back that he agreed with the Bureau—hydrochloric acid works fine. A top scientist—boss of the first two—broke the impasse by tearing himself loose from technical terminology and writing this letter:

"Don't use hydrochloric acid. It eats hell out of the pipes."

—As quoted by Mr. Clymer

422. When we are understood, it is proof that we speak well; and all your learned gabble is mere nonsense.

—MOLIERE

423. When two people talk to each other, a good deal of what is said is never heard. Too many people forget they must compete with the inner voice of the person they're addressing. To really be understood, we must learn to handle the emotional aspects of communication.

—DR. JESSE S. NIRENBERG, *Sales Management*

424. If we as communicators don't watch our P's and Q's someone will compile a glossary of communicationese, with such listings as:

2-way communications—standing in the middle of the week looking both ways for Sunday.

Feedback—vomiting unsavory or unpalatable ideas.

Committee report—a thousand words about nothing.

—C.M.B., *Journal of Communication*

425. The communication is too long. Brevity is not only the soul of wit; it is also the essence of good communication. The long-winded speaker doesn't realize that his speech didn't get across. He should have quit when he was ahead, but he added more and more and more. As a short speech it would have been a dandy; as a long speech it was a bore. The poor speaker quits when he is tired. The good speaker quits just before the audience gets tired. Turn off the flow of words when their cups are full.

No one can say just how long a message should be, but you rarely hear complaints about a speech being too short. The amateur worries about what he is going to put in his speech or article. The expert worries about what he should take out. An artistic performance is concentrated, has a central focus. Lincoln spoke for less than two minutes at Gettysburg but his message still tugs at the heart.

—EDGAR DALE, *The News Letter*

426. The role of communication has become a popular subject in recent times and it is an important factor in dissolving impasses. The inability to communicate effectively is high on the list of causes of sustained crisis.

—GEORGE BENNETT, *Partners*

427. Some years ago I heard a radio authority picturing the prospects of television, frequency modulation and other features we now enjoy. Yet as I listened I could not but remember what Henry Thoreau cynically said when he learned of the laying of the Atlantic cable. His caustic comment: "Yes, it's wonderful, but probably the first news that comes over will be that Princess Adelaide has the whooping cough." Our means of communication do sometimes seem to improve faster than what we have to say over them.

—DR. RALPH W. SOCKMAN, *Quote*

Competition

428. Never malign your competitors. If it weren't for them you'd be either self-satisfied or broke. They keep you alert to your faults and aware of your mistakes. They force you to do continually better work at lower cost. They serve as efficiency experts and charge you no fee. They're your friends in disguise. Don't curse them. Thank them—and show your gratitude by giving them even more to sweat about than they give you.

—*S F C Spotlight*

429. The only competition worthy of a wise man is with himself.

—W. ALLSTON, *Lutheran Digest*

Concentration

430. "I suppose," said the man to the boy applying for a job, "you have a host of schemes and employments of your own that will be a great deal more important than anything here. You are interested in ball games and ..." The boy replied promptly, "Yes, sir, I like ball first rate; and I play it for all I'm worth. But when I am here, I'll be all here. I ain't big enough to divide."

—*Moody Monthly*

431. Fifteen minutes a day devoted to one definite study will make one a master in a dozen years.

—EDWARD HOWARD GRIGGS, *Odd Moments*

Conservation

432. Suppose one day we took an axe and cut the parlor wall,
Then tore up Mother's potted plants and wrecked them, roots and all;
Then threw a lot of paper trash and food scraps on the floor—
Why—we would simply treat our homes as some folks treat outdoors!

Suppose we took a knife and carved initials on the chairs,
Then broke a window-pane or two and said, "Nobody cares!"
Or tossed around banana peels, tin cans and apple cores,
Why, we would simply treat our homes as some folks treat outdoors!

But outdoors is a lovely place, so pretty and so bright,
With grass and flowers and brooks and trees; folks ought to treat them right.
So when a call to camping trip, or jolly picnic comes,
Suppose we try to treat outdoors as we would treat our homes!

—*St. Nicholas*

433. As secretary for a soil conservation program, it was my job to compose and mimeograph the programs for our annual banquet. Deciding on a before-and-after gimmick for the program cover, I selected two pictures. One depicted a pitiful-looking cow standing on scrawny legs in a patch of eroding land; the other portrayed, in a field of verdant clover, a paragon of bovine perfection. I traced these side by side on my stencil and lettered below them the slogan, "Conservation Makes the Difference."

I felt sure my artistic effort would remind every farmer at the banquet the proper land use could perform miracles. Still, I was hardly prepared for the stir my cover page created. Program in hand and eyes a-twinkle, one landowner approached me with the query, "Is it really true that soil conservation can turn a cow into a bull?"

—ELIANA BEAM

Conventions

434. A dapper, middle-aged man sitting near me at the lunch counter observed my convention badge and asked, "Are you having a show?" Surprised by the question and not quite sure what he asked, I asked him to repeat his question. The second time he altered his question to "Are you attending a convention of some kind?" I answered, "Yes, I'm attending the American Association of Higher Education but it's no show, it's talks."

My chance acquaintance turned out to be the Director of the Midwest Beauty Show which attracted hundreds of beauty-care specialists to a multitude of demonstrations.

When he had gone it occurred to me that perhaps our educational conventions could have a little more "show" in them.

—M. DALE BAUGHMAN

435. Convention is a girdle which society wears with indifference and frequent discomfort.

—DOUGLAS MEADOR, *Matador Tribune*

436. As a veteran of the Convention Circuit we applaud with such energy as we are able to muster the ingenuity and enterprise of the Paint Industries Show in Cleveland. In connection with their 23rd annual exhibit the committee established what was termed a Pooped-People Parlor.

437. Convention: Where people pass a lot of resolutions but few bars.

—HAL COCHRAN, *NEA*

438. One superintendent declared that he was never going back to Atlantic City to a National meeting. "Why not?" asked a colleague, "It's a clean and friendly city."

"It sure is," came the sarcastic answer, "at my last convention there I was driving down main street, at high noon, and what do you think happened. I signaled for a left turn and some local citizen stole the olive right out of my martini."

439.   *Poem for Convention-goers*:
"Oh, 'tis easy to be gay and pleasant
With a lass and a glass and a song
But the man worth while
Is the man who can smile
When he takes his old lady along."

Conversation

440. The reason so few people are agreeable in conversation is that each is thinking more of what he is intending to say than of what others are saying, and we never listen when we are planning to speak.

—*Friendly Chat*

441. "Discreetly keep most of your radical opinions to yourself," once advised the lamented Grenville Kleiser. "When with people, be a listener a large part of the time. Be considerate in every word and act, and resist the tendency to say clever things. The best evidence of your culture is the tone and temper of your conversation."

—*Sunshine Magazine*

442. You can never hope to become a skilled conversationalist until you learn how to put your foot tactfully through the television set.

443. Good conversation like good champagne should sparkle and bubble at the brim.

—ASHLEY MONTAGUE, *House and Garden*

444. One secret of successful conversation is learning to disagree without being disagreeable. It isn't what but how you speak that makes all the difference. Ben Franklin used to remark diplomatically, "On this point, I agree. But on the other, if you don't mind, may I take exception?"

—JACK HARRISON POLLACK, Family Circle

Cooperation

445. The thing most needed in the United States is united notions.

446. John Ruskin: "When love and skill work together, expect a masterpiece."

—Friendly Chat

447. An old ferryman painted the word "Faith" on one oar and "Works" on the other. When asked the reason he explained: "To make a passage across the river you need both oars. See where 'Faith' without 'Works' takes us." The ferryman slipped one oar and turned with "Faith" only, and went around and around in a circle. Now let us try 'Works' without 'Faith.' We make just as little headway; and it is just the same in the journey of life."

—Wesleyan Methodist

Coordination

448. Definition: A coordinator is a guy who has a desk between two expediters.

449. There's need for better coordination when mother is sterilizing baby brother's bottle, while baby brother is eating the dirt out of the flower pot.

Courage

450. Remember you are your own doctor when it comes to curing cold feet.

—Brushware

451. Courage is a commodity that is never out of date.

452. A course should come to a beginning, not an end.

453. Too many people major in minors.

Courtesy

454. America can never be called an ill-mannered country. We pay more than ten million dollars every year in toll charges to add the word "please" to our telegrams.

455. The toughest problem some children face is that of learning good manners without seeing any.

456.   Hearts, like doors can ope' with ease
To very, very little keys
And don't forget that they are these:
"I thank you, sir" and "if you please."

—Author unknown

457. The man sitting in the street car addressed the woman standing before him:

"You must excuse my not giving you my seat—I'm a member of the Sit Still Club."

"Certainly, sir," the woman replied. "And please excuse my staring—I belong to the Stand and Stare Club.'

She proved it so well that the man at last sheepishly got to his feet.

"I guess, ma'am," he mumbled, "I'll resign from my club and join yours."

458. Horace had been properly taught to be polite and to say nice things to people.

At his first stag dance in junior high school he found himself struggling with a more than plump partner.

When his parents asked him how he enjoyed the evening, he was only half enthusiastic. After some prodding he finally admitted that he hadn't enjoyed his dance with the chubby miss. "But, dad," he hurried to explain. "I did say something nice to her."

"What was it, son?"

"I told her, 'You sweat less than any fat girl I ever danced with.' "

Creativity

459. The employment of analogy is creative and characteristic of the highly intelligent.

460. A more creative type of teaching could do much to remedy our nation's malady. As we all know from experience, too many of our teachers have been content merely to make us swallow the text book, and then cough it up.

—ALEX OSBORN, *The Creative Education Foundation*

461. Creativity lifts the monotony of the classroom into the exhilarating atmosphere of discovery and search.

462. In effect the brain is a sponge. Through absorption and retention we fill up the sponge; through judicial thinking and creative effort we "*squeeze* the sponge."

—RICHARD BUGELSKI University of Buffalo

463. You have to be an opportunist.

Consider Dorothy Mihlfred's problem, for example:

Outside her Magnolia School classroom windows, the track pullers were whanging and banging—creating more space for more traffic to make more common everyday noise.

Miss Mihlfred and her third graders considered the situation. Then they wrote a group poem and put it together like this:

Noise

I heard the noise outside!
Machine noise, loud noise,
Truck noise, hammering noise!
Headache-making noise, picking noise!
Drilling, rattling, bumping noise,
Shaking, banging, pounding noise,
And noise that makes me
Think of the dentist.

—Riverside City School Bulletin Board

464. The tragedy of life is not lack of brain power or education but doing so little with what we have.

—ROBERT P. CRAWFORD *The Techniques of Creative Thinking*

Criticism

465.   I have so many faults myself—
I seldom ever see

A defect in another's life
But what I see in me.
I make so many rash mistakes,
I feel condemned to find
A bit of fault in anyone
When I'm so far behind.

I used to censure everyone,
I was a Pharisee,
Until, quite unexpectedly,
I got a glimpse of me.
I tried to justify myself,
And frame some alibi,
But here I stood, caught by myself,
And I to me won't lie.

And now, whenever I'm inclined
Some others' judge to be,
I always go and take a look
At him whom I call "Me."
I find it is a splendid thing—
Just try it, and you'll see,
To keep from criticizing other folks
Let each "I" look at "Me."

—CALMER NEWLAND
Sunshine Magazine

466. Don't fear criticism. Ford forgot to put a reverse gear in his first automobile. Edison once spent $2,000,000 on an invention which proved of little value.

—*Friendly Chat*

467. Any fool can criticize. The man with a future is the one who can match his criticism with a cure.

—*The Lion*

468. If you are criticized, you have either done something worthwhile, or refrained from doing something foolish. So congratulations!

469. Criticism is the one thing most of us think is more blessed to give than to receive.

—*Society of Automotive Engineers Journal*

470. If criticism had any real power to harm, the skunk would be extinct by now.

—FRED ALLEN

471. Correcting faults is like tying a necktie; we can do it easier on ourselves than on anybody else.

—NCR Factory News

472. There are persons who constantly clamor. They complain of oppression, speculation, and pernicious influence of accumulated wealth. They cry out loudly against all banks and corporations and all means by which small capitalists become united in order to produce important and beneficial results. They carry on mad hostility against all established institutions. They would choke the fountain of industry and dry all streams. In a country of unbounded liberty, they clamor against oppression. In a country where property is more evenly divided than anywhere else, they rend the air shouting agrarian doctrines. In a country where wages of labor are high beyond parallel, they would teach the laborer he is but an oppressed slave. Sir, what can such men want? What do they mean? They mean nothing, Sir, but to enjoy the fruits of another man's labor.

—From a speech by Daniel Webster
in the U. S. Senate

473. I still firmly believe that criticism of the schools is a fine thing. In the first place, criticism is a hair shirt. It makes us scratch, keeps us from relaxing too comfortably on our laurels. Historian Arnold Toynbee's story of the North Sea fishermen illustrates the kind of thing I mean. Finding that too much of their catch was decaying before the ship could return to port, the fishermen installed sea water tanks to keep the fish alive; but that only substituted a new problem because, although now none of the catch perished, life was so easy for the fish that they became flabby, oily, and unpalatable. Then, the fishermen put into the tanks a few voracious cannibal fish and that paid off. True, some of the catch was eaten by the cannibals but the survivors became vigorous, healthy and very palatable. The critics are our cannibal fish.

—EARL HANSEN, Superintendent of Schools,
Rock Island, Illinois, "Don't Stop
Criticizing Us Teachers," Saturday
Evening Post

474.   "The stones that critics hurl with harsh intent
A man may use to build his monument."
—ARTHUR GUITERMAN

475. Heat hardens clay, but melts wax. It tempers steel but softens lead. The hot sun ripens fruit and grain, but withers and blasts the cut flowers and tender plants. Wintry blasts work havoc with summer annuals, but toughen the fiber of the mighty oaks. The difference in results is not with the external agent but with the inherent qualities of the receiving object.

Every person who attempts to do anything worthwhile has to learn to take criticism, constructive or otherwise. Often those who accomplish most in the long run come in for the most criticism.

Curiosity

476. An adult asks questions because he wants to do something with the answers; children ask questions and want to know just because they want to know.
—M. DALE BAUGHMAN

477. Progress travels on the sturdy back of the question mark. So long as men accepted the world as it was, it remained as it was. The individual who asks no questions rarely learns anything. Curiosity may have "killed a cat," but it has also created a generation of scientists.

One of the chief differences between the little businessman and the big one is the use which they make of the symbol for interrogation. The "small fry" in every vocation is more given to talking than to listening. He has much to say, but there is little which he cares to know. The big man has the questioning habit. He is always trying to learn something new.
—JOHN SCOTFORD, *Friendly Chat*

Curriculum

478. The Council for Basic Education, in Washington, has received the following definition of a "core curriculum" from a school superintendent, who says the author is unknown:

"A core curriculum is one in which the children bring apples to school and eat and plant the cores in the school grounds. They watch them sprout and grow into leaves and blossoms and then fruit. This is Science. They paste pieces of bark and twigs and leaves on paper and they paint pictures of the apples in a dish. This is Art.

"The children sit around under the trees singing 'In the Shade of the Old Apple Tree.' This is Music. The story of Johnny Appleseed is told them. This is Library Study. They climb up in the tree and pick the apples. This is Physical Education.

"They count the apples, 'taking away' the wormy ones. This is Arithmetic. In their own words, they tell what a tree is and what they felt when they saw the cores turn into trees. They also write letters to the National Apple Growers Association. This is Language Arts. The gifted children do enrichment research by reading Kilmer's 'Trees' or by finding out about Isaac Newton, the Apple of Discord, the Garden of Eden, William Tell and other apple-y events.

"They learn such words as arbor, l'arbre, apfel, baum, manzana. This is Foreign Languages.

"The boys build boxes to store the apples. This is Industrial Arts. And the girls bake them and sauce them and pie them. This is Homemaking. Then everyone eats them and learns about their nutritional value. This is Health Education.

"These activities have been performed without a textbook or a workbook.

"When all the apples are gone, they take the cores once again and plant them in the school grounds and watch them grow and flower and fruit. Pretty soon, you cannot see the school for the trees. This is called The End of Education."

—*New York Herald Tribune*

479. One morning of a spring-like day I spied a school-house by the way—the sort of school you seldom find—the little red, old fashioned kind. Upon the porch I chose to light, perchance to hear a class recite. But not a voice I heard intone; the only sound, a green-head's drone. I tiptoed close and gazed, intent. I saw each pupil closely bent above some lengths of tangled string, each striving to undo the thing. The master saw me watching there, and called me forward to a chair. "I wonder at this task," I said.

The master smiled and wagged his head. "I teach them how to read and spell, and names and dates and towns to tell. But once a week, from fall till spring, they practice at untangling string. No better labor can you find to breed a strong and patient mind. I

make them struggle with these strings, for life is mainly tangled
things."

—GEORGE L. KRESS, *Sunshine Magazine*

Decision

480. Did you hear about the parents who sent their young son
to camp to learn to make decisions of his own?
He did. The second day there he decided to come home.

481. "Do you have trouble making decisions?" asked the psychiatrist.
"Yes and no," came the reply from the couch.

482. Two farmers, working in a field, noticed a neighbor's barn
was on fire. One farmer wanted to rush over to aid the neighbor.
The other suggested, "Don't you think we'd better first ask him if
he wants the fire out?"

—LIDLEY J. STILES, Dean,
College of Education, University
of Wisconsin

483. Knute Rockne once told a newsman, "Give me a slow quarterback with fast decisions and we'll beat most teams around; give
me a fast one with that decisive ability and we'll beat them all."

—BILL ORMSBY, "Decisions . . . The
Thinking Man's Trouble," *Trained
Men*

484. Decision making is a lonely business, and the greater the
degree of responsibility, the more intense the loneliness.

—JACK C. STAEHLE

485. Edwin Markham wrote: "I will leave man to make the
fateful guess—will leave him torn between the 'no' and the 'yes'."

486. Writing in *Nation's Business*, April, 1956, Peter Drucker out-
lined four steps in decision making:
1. Define the problem
2. Define expectations
3. Develop alternative solutions
4. Know what to do with the decision after it is reached.
It occurred to me that school administrators who make as many

decisions as little league umpires can quite easily acquire great skill in applying the above steps merely by taking up the game of golf. It's difficult to say how many decisions a golfer makes in one round of 18 holes, but they must number in the hundreds. Here's one example: the object of swat lies there in the sand! The golfer *defines the problem*—how to remove the oval from its resting place to the cup according to the rules of the game; he then *defines his expectations*—to beat par or partner; he next *develops alternative solutions*—use the wedge and blast out or use another suitable instrument and pick the ball out delicately; finally, he must *know* what to do with the decision after it is reached—with confidence he blasts and surveys the results, knowing full well he followed the steps in decision making.

—M. DALE BAUGHMAN

487. Life is no corridor with only a single door opening out of the farther end. Unnumbered doors—some opening on the good, others on evil, and many on a puzzling mixture of both—open off the corridor all along the way.

—HAROLD A. BOSLEY, *Pulpit Digest*

488. It does not take much strength to do things, but it requires great strength to decide on what to do.

—*Friendly Chat*

Degree

489. "I hear Sam Tweedle turned down his divinity degree."
"Yeah, he didn't want to be called Tweedle, D.D."

—*Wall Street Journal*

490. I am surprised that in my later life I should have become so experienced in accepting honorary university degrees when, as a schoolboy, I was so bad at passing examinations. In fact, one might say that no one ever passed so few examinations and received so many degrees!

—WINSTON CHURCHILL

491. An Indian left the reservation to visit in New York City. He signed the Hotel register with an XX. The registration clerk asked, "What do the X's stand for?"
"The first X stands for Shooting Bull and the second for Ph.D."

Desire

492. Wise is the executive who can eliminate "ought" from his thinking about staff performance . . . unusually wise, the one who takes extra time and trouble to get a staff to "want" to do something.

—NORMAN G. SHIDLE, editorial,
Society of Automotive Engineers Journal

493. One hundred years ago it was figured that the average American had 70 wants. A similar survey taken recently showed his grandson had nearly 500 on his list.

—*Beveridge Paper Co. Newsletter*

494. If you don't get what you want, it is a sign either that you did not seriously want it, or that you tried to bargain over the price.

—RUDYARD KIPLING

Determination

495. Beware of what you set your mind on for that you will surely become.

—EMERSON

496. There is a big difference between a mere desire to do a thing, and a burning passion to do it—a determination to accomplish it at any cost. A mere desire is like warm water in a locomotive—it will never produce steam. It takes fire and force and enthusiasm to generate the things that propel the successful character.

—*Better Way*

497. Years ago new engineers in the lamp division of General Electric were assigned the impossible task, as a joke, of frosting bulbs on the inside. Each perspiring neophyte forgave the snickers greeting his failure. One day, however, Marvin Pipkin was initiated and he not only found a way to frost bulbs on the inside but developed an etching acid which gave minutely rounded pits instead of sharp depressions, thus materially strengthening each bulb. No one had told him it couldn't be done, and he took it so seriously that he did it.

—HARRY MCKOWN, *Fools and Foolishness*

498. No technique ever devised gets at that indefinable X called will power: the thing that's in you that makes you succeed with whatever intelligence, aptitudes, or even handicaps you might have.

499. There was once a man who was obsessed with the idea that there was a secret known to those who achieved success. To discover this secret he devoted years to study and research. Ancient Masonry, philosophy, astrology, psychology, salesmanship, religious beliefs, the various cults that have had their rise and fall—all these he studied long and diligently. Finally he gave his conclusion, and it came in two short words: "I will."

—Friendly Chat

500. A man asked his teen-aged son to explain where he was going with a pick, a shovel and a guitar.

"I'm going to see my girl," the lad said. "I promised to serenade her tonight."

"If that's the case," the father asked, "why are you taking a pick and shovel with you?"

"Because she wants me to serenade her under her window," the boy replied, "and she lives in a basement apartment."

—Wall Street Journal

501. Cato the Elder used to rise regularly in the Roman Senate to declare: "Carthage must be destroyed!" Partly because of this constant reiteration by a respected man, the ancient city eventually was leveled. That was determination in action.

If you will adopt your own slogan, will repeat it again and again and will act on the slogan, you can whet your skills and increase your capacity to become an executive in any field.

—LARSTON D. FARRAR, Partners

Discipline

502. The lad was dull at school you see; his dad took things to heart. He took the lad across his knee and there he made it smart.

503. Parents' discipline should be based on four F's: firmness, fondness, frankness, and fairness. Parents who cannot say no to a child often rear offspring who have contempt for authority. Parents who get too angry over minor infractions often fail to instill a sense of discipline in their children.

—ALEXANDER MARTIN, Survey Bulletin

504. At last we've discovered how to get the children to bed without arguments. Let them stay up as late as they want.

505. Experts have yet to find a system of raising children that will beat affectionate discipline.

—Sunshine Magazine

506. "We must remember, all of us, that children need and WANT discipline. They want to know what the right thing is to do and, given half a chance, they'll do it . . . Discipline, begun early and maintained, is a solution to hoodlumism. Surrendering the night is not one."

These are words from a letter to his colleagues by Herman L. Shibler, general superintendent, Indianapolis Public Schools, in which he refused to accede to requests for abandoning night football because of hoodlumism at the eighth annual Football Jamboree in Indianapolis a few years ago.

—Phi Delta Kappan

507. A child who has not been taught the meaning of the word "no" by the time he is 4 years old has spent 4 years in the academic school of crime.

—Survey Bulletin

508. Miss S. is a teacher who rang a bell with my friendship the day I stepped into her room. She was smiling and when the bell rang and the kids were seated, the sort of "rough-good-time boys" started talking and laughing it up. She stopped smiling, frowned, and set them down in their places with words so fast that they didn't recover for ten minutes. From that time on until now the classroom has been a place for learning as it should be, instead of a good community social hour. She didn't punish students but kept them busy, instead. She told them to do their work and they did.

—Wilmer A. Lamar, Teachers as Students See Them

509. An ex-wrestler, Mr. Hard Crust was a strong, violent-tempered man. He occasionally threw books at students, who were causing disturbances in his class. The books generally hit their mark. Once, he picked up two boys and knocked their heads together because they were talking.

—Wilmer A. Lamar, Teachers as Students See Them

510. When I first met this teacher, I was scared of her. I had been chewing gum when she came by my desk. She turned on her heel and pointed her finger at me and asked, "Are you chewing gum?" She scared me so badly that I swallowed the gum.
—WILMER A. LAMAR, *Teachers as Students See Them*

511. Undoubtedly, my seventh grade home room teacher was my most unforgettable. He was a very short and a very fat man. He was red-faced and bald-headed. When he went into one of his lengthy and frequent orations, he could be heard all over the entire school. As almost any of the students he had will tell you, the way they best remember him is after one of his lectures. His face would get fiery red and beads of sweat would rise from his forehead and roll down the side of his face. Then he would take out his handkerchief and mop off the sweat.
—WILMER A. LAMAR, *Teachers as Students See Them*

512. I had two teachers last year who never said a harsh word to anyone, yet the discipline in the classrooms were "under their little finger." In each case, the teachers were mannerly and respectful toward their students; therefore, the students were respectful toward the teachers. Both teachers had variety in their classes which made sitting and listening for an hour a pleasure.
—WILMER A. LAMAR, *Teachers as Students See Them*

513. Eight-year-old boy's description of his mother's punishment procedure: "After the storm comes a palm!"
—M. DALE BAUGHMAN

514. Control of discipline is like controlling a fire. If you catch it early, it is easy to handle.
—LLOYD W. WALLER, *California Journal of Secondary Education*

515. Andrew Manuel, who was county superintendent of schools in Brown County, Indiana from 1899 to 1903 was a rugged individualist and a self-made man. In build, appearance and temperament he might have passed for a twin brother of John L. Lewis. He had a lot of will power and self-determination.

Mr. Manuel related an incident which shows how parents may back up a teacher more than he realizes. Manuel said that he was teaching all grades at Christiansburg, Indiana; the enrollment was sixty, about 25 of whom were nearly young men and women, some as large in build as the teacher.

One day just after lunch the teacher decided that whispering had become a nuisance and should be stopped. He announced that there would be no more whispering and that the first one he caught at it would get a "whaling." Just before time to dismiss that evening he saw a young man whisper to a well-matured girl. He called the student by name and told him to remain after school. The boy asked why. He was told that it was because he had whispered. He readily admitted that he had whispered, but he pointed to the girl and said, "She whispered, too." One implicated another until fifteen young men and women admitted that they had violated the whispering rule.

Manuel thought it would be a man-sized job to "thresh" fifteen pupils in one afternoon so he decided to wait until next morning when he would feel fresh and sure of doing a good job. When he arrived at the school building next morning, Henry Anthony and Robert Wilson, parents of two of those to be punished, were already at the school building. Manuel assumed that they had come to defend their children. He greeted them very coldly and went about the business of preparing for the day and attempted to ignore the parents.

He opened school, weakened a little, and finally decided to wait until recess time to administer the punishment, hoping the parents would be gone by that time. However, they proved to be "stayers." At last he decided that he might as well get it over with. He sent out for four good healthy switches, and gave each one of the guilty fifteen a good "whaling" as promised.

By this time he had decided that he was in the proper frame of mind to talk to the parents. He stalked back to them with a set jaw, demanded, "And, men, just what is your business here today?" The spokesman answered, "Mr. Manuel, we heard you were going to 'thresh' fifteen of your pupils today. We came over to see if you had the nerve to do it. If you can't control our children, let us know and we will promptly take them in hand."

—GROVER G. BROWN, Retired
Superintendent of Brown County,
Indiana

516. You can bruise the human ego; you can bend it, you can fracture it. But as long as there is life, it will try to reassert itself . . . Don't constrict children and their world. Let them disagree.

Let them talk back once in a while. Let them show their animosity and get rid of the venom that is occasionally a part of the sweet sap of growing up.

—DR. PETER STEINCROHN,
Indianapolis Star

517. *Little Lad (between sobs)*: "It's not fair! It's not fair!"
Passerby: "What's not fair, little man?"
Little Lad: "Dad gave me a lickin'!"
Passerby: "Now you must not cry about it. All fathers sometimes must punish their children."
Lad: "But my dad plays the bass drum in the town band."

518. It is important that your pupils know what you stand for; it is equally important that they know what you won't stand for.

Discouragement

519. It is a healthy symptom when a man is dissatisfied without being discouraged.

520. There is a legend that Satan decided to get rid of a number of his tools, so he arranged an auction . . . There were envy, deceit, malice, sensuality, enmity, thoughtlessness and many other tools which Satan had used successfully (priced very low). One piece, marked very high, was labeled Discouragement.

"Why do you want so much for this tool?" asked one bidder.

"This tool," replied the old tempter, "has always been my most useful one. You can see it has had more wear than the rest. It is used as a wedge to get into a man's mind when all other means fail. Practically every human being has had this tool used on him, although very few know that I'm the one wielding it." . . . As it worked out, none could afford the price Satan demanded for Discouragement . . . so he is still using it.

—WILLIAM S. DEAL, *United Evangelical Action*

Duty

521. I slept, and dreamed that life was beauty; I wake, and found that life was duty.

—*Corrigenda*

522. A duty dodged is like a debt unpaid; it is only deferred and we must come back and settle the account at last.

—JOSEPH FORT NEWTON

523. "It doesn't matter what qualifications we have for a job, if we cannot be relied upon to do what needs to be done when it needs to be done," says Richard L. Evans.

—*Friendly Chat*

524. Yesterday I passed a building undergoing repairs. On one side workmen were removing large quantities of bricks which had crumbled away. Why, I mused, had some brick disintegrated and not others?

"Fifty years ago, when the building was erected," said the foreman, "there came a day when the laborers at the brickyard had trouble with one another. And now, long years after the failure of those men to work together for a single day, a moral is written in crumbling brick."

—*Friendly Chat*

525. It is seldom very hard to do one's duty when one knows what it is, but it is often exceedingly difficult to find this out.

—SAMUEL BUTLER, *Changing Times*

Education

526. Education, to be successful, must not only inform but *inspire.*

—T. SHARPER KNOWLSON, in *Originality*

527. Modern education does not give sufficient attention to individual tendencies. It is very difficult indeed to arrange any program that will remedy this defect. Boys and girls, and older students of both sexes, have to be dealt with in large groups and hitherto it has been found impossible to isolate individuals and detach a member of the staff to give them a special form of training. We regret we can offer no practicable scheme for relief. But the one aspect that concerns us here is this: we mercifully make special provisions for the crippled and the mentally defective—we make no such provision for the youth of talent.

In other words the weak get more attention than the strong.

—Anonymous

528. Education consists mainly in what we have unlearned.

—MARK TWAIN

Sure they both go . . . But one has to be pulled.

529. A good education consists in giving to the body and the soul all the beauty and all the perfection of which they are capable.

—PLATO

530. The regrettable weakness of an educational mystique which says to one child: "You by virtue of your genes and environment, are educable," and to another child, "And you by destiny's sin, are not," is simply that mortals are so very fallible.

531. Milk can be homogenized, but not children.

533. As far back as anybody can remember, most children learned exactly as much at school as they were compelled to.

—*Grit*

534. We must make people realize that success in business and in the professions is not geared to the lack of education. It is dependent on education! Abe Lincoln was not great because he was born in a cabin—but because he was able to get out of it.

—ELMER S. CROWLEY, *Idaho Education News*

535. Cumulative records are kept in most schools of the USSR. They are open to teacher, pupil, and parent. The ministries of Education fix the maximum amount of homework. One Soviet educator said: "The better the teacher, the less homework is required." He recommended no homework in the first grade; one hour and fifteen minutes for the middle grades; and four hours for the upper grades.

—Phi Delta Kappan

536. One of our correspondents sends us word of a fascinating 4-H Club program that took place recently in Riverton, Wyoming. The program was divided into two parts, the first half a talk and demonstration on whittling. The second half? "First Aid for Cuts."

537. People who complain that Americans spend more for alcohol than for education (says Teddy Randazzo) just don't realize how much you can learn at a cocktail party.

538. It's not our system against theirs (Russia). We have no real system but rather a variety of plans, perhaps more alike than different, for education.

539. I respect faith but doubt is what gets you an education.

—WILSON MIZNER, *Education Digest*

540. A child is being properly educated only when he is learning to become independent of his parents.

—ADMIRAL H. RICKOVER, *Phi Delta Kappan*

541. Palmer Hoyt, editor of the *Denver Post*, speaking before a lay group; "A number of people who ascribe to Dewey the so-called ills of present day public schools do not know whether it is Governor Dewey, John Dewey, or Admiral Dewey!"

—Phi Delta Kappan

542. As long as we pay Elvis Presley as much in one year as the combined salaries of the faculty members at a university, we're not going to solve the problems of American education.

—REPRESENTATIVE GEORGE S. McGOVERN

543. Education which is simply intellectual taxidermy—the scooping out of the mind and the stuffing in of facts—is worthless. The human mind is not a deep-freeze for storage but a forge for production; it must be supplied with fuel, fired, and properly shaped.

—WILLIAM A. DONAGHY, president, Holy
Cross University, Massachusetts

544. As any engineer knows, a structure may serve its intended purpose for many years, and inherent defects may not become apparent until the structure is subjected to unusual stresses and strains. It is my personal judgment that an analogous situation exists in our programs of organized education; they have served our needs very well until subjected to the stresses and strains of modern civilization. Now we are observing weaknesses of disquieting consequence.

—CARROLL V. NEWSON, president, New York
University, in Inaugural Address

545. Verbatim "howlers" from high-school students' college application folders collected by an admissions officer of an Eastern university:

One boy wrote: "You informed me you were sending me a copy of your catalogue. By some insight, it was never sent to me."

546. A philosophy of education cannot be crammed down people's throats; they must feel it to be true in the marrow of their bones and look with trust and approval upon the leaders who attempt to give it expression. It must catch and reflect their temper, not arouse their distemper.

—JOSEPH JUSTMAN, *School and Society*

547. Without ideals, without effort, without scholarship, without philosophical continuity, there is no such thing as education.

—ABRAHAM FLEXNER, *The Indiana Teacher*

548. To critics who have said that our schools are stressing quantity rather than quality, I wish to point out that with about 6% of the world's population, the U. S. has trained 21.6% of the winners in the 57-year history of the Nobel Prize awards.

—DR. LYMAN V. GINGER, President,
National Educational Association

549. America was discovered by a man trying to find a better way to go places. American education has been trying to do that ever since.

550. The object of the common school system is to give every child a free, straight, solid pathway by which he can walk directly up from the ignorance of the infant to a knowledge of the primary duties of a man and can acquire a power and an invincible will to discharge them.

—HORACE MANN, First Annual Report as
Secretary of Massachusetts School Board

551. The criticism and the answer: "Children don't learn as well as a generation ago."

They didn't then, either; and as we progress backward, generation by generation, what a super-intelligentsia our primordial progenitors must have been.

"Students avoid hard subjects."

Yes, the children of parents other than the critics.

"The high school diploma has lost its significance."

When we graduated from high school in 1913, it hadn't yet gained any significance for 90 per cent of our contemporaries.

"Schools are not properly preparing students for college."

A number of colleges have failed to prepare themselves for students.

"Modern schools cost too much."

So do refrigerators.

—*Idaho Education News*

552. There's only one thing that costs more than education today —the lack of it.

553. Education does not end in the afternoon; it does not end in the spring; it does not end. . . . until you do.

—M. DALE BAUGHMAN

554. Training is everything. The peach was once a bitter almond; cauliflower is nothing but cabbage with a college education.

—MARK TWAIN

555. In the process of education the teacher is a guide and a counselor. The real purpose is achieved when the student is inspired to find out things for himself. Reading is a basis in his intellectual progress, and books are his tools. The more they are comprehensible, the greater is his achievement. If he seeks them, knows how to use them, and let's them serve his needs, he has

acquired the essence of reading. A nation full of avid readers will
not become second-rate.

> —George Fisler, Adrian College, "Feeling the Need,"
> reprinted from the November 1958 issue of *Education*
> by special permission of the Bobbs-Merrill Co., Inc.,
> Indianapolis, Ind.

556. Real education belongs to the future; most of our education
is a form of tribal conditioning, a pilgrimage in routine and pre-
mature adjustment. When education stirs our innermost feelings
and loyalties, when it awakens us from the slumber of lethargy,
when it brings individuals together through understanding and
compassion, it becomes our foremost hope for lasting greatness.

> —Frederick Mayer, University of Redlands,
> "The Bases of Social Advancement," *Phi
> Delta Kappan*

557. The recruit had finished his physical and was being questioned by a sergeant, who asked: "Did you go to grammar school?"

"Yes, sir. I also went through high school, graduated cum laude
from college, completed three years of graduate studies, and then
received two years at Purdue, two at Vanderbilt, and two more at
Wabash."

The sergeant nodded, reached for a rubber stamp, and slapped
it on the questionnaire. It consisted of one word: "Literate."

> —*Rotary News*, Columbia, Tenn.

558. We want you (students) to come to the point where, in
every phase of your life, you will be able to make a moral and
responsible choice by asking, "What do I think?" rather than "What
does the book say?" or "What does the professor say?"

> —Dr. Alfred B. Bonds, Jr., president,
> Baldwin-Wallace College, at freshman
> convocation.

559. "Perhaps the most valuable of all education is the ability to
make yourself do the thing you have to do when it ought to be
done, whether you like it or not." Thus spoke Thomas Huxley, the
great scientist. That is a kind of education that comes from inside
us and very little from books or teachers. It is something that we
acquire from the example of good men and apply to our own actions as occasion arises. It is gumption at work.

> —*Sunshine Magazine*

560. Education is a controlling grace to the young, consolation
to the old, wealth to the poor, and ornament to the rich.

> —Diogenes

561. Teach the young to shoot craps? But does modern schooling really offer a course in gambling? A child said of the Ethical Culture School: "What I like best is Arts and Craps."

—Ethical Outlook

562.   "He who can learn to seek for facts
When facts there are to find,
And when opinions must be used,
Can keep an open mind,
Can feel respect, deep and sincere,
For those he differs from,
And yet can run full patiently
The path he entered on."

—Author Unknown

563. Whom, then, do I call educated? First, those who manage well the circumstances which they encounter day by day; and those who possess a judgment which is accurate in meeting occasions as they arise and rarely misses the expedient course of action.

Next, those who are honorable in their dealings with all men, bearing easily what is unpleasant or offensive in others, and being as reasonable to their associates as it is humanly possible.

Furthermore, those who hold their pleasures always under control, and are not unduly overcome by their misfortunes, bearing up under them bravely and in a manner worthy of our common nature.

Most important of all, those who are not spoiled by their successes, who do not desert their true selves, but hold their ground steadfastly as wise and sober-minded men, rejoicing no more in the good things that have come to them through chance than in those which through their own nature and intelligence are theirs since birth.

Those who have a character which is in accord, not with one of these things, but with all of them, these are educated—possessed of all the virtues.

—Sunshine Magazine

564. True education does not make all men alike. No human being worthy of the name is a common man; there is no magic and no virtue in commonness. Truth and virtue do not issue from undifferentiated mobs.

—Dr. Harold W. Dodds, president-emeritus,
Princeton University

565. At what age does a youngster really determine his future career? An outstanding farm scientist tells me he was 9 when he decided to become a chemist. A toy chemistry set aroused his interest. A survey among ornithologists showed that nearly all noted figures in this field were fascinated by bird studies at from 9 to 12 . . . I have an idea many of the more able young people know what they want to do even before they get to high school.
—WHEELER McMILLEN, *Farm Journal*

566. Learn to use your hands as well as your head, I am not belittling education. But the person educated entirely through books is only half educated. There is a kind of practical knowledge and good sense which can flow into the brain only through the use of the hands.
—WILLIAM S. KNUDSEN, quoted in *Wesleyan Methodist*

567. If the cost of a college education continues to snowball for many more years, a person can make a profit by remaining ignorant.
—*Grit*

568. A longer school day for Russian children is the latest Soviet educational experiment. Special grade schools will be established at which the pupils' day will be extended to conform to the working hours of their parents. Two meals a day will be served.
—*Education Summary*

569. What makes an educated man?
An educated man has been variously described.
One authority says Education is Modification of Behavior. Then the wag who chalked over the letters "Know Thyself" the words "Behave Yourself" might have a point.
Another says a man should be:
Literate and Articulate—
Informed and Curious as to the world of nature and the Diety—
Sensitive to Moral and Aesthetic values—
Able to see Relationship of man to man; past to present—
Oriented and Integrated.
There have been others. The process of bringing out what's in you. And the statement that college doesn't make fools, it develops them. All may be crude approaches to profound truth.
Studies of biography show that men who achieve usually have an aim—they sacrifice rest and pleasure and applause for that aim.

So Education seeks to give a man an aim; it seeks to get a man to think for himself, and to try for himself.

Salesmanagers say that a man who thinks he can't sell an article is usually right.

"If you say, my son, that it can't be done,
What you say, my son, is not true.
What you mean, my son, is it can be done,
Though it may not be done by you."

570. We so lead them to trust only the printed page. They are spared of the pain which accompanies that which they think out.

571. A lot of people are being scared by the Russians into hardening up our education or speeding it up. I am interested in toning it up.

—Robert Frost

572. Our own best schools are unsurpassed. We are confronted with the problem of how to spread the good practices of these best schools to all schools.

—Lawrence G. Derthick, U. S.
Education Commissioner

573. Unless Education promotes character making, unless it helps men to be more moral, juster to their fellows, more law-abiding, more discriminatingly patriotic and public spirited, it is not worth the trouble taken to furnish it.

—William Howard Taft

574. Thousands of high schools are doing a better job in many ways than ever before. Those that have been misled by *progressive education nonsense* are waking up and everywhere we see *work and discipline* coming back into elementary and secondary education. Right this minute the breast beaters and calamity howlers are saying that *right away-pronto*, they are going to be making Einsteins out of congenital dummies. It is to laugh. Hungry minded kids always become educated. Those who are born without their buttons will never be buttoned up anyway.

—Dr. Galen Starr Ross, president
Capitol College Oratory and Music
Columbus, Ohio

575. Education is man's going forward from cocksure ignorance to thoughtful uncertainty.

—Kenneth G. Johnson,
University of Wisconsin

576. Education by its nature is a slow, time-consuming process. Someone has said that where education is the only remedy, there can be no faster one. Here is the best answer we've found to the question, "How can I find time to take part in adult education?" There are 8,760 hours in a year. Work and sleep require about 5,000 hours. Allow 1,000 hours for dressing and eating. You have more than 2,500 hours left. Take half of that for recreation and you still have more hours a year than most college students use for classes and study.

—*Community Teamwork*, Adult Education
Newsletter, Purdue University

577. The man who graduates today and stops learning tomorrow is uneducated the day after.

—NEWTON D. BAKER, *Forbes*

578. A certain young man wanted to learn ballroom dancing. He went to a dancing school and took lessons. It so happened his instructor always started the lessons from a fireplace at one end of the studio.

After he finished the dancing course, the young man took a girl to a dance. But he couldn't dance. There wasn't a fireplace in the room!

How many of us go through life with that sort of education?

—*Quote*

579. Education is not to reform students or amuse them or to make them expert technicians. It is to unsettle their minds, widen their horizons, inflame their intellects, teach them to think straight, if possible.

—ROBERT M. HUTCHINS

580. A distinguished educator, when asked his opinion of the Midwest Airborne TV Project—which televises lessons from airplanes to 13,000 schools in six midwest states—made the following comment: "It's educational crop-dusting. You can't spray a mass audience with a subject."

—*Television Age*

581. The most important fact about America's educational system . . . is that it does not exist. What we have are 50 separate state systems of education, and over 50,000 school boards within those states which also set school policy. As a result, there is a vast diversity of educational standards, systems and facilities . . . and a vast diversity of educational problems and opinions on how to solve them.

It is generally conceded that the future of America—a future filled with fabulous opportunities—will be won or lost in our classroom.

—Saturday Review

582. It is possible to instruct a child in all the arts and sciences and at the same time neglect his education. To educate him means to lead him forth; to develop what is best in him; to lead him to the discovery of himself. To instruct him means to set up and arrange in order an array of facts within his mind. Instead of having the powers of his mind released the child is simply having his mind converted into a sort of filing case and filled with a more or less orderly assortment of facts and figures.

—S. S. MARQUIS

583. It is not what is poured into a student but what is planted that counts.

—JOEL HILDEBRAND, *Chemical Education*

584. The twin purposes of education—information and inspiration.

—SAY

585. Every man has two educations—that which is given to him, and the other, that which he gives to himself. Of the two kinds, the latter is by far the more valuable.

—JEAN PAUL RICHTER *Rosicrucian Digest*

586. Education is an admirable thing, but it is well to remember from time to time that nothing that is worth knowing can be taught.

—OSCAR WILDE

587. Vice Admiral Hyman G. Rickover, analyzing why Congress holds back on funds for education but spends billions for weapons: "If the Russians announced today they were going to send a man to hell, there would be at least two government agencies before the appropriations committee of Congress tomorrow, with their public-relations men, asking for money on the ground that we've got to get there first."

—*Quote*

588. A wagon is built that a load may be hauled, but it must have a body, a tongue, and four wheels, each of which performs a function and is necessary to the others. In like manner, the functions of the school comprise the vehicle for the realization of the school's purpose.

—Schools for a New World

589. Education fails unless the Three R's at one end of the school spectrum lead ultimately to the Four P's at the other—Preparation for Earning, Preparation for Living, Preparation for Understanding, Preparation for Participation in the problems involved in the making of a better world.

—NORMAN COUSINS, *Clearing House*

590. Spelling, punctuation and penmanship are not always mastered by school pupils. Letters from summer camp, according to some parents, bear a strong resemblance to ransom notes.

591. The bookkeeping student handed the teacher four neatly typed sheets with items and costs in their proper columns. She looked them over carefully. All was clear except one item which read ESP, $19.75. The puzzled teacher asked, "What does ESP mean?" "Error Some Place," the girl explained.

592. Real education must ultimately be limited to men who insist on knowing. The rest is mere sheepherding.

—Author Unknown

593. In the pursuit of quality in education people have tried faith, prayer, and old phonograph records. None has worked.

A few school districts are now trying *money* and they are achieving *remarkable* success.

—DR. PAUL MORT, in speech to APSS
representative in Mt. Eden, California

594. The great danger in public education today is that we have failed to see the difference between knowledge and wisdom. We train the head and let the heart run hog-wild. We allow culture and character to walk miles apart, stuffing the head with mathematics and languages—leaving manners and morals out of the picture.

—DR. THEO H. PALMQUIST, of Foundry
Methodist Church, Washington, in
vesper service talk opening annual
National PTA Congress

595. To my mind, there is a great story in education—a succession of stories. I think education is dramatic. It has everything in it to make it so; struggle, pathos, triumph, competition, good humor, and interesting people. Just as business needs more customers, education needs more enthusiasts. For my part I'll buy it, and what's more I'll bet we can sell the story.

—ERIC JOHNSTON, Address at Chicago
Regional AASA Convention

596. Quality education should aim to make better and more complete *men*—not better butchers or bakers and more complete bombmakers.

—HAROLD L. CLAPP, N.C.A. annual
meeting

597. Education should be as attractive as sin.

—DR. RICHARD E. MORLEY, *Partners*

598. A machine is a great moral educator. If a horse or a donkey will not go, men lose their tempers and beat it; if a machine will not go, there is no use beating it. You have to think and try till you find what is wrong. That is real education. The machine, furthermore, has made the present generation of average men more careful and conscientious than would have been thought possible in the Middle Ages. There are millions of engines, motors, and airplanes which are set going every day with human lives dependent on them. There are millions of workmen who, as a matter of course, look over these machines daily and see that their innumerable parts are in order. And we, the public, trust our lives to them without further thought, trusting that among all those workmen no one will have made any important mistake. That is a thing which should fill one with wonder.

—*Friendly Chat*

English

599. Tommy was asked the difference between prose and poetry. He pondered a while, then said, "There was a young man named Reeze, who went into a pond to his ankle. That's prose, but if the water had been a little deeper, it would have been poetry."

—*The Lookout*

600. *Mother (helping small son with his language lesson):* "What is a synonym?"

Small Son (smacking lips in pleasant memories): "Synonym is something you put in rolls."

601. *Teacher:* "Where's your pencil, Alfred?"
Alfred: "Ain't got one, teacher."
Teacher: "How many times have I told you not to say that? Listen: I haven't got one, you haven't got one, we haven't got one, they haven't got one—"
Alfred: "Well, gee whiz, teacher, where are all the pencils?"

602. During a study of verbs, the teacher read the sentence, "It was milking time," and then asked, "Johnny, what mood?"
Johnny: "The cow!"

603. My unreasonable facsimile, Burton Hillis, Jr., age 12, has again alienated his school teacher's affections. She asked him to name two pronouns, and he replied, "Who, me?" She punished him for being sassy before she realized his answer was correct.

—BURTON HILLIS, *Better Homes and Gardens*

604. The seventh grade was studying parts of speech and when they came to adverbs, the teacher explained, "I look lovely. Now lovely is an adverb."
One pupil piped up with "That's a supposition if ever I heard one."

—DEAN BERKLEY

605. Working with a grammar lesson, the teacher asked, "Willie, what is it when I say, 'I love you, you love me, he loves me?'"
Replied Willie, "That's one of those triangles where somebody gets shot."

—*Seng Fellowship News*

606. Two boys from different schools were discussing their progress in English. Their conversation went something like this:
"We're having the indicative mood and the abaltive absolution now. Ever had them?"
"Sure. We also had the subterranean conjection."
"That's nothing. We had the double genitive and the hysterical present."
"I'll bet you never had the passionate auxiliary."
"Sure did! We even had the spilled infinitive."
Suddenly a third boy, who was standing nearby, quietly spoke up. "At our school we have the extended recess. Ever have that?"

—*Scouting*

607. A favorite sport nowadays is to poke fun at the products of translating machines. For instance, a machine was supposed to put the English phrase "out of sight, out of mind" into another language and produced "invisible fairy." "The spirit is willing but the flesh is weak," when translated from English appeared as "the liquor is agreeable, but the meat is rotten." Things are getting so bad that I feel myself feeling sorry for those machines. After all, if everybody took pokes at you, your screws might get a little loose, too.

—George Arch

Enthusiasm

608. It is difficult to be emphatic when no one is emphatic on the other side.

—Charles Dudley Warner

609. Nothing is so contagious as enthusiasm; it moves stones, it charms brutes. Enthusiasm is the genius of sincerity and truth accomplishes no victories without it.

—Bulwer-Lytton

610. It could have been any educator or any preacher riding the train, but it happened to be Norman Vincent Peale. Peale was seated in the diner across from a fellow passenger, a stranger. He asked Peale his line and Peale asked his. "You really want to know?" he asked. Peale said yes, so he reached into his briefcase and pulled out, of all things, a fly swatter and put it on the table. "Yes, it's a fly swatter, but it's not an ordinary fly swatter. You've never seen one like this before. See that swatting end? It's smooth; it won't tear the curtains or the furniture fabric. It's bigger than most, and that makes it easier to kill flies. But the great thing about it is this," and he pointed to a place where there was a little tank. This is filled with perfume, and every time you swat flies you fill the air with perfume! Then he went on to tell how he was making the world a sweeter-smelling place with fewer flies. By the time he was through Peale was ready to buy.

Here a minister and a salesman had talked, but about the greatness of a new kind of fly swatter, not about the greatness of God.

The swatter salesman had practiced the art of enthusiasm!

Examinations

611. *Teacher:* "A fool can ask more questions than a wise man can answer."

Student: "No wonder so many of us flunk our exams."

—*The Lookout*

612. The college students were asked to comment on the course they had just completed. One student said, "It seems to be a well-rounded course. Everything not given in class during the semester was included in the final examination."

—*Texas Outlook*

613. Last spring I told my students that Easter occurred the first full moon after the vernal equinox.

Subsequently, I asked them on a test to give me the information. One answer I received: "Easter is the first Sunday after the first full moon after the infernal equinox."

—CAROL HANEY, *N.E.A. Journal*

614. When a volcano spits fire it is called saliva.

615. John Dewey once said of intelligence-testing, "It reminds me of the way they used to weigh hogs in Texas. They would get a long plank, put it over a crossbar, and somehow tie the hog on one end of the plank. They'd search all around till they found a stone that would balance the weight of the hog, and they'd put that on the other end of the plank. Then they'd guess the weight of the stone."

—ANNE SNYDER in "Letters to the
Editor," *The Saturday Evening Post*

616. One of my eighth graders listed these as state, federal and local taxes: gas tax, income tax and thumb tax.

—ETHEL KAISER, Greenlawn, New York
NEA Journal

617. Answers by junior high school pupils:

Caucus—the part of an animal left for the buzzards.
Excise—how big she was before she took "slim" pills.
Butte—the new girl next door.
Gorge—brother of the new girl next door.
Glacier—ice cubes which put Texas in second place.

Levee—one leg of a pair of levis.

Pocket Veto—deodorant for the traveling man.

—M. Dale Baughman

618. On a questionnaire asking: "What is the principal contribution of the automobile age?" the following answer was given by a college student: "It has practically stopped horse stealing."

619. A hamlet is an English dish consisting of ham and eggs cooked together.

Fiction are books which are fixed to the shelves and cannot be removed.

The Red Sea and the Mediterranean are connected by the Sewage Canal.

The chief occupation of the inhabitants of Perth is dying.

—*Laugh Book*

620. Definitions from examination papers in Hoban Heights, Pennsylvania: A blizzard is the inside of a fowl; a goblet is a male turkey; paraffin is the next order of angels above the seraphim.

—*NEA Journal*

621. Educators insist that the "crazy" answers that high-school students sometimes give to examination questions are not an indication of deliberate facetiousness—but it seems hard to believe. At any rate, here are a few comments from test papers:

Many Southern parents employed tooters for their children.

The hound rushed wildly over the moor, emitting shelps with every leap.

The man tried in vain, and was successful.

Shakespeare expressed in his play through the characters that something you gain through dishonesty you loose easily, as MacBeth lost his head in the end.

Salt Lake City is a place where the Morons settled.

Typhoid fever can be prevented by facination.

The teacher must be dressed simple. She should wear a commanding look on her countenance.

MacBeth is a typical husband, courageous and strong when away from home.

He sees everything at once, and writes them down in that order.

Gabriel Oak, with all his horse sense, is really a stable character.

Question—Name three Greek educators and tell what each one taught.

Answer—Socrates, Plato, and Aristotle. Socrates taught Plato, and Plato taught Aristotle.

—Sunshine Magazine

622. *Senior:* "They caught poor Wilbur cheating and they're kicking him out of school."
Junior: "Cheating? What was he doing?"
Senior: "Counting his ribs on a biology exam."

623. *Professor:* "Were you copying Smith's answers?"
Student: "No sir, I was only looking to see if he had mine right."

624. *Prof:* "The examination papers are now in the hands of the printer. You have three days in which to review the term's work. Are there any questions?"
Voice from the rear: " Who's the printer?"

625. "This examination," said the experienced professor, "will be conducted on the honor system. Please sit three seats apart and in alternate rows.

—The Balance Sheet

626. A seventh-grade history class, which had just finished studying colonial life, was having an examination. The first question read: "Discuss city life in colonial times." One boy wrote: "There were not many cities, and what there were, were out in the country."

627. A law school professor was telling his class what to expect of the final examination. "It will be twenty-five pages long, and it will take at least four hours to answer the questions," he said. Then, as the class groaned, he added consolingly, "Don't worry. All of you will be in the same boat."
At this a student spoke up. "Yeah," ahe said, "the Titanic!"

628. Answers: Germinate—Become a naturalized German.
Oboe—An English tramp.
Polygon—A heathen who has many wives.
Red and Mediterranean Seas—Two bodies of water connected by the Sewage Canal.

629. From a schoolboy's exam paper: Matterhorn was a horn blown by the ancients when anything was the matter.

—The Lookout

630. A gargoyle is something you swallow when you have a sore throat.

The Tower of Babel was the place where Solomon kept his wives.
Homicide is when a man kills himself in his own home.

631. According to testimony before the Congressional committee on atomic energy, "Boss Kettering of General Motors once gave the MIT entrance exam to fifty-seven of his top engineers. Exactly fifty-three of them flunked.

—*Quote*

Example

632. We are all of us more or less echoes, repeating involuntarily the virtues, the defects, the movements, and the character of those among whom we live.

—JOSEPH JOUBERT, French Essayist

633. All true teachers illustrate in person the running text of their teaching. The most spacious reasoning cannot dispose of an idea which is alive in human form. Hence the convincing power of example. The protest that a thing cannot be done falls flat in the presence of one who is doing it. Example is a type of practical philosophy more potent than oratory or logic.

—LYDIA ROSS, *Sunrise*

634.   A careful man I want to be—
A little fellow follows me;
I do not dare to go astray,
For fear he'll go the selfsame way.

I cannot once escape his eyes;
Whate'er he sees me do, he tries;
Like me he says he's going to be—
The little fellow who follows me.

He thinks that I am good and fine—
Believes in every word of mine;
The base in me he must not see—
The little fellow who follows me.

I must remember as I go
Through summer's sun and winter's snow,

I am building for the years that be
For that little chap who follows me.

—Lee Fisher, *Sunshine Magazine*

635. A certain psychology professor admonished his students, "Don't let school pupils get dependent on you: Make them think for themselves." After the lecture a graduate student came to the professor seeking an answer to a question. It seems that he was supervising some undergraduates who constantly troubled him with problems which could and should be solved by the students themselves. "What am I to do?" he wanted to know.

The learned professor cleared his throat and agreed that some students frequently tried to trap instructors into solving their problems for them. "Now what I would do if I were you," he went on, "is to————."

636. The Sociology professor had just returned term papers to the students in his class. Obviously perplexed one student hesitatingly approached the professor. "What is this you wrote on my paper?" he asked.

"I told you to write legibly," explained the professor.

637. There can be no striving for excellence without models to inspire emulation. There can be no greatness without the encouragement to ask much of oneself.

—Special Studies Project V,
Rockefeller Brothers,
The Pursuit of Excellence

638. The best way to show that a stick is crooked is not to argue about it, or spend your time denouncing it, but to lay a straight stick alongside of it.

—Dwight Lyman Moody

639. "Example is not the main thing in influencing others. It is the only thing!"

—Albert Schweitzer

640. A man had a Chinese plate he valued very much. One day it fell and cracked down the middle. He ordered 6 more made and to insure the exact pattern, he sent his broken plate as a copy. When he received the package from China 6 months later, he was astonished to find the Chinese craftsman had so faithfully followed his copy that each new plate had a crack right down the middle.

... If we imitate even the best of men we are bound to follow some of their imperfections.

—REVEREND A. PURNELL BAILEY, "Bread of Life," *Grit*

641. When Benjamin Franklin wished to interest the people of Philadelphia in street lighting, he didn't try to persuade them by talking about it; instead, he hung a beautiful lantern on a long bracket before his own door. Then he kept the glass brightly polished, and carefully and religiously lit the wick every evening at the approach of dusk. Thus recounts Cole D. Robinson in *World Horizons.*

People wandering about on the dark street saw Franklin's light a long way off and came under the influence of its friendly glow with grateful hearts. To each one it seemed to say: "Come along, my friend! Here is a safe place to walk. See that cobblestone sticking up? Don't stumble over it! Good-bye! I shall be here to help you again tomorrow night, if you should come this way."

It wasn't long before Franklin's neighbors began placing lights in brackets before their homes, and soon the entire city awoke to the value of street lightning and took up the matter with interest and enthusiasm.

—*Sunshine Magazine*

642. We capture attention, then by what we are. What kind of attention do we wish to capture? Interest, frank approval, enthusiasm? Then there must be in us the qualities that elicit these responses. We might call this the homogenic technique.

—HARRY OVERSTREET

643. We fool no one if our philosophy is, "Do as I say, not as I do."

Long before he begins to function as an educator, a teacher should resolve to live in harmony with standards set by the great teachers ... Let us learn what made great teachers great. Let us learn what is to be taught. Let us teach and practice what we teach.

—RAYMOND M. CASE, Elk Grove, California, *Phi Delta Kappan*

644. It is what people are that gets across, not what they try to inculcate.

—JOANNA C. COLCORD

645. Just attention is not enough. The teacher desires to secure her own kind of attention. Like begets like. This teachers and parents must know well.

646. "Alice," said mother, "I wish you and Billy would quit quarreling." Imagine her surprise when Alice said: "Mother, we're not quarreling. We're playing Ma and Pa."

647.
His little arms crept 'round my neck
And then I heard him say
Four simple words I shan't forget—
Four words that made me pray . . .
They turned a mirror on my soul,
On secrets no one knew.
They startled me, I hear them yet;
He said, "I'll be like you."
—HERBERT PARKER, Fredericksburg, Va.

648. "One example is more valuable than twenty precepts written in books."
—ROGER ASCHAM

649. When telling others what to do, I'm at no loss for speech. The thing that really gets me is to practice what I preach!
—EDNA H. HUNTINGTON
Sunshine Magazine

Executive

650. A person who wants to be an executive must learn how to grow, rather than to swell.
—LARSTON D. FARRAR, *Partners*

651. An executive is a man who can make quick decisions that are right sometimes.
—LARSTON D. FARRAR, *Partners*

Experience

652. Experience is a wonderful thing. It helps you to recognize a mistake when you make it again.

653. Experience is a comb which nature gives to men when they are bald.
—*Old Proverb*

654. Experience seems to be like the shining of a bright lantern. It suddenly becomes clear in the mind what was already there, perhaps, but dim.

—WALTER DE LA MARE

655. If a middle-aged school superintendent could only sell his experience for half what it cost him, he could live in retirement and luxury.

656. Experience is not what happens to you; it is what you do with what happens to you.

—HUXLEY

657. Sometimes it seems as if all I ever learn from experience is that I have made another mistake.

—BURTON HILLIS, *Better Homes and Gardens*

Facts

658. It's easier to believe a lie that one has heard a thousand times than to believe a fact that no one has heard before.

—*Grit*

659. British playwright John Tyndall said: "The brightest flashes in the world of thought are incomplete until they have been proved to have their counterparts in the world of fact."

660. Back in my divinity-school years the professor of elocution each year admonished the outgoing senior class: "Young gentlemen, in your sermon preparation, always remember that there is nothing so eloquent as a fact!"

—WILLIAM B. LIPPHARD, "As I See It," *Missions*

661. "Facts do not cease to exist because they are ignored."

—ALDOUS HUXLEY

662. First get your facts; and then you can distort them at your leisure.

—MARK TWAIN

663. Sit down before fact as a little child, be prepared to give up every preconceived notion, follow humbly wherever and whatever abysses nature leads, or you shall learn nothing.

—THOMAS H. HUXLEY, *Partners*

Family Life

664.   Dear Mother used to sit and sew,
While listening to the radio.
Our sox were darned, our buttons tight;
Neatly she mended every night.
Two buttons off Dad's shirt I see
—for who can sew and watch TV?

—*Sunshine Magazine*

665. I was going to spend the whole day in a nearby town so, before leaving, I pinned a note inside the front door for my teenage daughter. I returned earlier than expected and was upstairs when my daughter came in with a bevy of teenagers.

I heard one boy exclaim, "Is this where your mother leaves notes?"
She said, "Sure. Where does your mother leave yours?"
As if it made sense, he said, "In the refrigerator!"

—*Pueblo Chieftain*

666. To be honest, the real reason it's so hard to bring up children right is that they insist on imitating their parents.

667. The average man has probably thought twice about running away from home—once as a child and once as a husband.

668. It was Saturday morning and while they were having breakfast, Mr. Smith suddenly announced that he didn't have to go to the office that morning.

"Well, don't think," said his wife, "that you're going to run off to play golf today and leave me alone with all this work to do."

"Why, golf is the furthest thing from my mind," replied the husband, gnawing at his breakfast, "and please pass me the putter."

—*Wall Street Journal*

669. "Help your wife," advises one home economics specialist. "When she washes the dishes, wash the dishes with her. When she mops the floor, mop up the floor with her."

670. No nation has ever prospered in which family life was not held sacred.

—DEAN INGE, *Ladies Home Journal*

671. Oscar was careless about his personal effects. When his mother saw clothing scattered about on the chair and floor, she

inquired: "Who didn't hang up his clothes when he went to bed?"
A muffled voice from under the covers murmured, "Adam."

—MICKY MORAN, *Quote*

672. *Father to his teen-age son:* "I'm worried! Your mother isn't home! She could be lying unnoticed, seriously hurt in some bargain basement!"

—DICK TURNER, *Detroit News*

673. A henpecked husband finally put his foot down—he ordered his kids not to bother him while he was washing the dishes.

674. John was showing his girl friend the old family album. Pointing to a picture of himself as a small boy sitting on his father's knee, he asked, "How do you like that one?"
"Very nice," she replied. "But who is the ventriloquist?"

—*The Lookout*

675. Sooner or later every husband learns Home Geometry. Here are its main propositions:
Any wife and budget are together greater than a salary.
Any two children will together gang up on a third.
Any baseball season is equal to three broken windows.
The cost of any repair is equal to your worst fears.
The angle of a borrowing neighbor is acute; to lend to him is obtuse; to say no is the right angle.

—DAVID SAVAGE, *Wall Street Journal*

676. A couple of teenagers, a sister and brother, were overheard talking about their father's birthday. "What do you think we ought to get him for a present?" asked the boy.
"I know," said the girl. "Let's let him drive the car."

—HAROLD HELFER, *Laugh Book*

677. The businessman was showing his daughter, just returned from finishing school, around the newly completed mansion. At the swimming pool they stopped to watch several young men diving and stunting.
"Oh, Daddy," exclaimed the girl, "and you've stocked it just for me!"

—*Brushware*

678. "Daughter, I don't mind that young man coming over here every evening, and staying up half the night with you, nor standing on the porch for a couple of hours saying good night, but please ask him to stop taking the morning paper when he leaves."

—Pelican

679. "We take liver tonic every day," said Maisie. "For every spoonful Mom gives us a nickel, which we save."

"That's good!" said the neighbor. "You probably buy something nice for the money you save."

"No," said Maisie, "for the money we save Mom buys more liver tonic."

—PAL

680. A local dad complains about the time his kids spend watching TV: "I have an eight-year-old son who knows only one word— 'Shhh!' "

681. The right temperature at home is more surely maintained by the warm hearts and cool heads of those who live there than by electric thermostats.

—Treasures

682. Happy laughter and friendly voices in the house are the best health tonics a child can have. No clinical thermometer or aspirin bottle can replace these.

—Eugene P. Bertin, *Pennsylvania School Journal*

683. A Chicago wholesaler has trained his pet crow to shout "Spend money!" when a customer walks in. We could use one at our house that yells, "Hang up your coat!"

684. In a movie the leading man suddenly slapped the heroine in the face. In the silence that followed, a little voice piped up and said, "Mom, why don't she hit him back, like you do?"

—Pinky Curran

685. *Husband:* "My dear, those cakes were as tough as iron."

Wife: "I know, that's why I said, 'Take your pick.' "

—Canadian High News

686. Nowadays, a family is a group of people who have keys to the same house.

687. Little Alice was helping her mother serve the dessert. She gave the first dish of pudding to her father, who offered it to the guest on his right. Returning with another dish and seeing that her father had none, she served him again. He in turn handed it on to his left.

When Mary came in with the third dish, she placed in it front of her father and said, "Daddy, you might as well keep this one. They're all alike."

—Sunshine Magazine

Fear

688. An old railway watchman was testifying for the defense in a suit having to do with a collision between a train and an automobile at the crossing he guarded. He was being cross-examined by the plaintiff's lawyer and appeared ill at ease.

"You kept waving your lantern," his questioner bellowed, "but my client kept approaching despite everything?"

"Yes, sir! Yes, siree!" the old man kept repeating until he was finally told to step down.

"What's got you all upset?" the railway's lawyer asked. "You had no reason to be afraid."

"Sez you!" the watchman retorted. "I was afeered he was gonna ask me if I had my lantern lit when I was waving it!"

—Townsend National Weekly

689. An oriental legend tells of the desert traveler, who, one night met Fear and Plague, going to Baghdad where they expected to kill 10,000 persons.

The traveler asked Plague if he would do all the killing and Plague answered, "Oh, no, I shall kill only a few hundred and my friend Fear will kill the others."

—R and R Magazine

690.   Don't be afraid of anything;
Through life just freely roam.
The world was made for all of Us,
So make yourself at home.

—Lutheran Digest

691. If a man harbors any sort of fear, it percolates through all his thinking, damages his personality, makes him landlord to a ghost.

—LLOYD DOUGLAS, Lutheran Digest

And classroom facilities are just as bad.

Football

692. Beware the feather-brained football player who also has lead in his bottom—he has to be unbalanced.

693. Perhaps the most humorous item in gridiron history concerned famed Jim Tatum, in 1946, when he was coach at the University of Oklahoma. Pacing in front of a bench full of substitutes that November afternoon, Tatum watched Army giving his boys a 21 to 7 lesson. Close by sat punter Charlie Sarratt, his ankle sprained and his foot lodged in a bucket of ice in the wan hope of repairs to get him back in the game.

Suffering with his team on the field made Tatum's throat dry. Without shifting his eyes from the play he reached down and drew Sarratt's foot out of the ice pail. While the substitutes blinked their astonishment Tatum lifted the pail, took a swig of melted ice and, still absorbed in the game, put the pail down, gently replaced Sarratt's foot and resumed his pacing.

—LAWRENCE A. KEATING, *Columbia*

694. Only one instance is on record of a kicker being told to punt on every first down. Coach Bill Alexander, of Georgia Tech, gave the order to avoid an astronomical score against a sadly outclassed opponent.

Every first down, Alexander's man kicked. But fate remained hard on the visitors, who soon fumbled on their own two yard line. Georgia Tech recovered and, true to his instructions, the back punted. That ball hasn't been seen since and the game proceeded to a rout.

—LAWRENCE A. KEATING, *Columbia*

695. At the training table luncheon before a bowl game a football player refused to eat a portion of quivering gelatin.

His explanation was to the point, "I just can't eat anything that's more nervous than I am."

696. "I've been asked for a reference on our last football coach," the superintendent explained to the high school principal. "Among other things I said he was lazy, disorganized, and impertinent. Isn't there something good I can write about him?"

After a moment of silence the principal offered a suggestion, "Why don't you just say he relaxes well and eats well in the best restaurants when he 'scouts' on the expense account?"

—M. DALE BAUGHMAN

697. A football player was invited to a dance. Having been accepted by a pretty girl as a partner, it soon became evident that he didn't know even one dance step. When the music finally stopped he bowed and said: "It was lovely, and I shall always remember it."

"I don't doubt it," answered the foot-sore girl. "Elephants never forget."

—*Arizona Kitty Kat*

698. "Uncle Robert, when does your football team play?"

"Football team? What do you mean, my boy?"

"Why, I heard father say that when you kicked off we'd be able to afford a big automobile."

—*Boston Transcript*

699. The football player for a southern school was having trouble with his grades. Since his services were needed, he was called into the president's office for re-examination. A one-question examination was decided on. The question was, "What is the capital of Florida?" The lad sweated over the question and finally wrote "Monticello." He passed. The officials, in checking the answer, said that 100 was perfect, and Monticello is 25 miles from Tallahassee. 25 from 100 leaves 75 and 75 is passing.

—*Florida School Bulletin*

700. A doctor who was a prominent alumnus, was asked to give the boys a pep talk at a rally before the first football game of the season.

The doctor was most enthusiastic. Throughout the speech he interspersed the following statements: "Give 'em hell boys . . . . When you get in that game, you want to give 'em H-E-L-L."

The next speaker was a mild-mannered minister. He arose and in a small voice said, "Give them what the doctor ordered."

—*A.M.A. Journal*

701. Here again is the bobtailed limerick presented in *The Rotarian* for November:

A quarterback speedy and strong
Hugged the football as he ran along,
But as he passed the ball,
He found no ends at all,
His aim, not his signal was wrong.

—*Rotarian*

702. "I have bin coachin' at Splinter Ridge and the work ain't stiddy—they shoot you if you don't win . . . I allus train my boys on this skedule: (1) Feed 'em Mexican beans and frogs' legs to make 'em jump . . . (2) For open field runnin', I send 'em out to snatch watermelons on bright moonlight nights. In dodgin' shotgun blasts they larn in a hurry how to git—or be got' . . . (3) Fer line work, I turn 'em loose in the barnlot with a bunch of onery ol' goats. Buttin' heads is also good trainin' fer what they'll meet when they git out of college . . . (4) I give 'em a leetle corn-squeezin's in their water. Once—fer fun—the boys poured some of this squeezin's in the gas tank of my old Model T. When I cranked up, it got clean away, an' when I caut up with it, it was

at the intersection darin' a Greyhound bus to cross Route 66 . . .
My onlie weakness is english."

—Earle Wilson, Champaign News-Gazette

703. After his team had lost an important game, football coach
Hugh Duffy Daugherty of Michigan State told a gathering of
disgruntled alumni: "I appreciate the wonderful support given
me by this group. I shall always treasure your telegram, 'We are
with you, win or tie!' "

—David Condon, Chicago Tribune Magazine

704. All sports fans know the dangers of football officials. Some
have been known to suffer physical injury. One South American
referee recently bought an old army tank which he uses for refuge
when violence erupts.

705. Second thoughts are best but the quarterback seldom gets a
chance to prove it.

—M. Dale Baughman

706. Describing the campus atmosphere after his team had lost 7
straight football games, the coach said, "I didn't see any dummies
where they had hanged me in effigy—I soon learned why. They
were waiting for the real me."

707. Ron Gibbs, well-known pro football official, likes this letter:
"Mr. Gibbs," it read, "I think you and your crew do a perfect
job every game you officiate. Please excuse the crayon as I am not
allowed to have any blunt instruments."

—T. O. White

708. That Texan who proved his fast draw was an ardent follower
of Southern Methodist and evidently feared Texas U would run
back a punt to overcome Methodist's 6 to 0 lead. At sound of his
pistol the ball collapsed like a duck shot from a blind. A new ball
was produced and another punt made—without shooting and without changing the score.

A Dallas paper reported next day that each of seven Southern
Methodist fans hinted he was the pistol-toter who had winged the
punt. None, however, would give his name, perhaps because nowadays there is a law east of the Pecos.

—Lawrence A. Keating, Columbia

709. "What would happen," Bert Bell, pro football czar, was
asked at a luncheon, "if a team was trying to kick the extra point

and the ball burst in the air with half going over the bar and half under it?"

"The way I see it," remarked Bell, after cogitating for a moment, "the team would be out eighteen bucks."

—Scholastic Coach

710. Self-interest, too, can prompt mercy in football, as when Stanford played Southern California in 1935. Noticing that a Southern California man was injured, Jimmy Coffis, a Stanford back, rushed to him and applied a vigorous leg massage. The Trojan recovered and thanked Coffis and went back in the game.

"I had to keep him in," Coffis explained later. "The sub they'd have sent in is the toughest man to block I've ever seen!"

—Lawrence A. Keating, *Columbia*

711. The football talent scout has his disappointments, too. After chatting with a potential college tackle, he wrote on his interview card: Chest 44—IQ to match.

712. *Football coach, to new player*: "You're great! The way you hammer the line, dodge, tackle your man, and worm through your opponents is simply marvelous."

New player, modestly: "I guess it all comes from my early training, sir. You see, my mother used to take me shopping with her on bargain days downtown."

713. The referee who worked the famous 1959 game in which Billy Cannon's 89-yard kickoff return beat Ole Miss 7-3 tells this one: "When Cannon started his run, flags went down. I was running with him and as I heard that howling mob of 70,000 going crazy, I said to myself: 'If that penalty is against LSU, I'm going to keep right on running through that gate.' Fortunately, it was against Ole Miss."

—Wilton Garrison, *Charlotte Observer*

714. The football game was being played in torrents of rain. The teams were ankle deep in mud. At half-time the local team were two goals down and everything seemed to be going against them.

"Come on, lads," called a voice from the crowd, "the tide's with you now!"

—Laugh Book

715. Comedian Milton Berle, who admittedly pilfers gags anywhere he can find them, tells the one about Army playing Notre Dame in football.

"The Cadets were getting nowhere against the Irish," Berle says. "In desperation, the Army quarterback said in the huddle, 'I'm going to call the signals in Yiddish.'

"As the teams lined up, he began to shout: 'Ein, Zwei, Dri. . . .'

"The linebacker of the Fighting Irish leaned across and hollered: 'It von't do you a beet of goot!' "

716. A star football player with a keen sense of humor suffered a severely twisted knee in a bitterly contested game. Upon examination it was found that there was a torn cartilage.

The football star in all seriousness asked the doctor, "When my knee heals, will I be able to do the tango?"

"Of course you will," comforted the doctor.

"Then you're a miracle healer, Doc," exclaimed the footballer. "I never could before."

717. Many a college quarterback has found his best pass receiver on the bench—in the moonlight.

—FRANK F. PEPE, *Quote*

718. Though a deeply religious person, the football coach also was something of a realist. Before the big game against his rough, tough, traditional rival, he gathered his squad around him and warned them about the rough stuff the opponents would throw at them.

"Now, fellers," he said, "the Good Book tells us that if an enemy smacks you on the cheek, that's all right. Turn your other cheek. And if the opponents smack that cheek too, it's still all right. But, gentlemen, the third lick—the third lick, I say, belongs to you!"

—*Scholastic Coach*

719. At the annual press-radio-television banquet the football coach predicted his next year's team would have a perfect 9-0 season.

Such optimism rarely revealed by a football mentor brought to attention the 200 guests.

Then the coach went on. "However, should we lose any, I will have three good reasons—incompetent assistants, poor personnel, and bad weather."

Fishing time . . . But what would be the best bait?

720. A famous football coach, "Hurry Up" Yost, of the University of Michigan, once rebuked a confident player who said their team would win because it had "the will to win."

"Don't fool yourself," said Mr. Yost. "The will to win is not worth a nickel unless you have the will to prepare."

—HALFORD E. LUCCOCK, *Christian Herald*

Future

721.

With the day skimming by,
Its tasks crowding thickly
Which we're goaded to try
To accomplish too quickly,

It's because we forget
There are hours to borrow.

> There's time—an as yet
> Untouched whole tomorrow.
> —MAY RICHSTONE, *Rotarian*

722. The only way to get rid of a past is to get a future out of it.
—PHILLIP BROOKS, *The Lion*

723. Geologists say that in ten thousand years Niagara Falls will be dry, if something isn't done about it. In ten thousand years all of us will be dry, in spite of anything we can do about it.
—*Nuggets*

724. What the future has in store for you depends in a large measure on what you place in store for the future.

725. The best thing about the future is that it only comes one day at a time.

726. Whenever I think of the future, I think of R E Olds, who made the Oldsmobile and the Reo cars. About 1902 he announced a new model which he called his Farewell Car. He implied that this automobile was the ultimate, that after it, nobody could ever bring improvement to the motorcar. How wrong he was! There's always more to be done. You can never catch up. You can never finish.
—BROOKS STEVENS, industrial designer,
quoted by Karl Prentiss, "He Has
Designs on Your Dough," *True*

727. There is no future in any job—the future is in the one who holds the job.
—*Friendly Chat*

Geography

728. Mary E. Coots, teacher of a 4-5 combination at Ben Lomond, passes this one along:
Question: Describe New Amsterdam.
Answer: New Amsterdam is the largest dam in the U. S.
—*The Pointer*, Covina School District,
Covina, California

729. *Teacher:* "Johnny, where is Brazil?"
Johnny (stalling): "Where do you think it is?"
Teacher: "I don't think, I know."
Johnny: "I don't think I know, either."

730. Billy went to sleep in geography class. His teacher woke him up. "Billy," she cried, "I'm ashamed of you! Were you really sleeping?"

"Yes, ma'am," replied Billy, "but I was dreaming I was doing my geography."

—*PAL*, Concordia Publishing House

Golf

731. "Golf is the game that turned the cows out of the pasture and let the bull in," informs the *Beecher City Journal*.

—T. O. WHITE, *Champaign-Urbana News Gazette*

732. *Small girl (as golfer in bunker pauses for breath):* "He stopped beating it, Mummy. I think it must be dead."

—*Cambridge Daily News*, England

733. From up New England way comes word of the first casualty from one of those powered golf carts. Fellow wasn't badly hurt, it seems. But he just about wrecked a wisecrack coined by *Changing Times:* "The advantage of golf is that it gives a person a chance to be a pedestrian without the danger of being run over."

734. Golf is a lot of walking, broken up by disappointment and bad arithmetic.

—*Scholastic Coach*

735. I think that I shall never see a hazard rougher than a tree— a tree o'er which my ball must fly if on the green it is to lie; a tree which stands that green to guard, and makes the shot extremely hard; a tree whose leafy arms extend to kill the mashie shot I send; a tree that stands in silence there, while angry golfers rave and swear. Niblicks were made for fools like me, who cannot ever miss a tree.

—*Detroit Purchasor*

736. An inebriated golfer staggered up to the first tee and asked the caddie, "Whisch way is the hole?" Pointing toward the flag, the caddie handed him his driver.

"No, no!" said the golfer. "Gimme m' trusty brassie." He took a big swing, and the ball dribbled a short distance down the fairway.

The drunk insisted on using his brassie again. This time he swung with all his might. The ball hooked into the woods, ricocheted off a tree, landed square on the green and rolled into the cup.

The caddie ran toward the flag, with the drunk stumbling after him. When they reached the green, the caddie pointed to the ball nestling in the hole and shouted, "Look, sir!"

The drunk looked "We're in a hell of a fix," he mumbled. "Gimme m' niblick."

—Philip C. Humphrey

737. Once, when General Ulysses S. Grant was visiting Scotland, his host gave him a demonstration of a game, new to Grant, called golf. Carefully, the host placed the ball on the tee and took a mighty swing, sending chunks of turf flying but not touching the ball.

Grant watched the exhibition quietly, but after the sixth unsuccessful attempt to hit the ball, he turned to his perspiring, embarrassed host and commented: "There seems to be a fair amount of exercise in the game, but I fail to see the purpose of the ball."

738. "Why don't you play golf with George Roberts any more?"

He: "Would you play golf with a man who cheats—who falsifies his score and picks up his ball when your back is turned?"

She: "Of course not."

He: "Well, neither will George Roberts."

739. Over in Africa some of the native tribes have the custom of beating the ground with clubs and uttering spine-chilling cries. Anthropologists call this a form of primitive self-expression. Over here in America, we call it golf.

740. Sweet old lady (to golfer vainly searching for his ball): Would it be cheating if I told you where it was?

—*The Lookout*

741. *Golf Clerk:* Here's your dozen golf balls. Shall I wrap them up?

Golfer: Never mind, I'll drive them home.

—*The Lookout*

Grammar

742. Our little girl does not yet know that prepositions should never be used to end sentences with. Sick in bed for a day or two, she greeted me last night with—"Daddy, what did you bring that old book I didn't want to be read to out of up for?"

—BURTON HILLIS, *Better Homes and Gardens*

743. Bobby was having much difficulty with his grammar. Finally one day he ran into the house to his mother, and throwing his books on the table said: "I got it straight now. Hens set and lay, but people sit and lie."

—*Hoard's Dairyman*

744. A certain young man never knew just when to say whom and when to say who. "The question of choosing," he said "is confusing." I wonder if *which* wouldn't do.

—*Guide to Modern English*

745. A sign on the desk of Representative Dave Campbell in the Arizona legislature reads:

"Don't ask me for information. If I knew anything, I wouldn't be here."

—*Daily News Wire Services*

Guidance

746. *Vocational advisor to youth:* "Your vocational aptitude test indicates that your best opportunities lie in a field where your father holds an influential position."

747. Each generation has its own outlook, its own problems, its own environment . . . one expert who studied over a thousand autobiographies of college students writes, "The youth of today has faced more moral alternatives by the time he is 20 years of age than his grandparents faced in a lifetime.

—*Changing Times*

748. Did you hear about the young college graduate who couldn't get a job because he had prepared in a field where there was a decreasing demand? He finally drifted into vocational guidance.

—M. DALE BAUGHMAN

749. "It is reported that all presently known methods of counseling are to be abandoned in favor of a single technique. This approach will employ only a picture of a cow and the only unusual feature of the picture will be that the cow's tail will be more prominent than usual. The question the counselor will ask of any counselee will be, 'If we call the cow's tail a leg, how many legs does a cow have?' If the counselee says 'Five,' the counselor will know he is good at figures and has an exacting mind and can be directed into math. If the counselee says, 'It doesn't make any difference what you call the tail, it is still a tail and the cow still has only four legs,' the counselor can assume a mind that is after facts, proof, and direct the person into science. If the counselee says 'It could be four, it could be five, or it could be one of several other numbers since the cow has several other appendages,' then the counselor will recognize an artistic, creative mind and so direct the person into an allied field. However, if the counselee says, 'I don't know about this, I'd better think it over and let you know tomorrow,' you have a bonafide candidate for a school administrator and should so direct his study."

Habit

750. We are all creatures of habit. Once we get the habit of doing things a certain way, it is difficult for us to change . . . since habits become so deeply rooted we should be more careful about forming them . . .

Intelligently formed habits work for us by helping us avoid the mistakes which break down our confidence and destroy our effectiveness . . . A habit, according to Aristotle, begins with the first conscious performance of an act and is strengthened by every repetition. A tendency to act in a certain way becomes ingrained in us in proportion to the frequency with which the action actually occurs.
—CARL HOLMES, *Sunshine Magazine*

751. There is no habit that cannot be overcome by the implantation of a desire that is greater than the desire for the satisfaction of the habit. The great antidote for bad habits is good habits.
—RICHARD LYNCH, *Mind Makes Men Giants*

752. A habit cannot be tossed out the window; it must be coaxed down the stairs a step at a time.
—MARK TWAIN

753. *Horace Mann:* "Habit is a cable; we weave a thread of it each day, and at last we cannot break it."
—*Friendly Chat*

754. Habit is the enormous flywheel of society, its most precious conservation agent. There is no more miserable human being than one in whom nothing is habitual but indecision. Fully half of the time of such a man goes to the deciding, or the regretting of matters which ought to be so ingrained in him as practically not to exist for his consciousness at all.

—WILLIAM JAMES, *Quote*

755. They were honoring Lord Macauley in London for fifty years of distinguished service to the crown. Macauley began his speech of acknowledgement with these sad words: "Gentlemen, I understand that Man inherited three basic vices. I must report to you that I quit one, and one quit me—but I still smoke."

Health

756. Joy and Temperance and Repose
Slam the door on the doctor's nose.

—HENRY WADSWORTH LONGFELLOW

757. Early to bed
And early to rise
And you'll never have red
In the whites of your eyes.

—*Manning Monitor*

758. A bunch of germs were hitting it up in the bronchial saloon; two bugs in the edge of the larynx were nazzing a ragtime tune. Back in the teeth, in a solo game, sat dangerous Ack-Kerchoo; and watching his pulse was his light of love, the lady who's known as Flu.

759. To get his Wealth, he spent his Health
And then, with might and main,
He turned around and spent his Wealth
To get his Health again.

760. Lady friend of ours, about 40, went to her doctor the other day. "I just don't know," she said. "I just don't feel too well when I get up in the morning."

The doctor fixed a weary eye on our lady friend, and demanded, "Who does?"

—*Milwaukee Journal*

761. "When we sleep," said the teacher, "every part of us is completely at rest."

"Not with my uncle," said Ellen.

"How so?" asked the teacher.

"When my uncle sleeps, his mind and eyes are resting," admitted Ellen. "But his nose and mouth are working overtime."

—PAL

History

762. The past is valuable as a guidepost, but dangerous if used as a hitching post.

—Indiana Parent-Teacher

763. *Teacher:* "What distinguished Washington from his fellow Americans?"

Pupil: "He didn't lie."

764. My fourth grade teacher didn't teach history; she was so old she remembered it.

765. *Teacher to class:* "Name the outstanding accomplishment of the Romans."

Small voice from back of the room: "They understood Latin."

—The Lookout

766. *Teacher:* "In what battle did General Wolfe cry, 'I die happy!'"

Billy: "His last one."

767. *Teacher:* "Can you give me Lincoln's Gettysburg Address?"

Fred: "No, but he used to live at the White House."

768. The teacher was trying to impress upon her class the advantages of peace and disarmament. "How many of you object to war?" she asked.

Up went several hands. "Jimmy, tell us why you object to war."

Jimmy replied soberly, "'Cause wars make history."

769. In a fashionable school in New England the history teacher was telling the story of the settlement of the country.

"Miss Cabot," she said, "can you tell me who came over in the *Mayflower?*"

"Yes," said the girl, "I can. My ancestors and a few other people."

—Journeyman Barber

770. *Teacher:* "Why haven't you studied your history?"
Willie: "Well, you said the world kept changing. I thought I'd wait until it settled down."

—The Lookout

Home Economics

771. The teacher finding a pupil in tears, asked what was wrong. "I baked a cake and put it in the freezer an hour ago," lamented the naive pupil, "and there's no frosting on it yet."

772. A happy seventh-grader came home from the first home economics class in which she had done some cooking.
"Oh, mother," she bubbled, "I got an A in applesauce."

—Laugh Book

773. Sixteen-year-old Elsie was telling her mother about the home economics class at high school.
"Do they let you eat what you cook?" inquired mama.
"Let us?" Elsie exclaimed. "They make us!"

Homework

774.   I am neither old nor stubby
          I was tutored past McGuffey
          And I cut my second dentals
          On the good old fundamentals.
          But, dear teacher, have a care
          You are giving me gray hair.
          Please ease off this mighty domework
          I must do on Johnny's homework
          I tell you it must stop
          Or I'm bound to blow my top.

775. The ten-year-old son of a friend has been duly impressed in school that he must study alone. He owns a sign hanging from a hook on his door which says: "Do Not Enter Without Knocking."
One evening, when his father had reprimanded him about something, he retired to his room after he had added the following to his sign: "Do Not Even Knock."

—Emily Lotney

776. "That lump on the side of Willie's head," little Willie's sister informed the teacher, "that's where Daddy helped him last night with his arithmetic lesson."

—*Newsletter*, Oklahoma School Bds. Association

777.   Two heads are better than one, they say,
I thought so too until the day,
Gropingly I tried to lick
My 12-year-old's arithmetic.

—JEAN CONDER SOULE, *N. E. A. Journal*

778. *Harry:* "Teacher, would you scold a boy for something he didn't do?"

Teacher: "Of course I wouldn't."

Harry: "That's good. I didn't do my homework."

—FAY LEMITY, Junction City, Ohio

779. The teacher was examining the homework. "Tommy," she said. "This looks very much like your father's writing to me."

"Well!" replied Tommy after a pause, "Come to think of it I did use his fountain pen."

Human Relations

780. A man was putting up a sign, Puppies for Sale, and before he had driven the last nail there was a small boy standing at his side. That kind of sign seems to attract small boys. The youngster wanted to know how much the puppies were going to cost. The man told him they were very good dogs and that he didn't expect to let any of them go for less than thirty-five or fifty dollars. There was a look of disappointment, and then a question: "I've got $2.37. Could I look at them?"

The man whistled and called "Lady!"—and out of the kennel and down the runway came Lady, followed by four or five little balls of fur, with one lagging considerably behind. The boy spotted the laggard and, pointing, asked, "Whats wrong with him?" The reply was that the veterinarian had said that there was no hip socket in the right hip and that the dog would always be lame. The boy's immediate rejoinder was, "That's the one I want to buy. I'll give you $2.37 down and fifty cents a month 'til I get him paid for." The man smiled and shook his head. "That's not the dog you want. That dog will never be able to run and jump and play with you."

The boy, very matter-of-factly, pulled up his little trouser leg and revealed a brace running down both sides of his badly twisted right leg and under the foot with a leather cap over the knee.

"I don't run so well myself," he said, "and he'll need somebody that understands him."

Yes, just a boy and a dog, but they stand for a great truth of our time. What we need desperately is the desire and the concern to understand.

—MATTHEW HILL, Judge, Supreme Court,
State of Washington, *National Parent-Teacher*

781. If you would stand well with a great mind, leave him with a favorable impression of yourself; if with a little mind, leave him with a favorable opinion of himself.

—*Wisconsin Journal of Education*

782. Some 50 years ago the symbol of human relations was all too often physical force—the fist! Twenty-five years later, it became verbal abuse—the tongue! Current-day thinking has changed the symbol—to the mind!

—SAUL SILVERSTEIN

783. Most young folk are familiar with such Indian expressions as "burying the hatchet" and "smoking the peace pipe." But how many ever heard of "setting up sticks" to settle a quarrel?

If two Seneca boys fell to quarreling, the mother would say to them, "Go and set up your sticks." The boys knew what this meant. They were to go some distance from the lodge and set up three sticks in tripod form. The quarrel must then be left with the sticks for one moon (month). At the end of that time the position of the sticks would determine who was right, but they must be sure to leave the quarrel with the sticks, and in the meantime the boys would have to go back to their work or play. They might have agreed that if the sticks at the end of the moon leaned toward the rising sun, Running Deer was right, but if they leaned toward the setting sun, Flying Squirrel was right. But if they had fallen down, neither one was right. Because of the action of the wind and the rain, the sticks usually did fall down.

—*Sunshine Magazine*

784. If you ride a horse, sit close and tight; if you ride a man, sit easy and light.

—BEN FRANKLIN, quoted in *Indianapolis Star Magazine*

785. Fred Nauheim offers a correspondence tip for letter writers: "Don't answer letters—answer people."

—*Executive's Digest*

786. It makes absolutely no difference how much you know, if you can't tell anybody about it and be persuasive, it won't do.

—CLARENCE RANDALL, quoted by Lionel Crocker, Professor of Speech, Denison University, *Vital Speeches*

787. *Henry David Thoreau:* "I had three chairs in my house—one for solitude, two for friends, and three for society."

—*Friendly Chat*

788. A narrative in the twelfth chapter of Judges related how Jephthah, judge of Israel, found himself faced with an attack by Ephraimites. After the Ephraimitish army had crossed the Jordan, Jephthah executed a flanking movement, getting a portion of his army between the Ephraimites and the Jordan. He thereby secured control of all of the fords or, as the King James Version puts it, "the passes" of the Jordan. This was to cut off the retreat of the Ephraimites in the event that Jephthah and his men of Gilead were successful in the battle.

To distinguish friends from enemies, Jephthah chose "Shibboleth" as a password, knowing that the Ephraimites had difficulty with the "sh" sound and "could not frame to pronounce it right."

The Ephraimites were defeated, and they came rushing pell-mell back to the Jordan in an effort to get to their own country. When they found Jephthah's men in command of the passes, they denied that they were Ephraimites. But when they were confronted with the challenge, "Say now Shibboleth," they said "Sibboleth." That trifling defect proved them to be enemies. "And there fell at that time of the Ephraimites forty and two thousand."

You may perhaps be wondering what this tale out of the Old Testament has to do with our problems today. The answer is very simple. The Ephraimites were confronted with a challenge—"Pronounce or perish." They could not pronounce, so they perished. It is my belief that we too are confronted with a challenge of "Pronounce or perish," that our learning, our skills and techniques will avail us nothing if we are unable to meet it. The word we must pronounce is the personal pronoun we.

It is not the phonetics of pronunciation but the connotation which we give the word that is of vital importance in our times. When we say we, we are ordinarily using it as a term of exclusion, as something that separates us from somebody else. It is "We, the Democrats," and "We, the Republicans"; "We, industry," "We, labor." We need an all-inclusive we.

Before we can pronounce the pronoun *we* as such a term, we must be able to pronounce certain other personal pronouns. We must be able to pronounce the pronoun *I* with a nice sense of balance between responsibility on the one hand and humility on the other—a humility that recognizes our obligation to those who have gone before and appreciates the heritage of liberty, freedom, and justice which they bequeathed to us.

We must be able to pronounce other pronouns too, such as he, she, and they, with some understanding of his, her, and their hopes, aims, and aspirations. Understanding coupled with concern is surely one of the great needs of the hour.

> —MATTHEW HILL, Judge, Supreme Court,
> State of Washington, *National Parent-
> Teacher*

789. Make other people like themselves a little better and rest assured they'll like you very much.

> —*Secretary*

790. One sign of maturity is the ability to be comfortable with people who are not like us.

> —*Christian Advocate*

791. When the Italian poet Tasso attained the zenith of his career, he was told that he was then in a position to take revenge upon a man who had hurt him greatly, relates Thomas Drier, philosophic writer.

"I do not desire to plunder him," the poet replied, "yet there is one thing I would like to take from him."

"His honor, his wealth, his life?" Tasso was asked.

"No," came the gentle reply. "What I desire to take from him I will try to gain by the exercise of kindness, patience, and forbearance. I will try to take away his ill-will!"

> —*Sunshine Magazine*

792. Four little words, too seldom heard, are: "You may be right."
—*Worcester* (Mass.) *Telegram*

793. Feuding staff members may suffer the fate of the Kilkenny cats; each thought there was one cat too many; so they scratched and they fit and they tore and they bit, 'Till instead of two cats, there wasn't any.

—M. DALE BAUGHMAN

Humor

794. It is probable that we will never see another Will Rogers during our lifetime. And this in itself could be tragic. Never, perhaps, in our country's history have we needed someone who could make us laugh—make us laugh by laughing at ourselves—as critically as we do now.

—BILL PROUTY, columnist, *Chapel Hill Weekly*

795. Good humor is a tonic for mind and body. It is the best antidote for anxiety and depression. It attracts and keeps friends. It lightens human burdens. It is the direct route to serenity and contentment.

—GRAVILLE KLEIRSER, *Think*

796. It has been observed that he who laughs, lasts.

797. Wit is the salt of conversation, not the food.

—WILLIAM HAZLITT

798. I don't make jokes—I repeat others or sometimes I just watch people and report the facts.

—M. DALE BAUGHMAN

799. Even a poor wisecrack often outlives a good sermon.

—GRACE PULLMAN

800. An ounce of clean humor is often a greater attention getter and thought provoker than a pound of serious approach.

—JOHN S. LORR, Instructor of Arts and Crafts, Fremont High School, Sunnyvale (Cal.), "Brains Can Be Exciting," *Teaching Tools*

801. The man who laughs at the boss's jokes does not necessarily have a sense of humor, but he surely has a sense of direction.

802. Laughter, it has been said, "is more than a defense mechanism, it is a means of adjusting to circumstances, a safety-value against tyranny—it is an agency in creative enterprise." So what's wrong with being funny? Isn't it preferable to be kept awake by a deft (though possibly undignified) bit of humor than to be put to sleep by unrelieved (though dignified) seriousness?

—JOSEPH STOCKER, "What's Wrong With
Being Funny?" *Kiwanis Magazine*

Ideas

803. What would your reaction be if a business associate told you he knew how to make a square bubble? You will probably find you don't really want to hear about such a (preposterous) idea. Our historic past is strewn with records of men scorned or persecuted for new ideas—Jesus, Columbus, Darwin, etc. (Yet) these new ideas changed the course of civilization.

. . . The ideas that will carry us forward to lasting prosperity are to be found among us today. But to harvest such ideas, a new dimension must be added to every man's equipment—a readiness to accept ideas as startling and new as that square bubble.

—*Client's Service Bulletin*
American Appraisal Co.

804. Don't let a warm idea freeze to death.

—*Client's Service Bulletin*
American Appraisal Co.

805. Ideas are like beards: men do not have them until they grow up.

—VOLTAIRE

806. The Greeks, who long have been concerned about how to save the ruins of the Parthenon from ultimate destruction by souvenir-seeking tourists, have hit upon a brilliant idea which is working admirably, according to reports. Every night a load of cracked marble is brought from nearby quarries and scattered about the ruins. This permits tourists to steal all the souvenir marble they want without doing any damage to the Parthenon itself!

807. An American religious leader recounts the story of a businessman from this country who had been sent to China to make some contracts with Chinese businessmen for an American firm which he represented.

After the business had been transacted, the ever polite Chinese asked the American if there was anything in particular that he would like to see while in China. The American expressed a desire to watch the coolies at the water front carrying their heavy burdens. He had heard of the tremendous loads they can carry, and he wanted to see them at work with his own eyes.

Thereupon, the American and the Chinese businessmen went down to the water front. Almost immediately the American's interest was attracted by two coolies who were engaged in a fierce quarrel. Words were being exchanged rapidly and in heated tones, fists were clenched and poised threateningly in the air, and a fight appeared imminent.

The American waited, expecting that a tremendous fist fight would break out at any moment. But after some minutes had elapsed and neither contestant had struck a single blow, he became a bit impatient. Turning to his Chinese associate, he asked when the fight would begin.

"Oh," replied the Chinese, smiling, "I cannot say. You see, the man who strikes the first blow admits that he has run out of ideas!"

—*Sunshine Magazine*

808. Let our teaching be full of *ideas*. Hitherto, it has been stuffed only with facts.

—ANATOLE FRANCE

809. When I got on a hunt for an idea I could not sleep until I had caught it.

—ABRAHAM LINCOLN

810. Ideas are very much like children—your own are very wonderful.

811. Every time a man puts a new idea across, he finds ten men who thought of it before he did—but they only thought of it.

—*Advertiser's Digest*

812. Some men have ideas; other men have notions. How easy it is to mistake one for the other.

—W. D. HOARD, *Hoard's Dairyman*

813. A group can spark an idea, but only an individual can have one. As Pres. Griswold of Yale, has so aptly asked: "Could Hamlet have been written by a committee? Or the Mona Lisa painted by a club?"

—W. JOHN UPJOHN, addressing 3rd
Annual Communications Conference, New York Art Directors Club

814. Imagination . . . provides the way to new ideas, new processes and new things. If we did not have imagination, we would plod along each day, seeing the same old things, going through the same old thoughts.

—York Trade Compositor

815. Idea: The result of careful thought and experience, when you have it. When somebody else has it, it's a lucky hunch.

—Phoenix Flame

816. The more ideas a man has the fewer words he takes to express them. Wise men never talk to make time; they talk to save it.

817. Greater than the force of marching feet is an idea whose hour is come.

—Victor Hugo

818. Summer is a good time for you to go fishing—for ideas with which you can awaken the zest for learning. Remember, an idea doesn't care who has it.

—M. Dale Baughman

819. There is a story of a certain sea captain and his chief engineer, who disputed as to which of them was the more important to the ship. Failing to agree, they resorted to the altogether unique plan of swapping places.

The Chief ascended to the bridge, and the Captain dived into the engine room.

After a couple of hours the Captain suddenly appeared on the deck covered with oil and soot. One eye was swollen shut, and he was very much the worse for wear. "Chief!" he yelled, wildly waving aloft a monkey-wrench. "You'll have to come down here; I can't make 'er go!"

"Of course you can't," replied the Chief, "she's ashore!"

—Sunshine Magazine

820. Aesop's Fly, sitting on the axle of the chariot, has been much laughed at for exclaiming: What a dust I do raise!

—Thomas Carlyle

Individuality

821. The people who have contributed most to our lives and well being of our country have been the individualists, and you can

start the list with Samuel Adams, who was considered somewhat
of a crackpot by his countrymen . . . There will always be leaders—
and the led. What this country can use—or in fact needs desperately
—is more individualists, more characters in every level of endeavor.
Bring on the characters, we say—and the more the better!

> —Louis E. Ball, *Farmington Valley
> Herald*

822. On developing individuality . . . Elementary teachers, especially, can appreciate what Goethe said: "Let none be like another;
yet each be like the Highest, How can that be? Let each be perfectly himself."

823. Every wheel ought to turn on its own axle.

Influence

824. "One rotten apple spoils a whole barrel," may be accept-
able counsel for a fruit-vendor. But if one bad child can spoil a
group of children, then that one child has been better schooled in
badness than the others have been tutored in goodness. And that
is a pretty serious indictment of us adults, both individually and
collectively.

> —George St. George, addressing a PTA
> meeting in Pittsburgh, Pa.

825. No sale is ever made until a buyer believes in the integrity
of a seller.

No pupil is taught until the teacher has won the confidence of
the prospective learner.

> —M. Dale Baughman

Initiative

826. The English essayist and divine of the 19th century, Sydney
Smith, had this to say about initiative and courage: "A great deal
of talent is lost in the world for want of a little courage. Every day
sends to their graves obscure men who timidity prevented from
making a first effort; who, if they could have been induced to
begin, would, in all probability, have gone great lengths in the
career of fame. The fact is, that to do anything in the world worth
doing, we must not stand back shivering and thinking of the cold
danger, but we must jump in and scramble through as well as we
can.

"A man waits, and doubts, and consults his brother, and his particular friends, till one day he finds that he is sixty years old, and that he has lost so much time in consulting that he has no time to follow their advice."

827. One story which illustrates the kind of talent we like to have is about General MacArthur who called in one of his Army engineers during the war and asked: "How long will it take to throw a bridge across this stream?"

"Three days," the engineer told him.

"Good," snapped General MacArthur. "Have your draftsmen make drawings right away."

Three days later the General sent for the engineer and asked how the bridge was coming along.

"It's all ready. You can send the troops across right now if you don't have to wait for the pictures. They ain't done yet."

—B. F. Coggin, Vice President
of Convair

828. Do we know how to use our information and knowledge? Once upon a time there was a ticket agent on a railroad in India. He knew all about selling tickets. He knew all about when the engine was coming and when it was not. But one day, he sent a telegram to New York to the people who owned the railroad, and it went something like this: "There is a tiger on the platform eating a customer. Please wire instructions."

—Roger G. Imhoff, Clergyman

829. Thomas A. Edison, the great inventor, was talking one day with the governor of North Carolina, and the governor complimented him on his inventive genius. "I am not a great inventor," said Edison.

"But you have over a thousand patents to your credit, haven't you?" queried the governor.

"Yes, but about the only invention I can really claim as absolutely original is the phonograph," was the reply.

"Why, I'm afraid I don't understand what you mean," said the governor.

"Well," explained Edison, "I guess I'm an awfully good sponge. I absorb ideas from every source I can and put them to practical use. Then I improve them until they become of some value. The ideas which I use are mostly the ideas of other people who don't develop them themselves."

—Adapted from *Just a Moment*

In-Service Education

830. Recipe for a successful workshop:

4 cups Intelligence	1¾ cups sifted Initiative
1½ cups Responsibility	3 cups Ambition
2 cups Open-Mindedness	2 cups unbeaten Patience
1 quart Understanding	1 cup Tactfulness
2½ teaspoons Attitude	4 cups Ability

Dash of Judgment

Have all ingredients at body temperature. Sift Intelligence, Ambition and Understanding together. Mix Cooperation, Attitude and Open-mindedness until dissolved. Add gradually Ability, Tactfulness and Responsibility. Stir Initiative and Judgment thoroughly. Beat Patience until smooth. Blend all ingredients well; sprinkle liberally with Cheerfulness and bake in an oven of Determination. When absorbed thoroughly, cool and spread with Common Sense.

–L. H. GLOVER, Cook County, Illinois
Education Digest

831. Many factors aid in the production of a good institute. One of the greatest of these factors is the instructor. He can make the best organized institute worthless. He can make a poorly planned institute very good. His attitude is a matter of supreme importance.

The instructor may be a man of great scholarship well known as a college president or professor. If he comes to the teachers with an attitude of superior wisdom, he places between himself and them an impassable gulf. They soon feel that his heavy cargo of knowledge is entirely beyond their reach. . . . His subjects look well in print and are intended to imply great wisdom. No one can guess from the title what the lecture will be about. These lectures fail to touch in a remote way either the course of study or the simple pedagogy of the common schools. The destructive power of such an instructor is great. Time and money given to him are worse than lost. It is stolen. An occasional instructor assumes that the institute exists for the sole purpose of amusement. He feels that his period of forty-five minutes is a failure unless in it he produces forty-five laughs. He has no respect for age, and uses freely alleged funny things that smell of the bilge water of the ark. . . . This type of instructor is never so happy as when the fame of his jokes goes outside the institute room and the men of the town crowd in to hear him. This sort of work sometimes produces a noisy interest that is mistaken for enthusiasm. That its value is below zero needs no argument. It is a hopeful sign that in many counties the teachers rebuke the amusement instructor by silent contempt and a refusal to laugh.

A rather large number of instructors spend much time in destroying straw men. This is especially true of some of the men who come to us from beyond the borders of our state. They become greatly distressed as they vividly describe a horrible state of educational affairs. They grow eloquent as they tell how these pedagogical wrongs are to be righted. We listen, and restrain ourselves, for the matter under discussion is ancient history.

The ground was fought over and the issue settled twenty years ago. Of course, bowling things over is a fascinating exercise. The straw-man killer is harmless and his work, is almost, if not entirely, useless.

Occasionally, a man appears in an institute with an attitude of indifference to everything except his pay. He has no aim and cares nothing for results. He works wholly for money and tries to get that with as little effort as possible ... He is a disorganizer. By the end of the second day he brings chaos into the institute and produces indifference in every teacher. He spells failure in letters so large that he ought to be prohibited by law.

There are instructors that really hardly have time to attend the institute. The representative of this class impresses upon the people at his hotel that he must have very prompt service as his time is valuable. He appears at the meeting place just at the time for his lecture to begin. At its close he rushes from the stage and hastens to the hotel.... He never gets into the spirit of the meeting and has no conception of what his co-workers are trying to do. He is generally a high priced man, getting for his services a sum out of all proportion to his worth.

It occasionally happens that clergymen or professional lecturers break into the institute field. These men attempt to play upon the emotions of their hearers by a cheap sentimentalism. They tearfully proclaim the beauties of the sacrificial life of the teacher. They touch the heart with beautiful stories of the innocence of childhood. ... They treat their hearers with condescension and disgust them with trivialities.

—PROFESSOR ROBERT J. ALEY, Indiana University, speech at the Indiana State Teachers Association Convention, 1908

Inspiration

832. Inspiration should be as the green of a fertile meadow on a warm evening after rain: a rich soil from which a breathtaking fragrance rises in a spiral of color. Inspiration can be chiseled like an antique dagger, or rough as a block of prime matter in the mind of a philosopher. It can caress you like a woman or hit you with the punch of a prizefighter. Inspiration is the certitude that, out of nothing, something is going to happen.
—SERGE DE GASTYNE, "Inspiration,"
Music Journal

833. Bruce, with eyes growing wider, watched a persevering spider, then rose and swiped the English army on the nose.

Newton, sitting on a wall, watched an autumn apple fall, and found that gravity brought apples to the ground.

Watt, observing someones kettle boiling near the chimney settle, designed a patent engine that amazed mankind.

I have looked at spiders toiling, apples falling, kettles boiling. My hat! If I could only think like that!
—*Sunshine Magazine*

834. Good teachers have the ability to arouse interest of pupils in subject matter and to shape wholesome attitudes while imparting facts and interpreting these facts. This ability to inspire includes a sense of the dramatic, even on a mild scale, such as might be used in approaching the solution of a geometry problem. The use of the dramatic, however, should not involve misinterpretation of fact.
—HOMER T. ROSENBERGER, *Bulletin, NASSP*

835. It is rather widely known that Mark Twain was somewhat profane at times. On the other hand his wife was quite refined. She devised a scheme which she thought might change his habits. She met him at the door once and immediately uttered a string of oaths. Mark was momentarily stunned but quickly recovered and saw through the ruse. He waited in silence while she finished her tirade and then said softly, "My dear, you have the words but not the music."

836. A young artist, who was studying under a great master, came one day to the studio to beg for permission to use his master's brush. The request was granted, and with a singing heart the young man went away to his own painting, thinking that now his work would be much better.

A short while later he returned with the brush, complaining that he could do no better with it than he could with his own brush. An assistant in the studio, hearing the young man's complaint, said to him: "Friend, it is not the master's brush you need, but the master's devotion, the master's spirit."

—Sunshine Magazine

837. Henry Ford once said that the ability to encourage others is one of life's finest assets. The auto inventor and manufacturer knew the power of encouragement. He had learned of it as a young man.

Memorable to him was the time, at the beginning of his career, when he made a drawing of his newly built engine for Thomas A. Edison. Young Ford had endured criticism and ridicule. Most mechanical experts of that day were convinced that electric carriages would be the popular passenger cars of the future.

But attending a dinner one evening at which Edison was present, Ford began explaining his engine to men nearest him at table. He noticed that Edison, seated several chairs away, was listening. Finally the great man moved closer and asked the young inventor to make a drawing.

When the crude sketch was completed, Edison studied it intently, then suddenly banged his fist on the table. "Young man," he said, "that's the thing! You have it!"

Years later, Ford recalled, "The thump of that fist upon the table was worth worlds to me."

—Jack Kytle, Partners

Intelligence

838. Intelligence has been defined by the psychologists as the capacity to learn. That is nonsense. Intelligence is the capacity to wonder.

—Hy Sherman, Flying

839. It is a mark of intelligence, no matter what you are doing, to have a good time doing it.

—V. W. Cochran

840. If a ship sinks, an intelligent rat gets off but a wise rat doesn't get on in the first place.

841. Like the X-ray, intelligence tests can bless or burn.

842. Not all gifted children are bookworms. Some may be found among the black-leather jacket and hot-rod set, says Dr. Elizabeth M. Drews, Michigan State University education professor. She groups gifted students in four categories: studious "A" scholars who are conformists and know how to work for good grades; social leaders who "choose to make their impact felt in the realm of people" and grow up to become executives and club women; "intellectuals," whom teachers do not always like, but who are the future scientists, artists and writers; and rebels, who may have high IQ's but low grades.

—Quote

Interest

843. Interest is like a kite. Under proper conditions it soars upward and is difficult to pull down.

844. Just as there is an attention span there is an attention-interest boundary line which the speaker or writer must cross to get to paydirt.

—M. DALE BAUGHMAN

Judgment

845. Snap judgment has a way of coming unfastened.

846. While on a walk one day, I was surprised to see a man hoeing his garden while sitting in a chair. "What laziness!" I thought. But suddenly I saw, leaning against his chair, a pair of crutches. The man was at work despite his handicap. The lesson I learned about snap judgments that day has stayed with me for years now: the crosses people bear are seldom in plain sight.

—ANNETTE ASHE, *Guideposts*

847. There was one who thought himself above me, and he was above me until he had that thought.

—ELBERT HUBBARD

848. We judge ourselves by what we are capable of doing; others judge us by what we have done.

—LONGFELLOW

849. Shakespeare was so right when he said: "Take each man's word, but reserve thine own judgment."

Junior High School

850. The two older types of organization, K-8 and 9-12, need to be united by a flexible coupling or universal joint rather than by a rigid shaft.

851. May I remind you of an old Talmudic legend which tells about a heathen who once came to Hillel, Hillel being an ancient and well known rabbi, and said to him, "I will convert to Judaism if you will tell me what it is about while I stand on one foot," and Hillel being a very clever man, said, "The whole of Judaism is that thou shalt love thy neighbor as thyself."

Now, I am much less clever than Hillel but if I were asked to tell the junior high school story while my skeptic questioner stood on one foot, I would say simply, "It means a square deal for pupils of the awkward age."

—M. Dale Baughman

Juvenile Delinquency

852. Juvenile Delinquency is proving that some parents just are not getting at the seat of the problem.

—Kenneth J. Shively

853. In science, thinking begins with a problem. In juvenile delinquency a problem begins with a thought.

—M. Dale Baughman

854. When adults act like children, they're silly; when children act like adults, they are delinquent.

—Elkhorn Independent

855. Prescription for curing incipient juvenile delinquents: affection, good food, fresh air and plenty to do.

—Dr. Randel Elliott, American Mercury

856. We read in the paper and hear on the air,
Of killing and stealing and crime everywhere.
We sigh and we say, as we notice the trend,
"This young generation, where will it end?"

But can we be sure that it's their fault alone,
That maybe a part of it isn't our own?
Are we less guilty, who place in their way,
Too many things that lead them astray?
Too much money to spend, too much idle time;
Too many movies of passion and crime;
Too many books not fit to read;
Too much evil in what they say.
Too many children encouraged to roam;
Too many parents who won't stay home.
Kids don't make the movies, they don't write the books,
That paint gay pictures of gangsters and crooks;
They don't make the liquor, they don't run the bars,
They don't make the laws and they don't buy the cars.
They don't peddle drugs that addle the brain,
That's all done by older folks, greedy for gain.
Delinquent teen-agers, Oh! how we condemn,
The sins of the nation and blame it on them.
By the laws of the blameless, the Saviour made known,
Who is there among us to cast the first stone?
For in so many cases, it's sad; but it's true,
The title "DELINQUENT" fits older folks too.

—JAMES SCALES, *Laugh Book*

857. Another way to reduce juvenile delinquency would be to quit coddling hard-boiled eggs.

—*Grit*

858. A juvenile delinquent is a teenager who wants what he wants when he wants it and won't wait to get it.

—CONSTANCE F. MURPHY, *Massachusetts Teacher*

859. Juvenile delinquency sets in when a youngster stops asking adults where he came from and starts telling them where to go.

—*Basic Blast*

860. The whole reason for juvenile delinquency is mental unemployment.

—*Jackie Gleason*

861. Primitive country: One that has no taxes to handle juvenile delinquency, in case it gets civilized enough to achieve it.

—*In a Nutshell*

862. The University of Hartford inaugurated a new night school course—Juvenile Delinquency. It's for adults only.

—Daily News Wire Services

863. Juvenile Delinquent: A teenager with a false sense of maturity.

—A. BOWMAN WEAVER, *Sales Management*

"Hurt hell . . . Somebody's gonna get sued."

Kindergarten

864. For several days the 84 boys and girls "graduating" from a kindergarten class were drilled to say "thank you, Mr. Nevins," when Superintendent Vincent Nevins presented them with diplomas.

But Nevins was unable to attend the ceremony Wednesday, and Miss Lillian L. Hannan, the principal, substituted for him.

The first 83 children in line said "Thank you, Mr. Nevins," when Miss Hannan presented the diplomas.

The 84th said, "Thank you, Mrs. Nevins."

865. Peering over Johnny's shoulder, the kindergarten teacher asked, "What are you drawing?"

"I'm drawing a picture of God," answered Johnny.

"But," the teacher explained, "nobody knows what God looks like."

"They will when I get through," proudly announced Johnny.

866. Freckle-faced Tommy brought his little red fire engine to "Show and Tell" session in kindergarten for what seemed to one little miss, the umpteenth time. When he presented it, she was heard to complain, "Oh, no, not again!"

867. Observing one of my little girls coming from the boys' lavatory, I explained to her, "Honey, don't you know that's *private*—just for the boys!" The surprised little red-head answered, "Why, Miss Pat! I know that! I just went in to borrow their soap."

—Miss PAT, Kindergarten Teacher,
Bay City, Michigan

868. Jeff, enamored of his blonde kindergarten classmate, told his mother the romance was making progress.

"Sally spoke to me," he said.

"What did she say?" inquired Mom.

"I hit her and she said, 'Stop that.'"

—*Omaha World-Herald*

869. Little Jimmy seemed to like kindergarten but showed no signs of being an outstanding student. One day, however, he came home with a big gold star. Asked why he was rewarded, he said, "Well, it's like this—every day we have to rest, and I rested the best."

—*Florida School Bulletin*

870. *Mother* (*to five-year-old child who has had a substitute teacher in kindergarten*): "How did you like your new teacher?"

Child: "Oh, she's smarter than Miss Jones. When we sang, she played the piano with one finger; and Miss Jones has to use two hands when she plays."

Knowledge

871. Whoever acquires knowledge but does not practice it, is like one who ploughs a field but does not sow it.

872. Knowledge is a torch of smoky pine that lights the pathway but one step ahead, across a void of mystery and dread.
—GEORGE SANTAYANA, quoted in
Science Digest

873. Oddly enough, it's the person who knows everything who has the most to learn.
—*Service for Company Publications*

874. If a man empties his purse into his head, no man can take it away from him. An investment in knowledge always pays the best interest.
—B. FRANKLIN

875. "Wear your learning, like your watch, in a private pocket; and do not merely pull it out and strike it; merely to show that you have one."
—PHILLIP D. STANHOPE,
EARL OF CHESTERFIELD

876. Those who know how to do a thing, says a Chinese proverb, do not find it difficult; those who find a thing to be difficult, do not know how to do it.
—*Odd Moments*

877. Everybody knows more than anybody.

878. Knowledge is like money—if you keep quiet about it, people will think you've got more than you have.
—"Seasoned with Sage," *Partners*

879. It is said that a professor is not smarter than other people; he just has his ignorance better organized.
—EDGAR DALE, "What Is the Image of
Man Tomorrow?", *Childhood Education*

880. If a little knowledge is dangerous, where is the man who has so much as to be out of danger?
—THOMAS HUXLEY, quoted in *Cuna
Mutual Newsletter*

881. "When a man's knowledge is not in order, the more of it he has the greater will be his confession."
—HERBERT SPENCER, quoted in
The Kiplinger Magazine

882. Thinking it can't be done is a great time waster; knowing it can't be done is a great time saver.
—FRANCES RODMAN, *Partners*

Laughter

883. Laughter, of course, is an activity not of the jaw muscles, but of the mind; indeed, silent laughter is usually the most fitting and satisfied form of mirth with which to confront matters of the profoundest import. The ability to laugh, silently or aloud, at moments of ultimate crisis is a sublime attribute: an expression of everything in us that is human and most civilized.

> —JULIUS NOVICK, "The Gift of
> Laughter," *Harper's Bazaar*

884. A psychologist, observing the behavior of men aboard an atomic submarine which was submerged for weeks at a time, noted that as tension increased so did a kind of earthy humor—horseplay, practical jokes, comical insults. Instead of choking up on their feelings of fear and boredom, the men broke the tension with laughter. Instead of putting a cork on their abhorrence of the situation and stewing it into a hostility for each other, the men openly ridiculed and insulted one another, and in doing so shared by laughter their common feelings.

> —*Capsuled Comments*

885. Of all God's gifts to man, laughter is one of the most subtle and is one of the most precious. It has neither nationality nor religion. As an equalizer, it has no equal. Even science which can do so many things can't teach us to laugh. Mirth is from God, dullness from the devil. When we laugh we agree with God that all is good.

> —*Office Gal*

Leadership

886. No man can exercise vigorous leadership who lacks the gift of transmitting thought.

> —CLARENCE B. RANDALL, "The Myth of
> the Wicked Politician," *Dun's Review*

887. The strong leader can be popular in a general way but he has few, if any, really close friends. He understands his subordinates but cannot be clearly understood by them. His position tends to isolate him. In general he is a "father image" to his subordinates and they admire, respect, fear or hate him as dictated by their childhood patterns.

> —JACK S. STAEHLE

And you can be the skipper.

888. Little Mary arrived home one day with a mongrel female dog. She thought the animal was beautiful, but try as she might, she couldn't persuade her mother to keep the dog.

The climax of the debate came one day a week later. When Mary arrived home from school, she found the dog running about the yard, closely followed by a pack of male dogs.

Mary, her eyes shining with pride, ran into the house. "Mommy," she called, "come to the window. Our dog is just a natural born leader."

—Journal of the American Medical Association

889. An anatomy of leadership: *Princes, Heroes, and Supermen* is a significant book in an unheroic age. It is a description and critical appraisal of contemporary concepts and behavioral patterns of leadership. The author, Eugene E. Jennings, defines three main types of leaders: "princes," or men driven to dominate others, "heroes," or men wholly dedicated to noble causes, and "supermen," or iron-willed individuals who destroy old values and create new ones. All great leaders combine these characteristics.

890. "Nothing is as difficult to explain as the knack of leadership," says Ludwig Hause. "But it's very easy to demonstrate. Place a 6-inch piece of string on top of your desk. Take hold of the back end of that string, and try to push it across the top of the desk. No luck? Now grab the front end and pull it. That's leadership!"

—Horizons

891. People will follow your footsteps more readily than they follow your advice.

—Survey Bulletin

892. A good leader inspires other men with confidence in him; a great leader inspires them with confidence in themselves.

—Origin Unknown

893. The ability to keep a cool head in an emergency, maintain poise in the midst of excitement, and to refuse to be stampeded are true marks of leadership.

—R. Shannon, Illinois Medical Journal

894. "The normal person," says a learned psychologist, "is also a mediocre person." Organizations, unfortunately, tend to select their leaders from men who think alike and act alike, according to the pattern of normality. "If we persist in penalizing people," he warns, "for having more than their share of intelligence, imagination, and energy—because they don't conform to the norm—we'll wind up with a group of happy nonentities for leaders."

—Phoenix Flame

895. He who cannot lead and will not follow, at least makes a dandy road block.

—Nuggets

896. Every great leader has had excellent reason to fulminate about the recalcitrance and stupidity of man.

—John W. Campbell, Jr.,
Independents Star Magazine

897. The chief responsibility of an executive is to set up targets at which to shoot.

—Thoughts for Today

898. Six centuries before Christ there lived a wise Chinese philosopher who gave us these three precious principles of leadership. As you read the pages of history you will find that the greatest men followed these simple principles. "I have three precious things which I cherish and prize," said the sage. "The first is gentleness, the second is frugality, and the third is humility. Be gentle and you may be bold; be frugal and you may be liberal; avoid putting yourself above others and you may become a leader."

—Supervision

899. It was obvious he was cut out to be a leader. He was just sewed up wrong.

900. All great leaders have deliberated with caution but acted with decision and promptness.

—Royal Bank of Canada Monthly Letter

Learning

901. The mere act of listening to wise statements and sound advice does little for anyone. In the process of learning, the learner's dynamic cooperation is required.

—CHARLES I. CRAGG, Harvard Business Bureau, Wealth of a Nation

902. Self-directed learning is desirable but we have only a few teachers who can keep the pot boiling when the fire is removed.

—M. DALE BAUGHMAN

903. Receptivity must be present in each student or he will not learn. (At times I have wondered whether learning on the part of eager students is not almost independent of teaching methods.)

—EDGAR COLLINS BAIN, "Russian Lesson for Americans," Education Digest

904. If the learner sits and lets knowledge flow over him like water over a rock, nothing is going to happen to him.

It is only when a genuine interaction between the learner and the "stuff" of education takes place does any observable change occur.

—GRAMBS AND IVERSON, Dryden Press, Modern Methods in Secondary Education

905. A young man came to Socrates one day and said, in substance: "Mr. Socrates, I have come 1,500 miles to gain wisdom and learning. I want learning, so I come to you."

Socrates said, "Come, follow me." He led the way down to the seashore. They waded out into the water until they were up to their waists, and then Socrates seized his companion and forced his head under the water. In spite of his struggles, Socrates held him under. Finally, when most of his resistance was gone, Socrates laid him out on the shore and returned to the market place. When the visitor had regained his strength, he returned to Socrates to learn the reason for this behavior.

Socrates said to him, "When you were under the water, what was the one thing you wanted more than anything else?"

He said, "I wanted air."

Then Socrates said, "When you want knowledge and understanding as badly as you wanted air, you won't have to ask anyone to give it to you."

—STERLING W. SILL in *Miracle of Personality*

906. Learning is aided by teaching—only "aided"; it is an active, not a passive process.

907. The common good of the group is a social aim of democracy. A proper balance should be maintained between the development of the independent individual and the social individual.

-WILLIAM BURTON, *Phi Delta Kappan*

908. Some of the best places to eat have no gaudy menu sign. Some of the best learning troughs have no glittering facades.

—M. DALE BAUGHMAN

909. The optimum learning state is relaxed in body and alert in mind.

910. Our chief task, really, is to arouse the more important but slumbering wants into action.

—H. A. OVERSTREET

911. You cannot learn when your mouth is working. You learn when your ears are working and your mouth is closed. Before you say it, write it; for then, if you do not like the way it looks, you can erase it on paper.

912. Everybody needs to learn but let's admit it—there are many who find it hard enough to hang on to what they already know.

—M. DALE BAUGHMAN

913. Learning is like mercury, one of the most powerful and excellent things in the world in skillful hands; in unskillful the most mischievous.

914. He who has imagination without learning has wings but no feet.

—JOSEPH JOUBERT

915. Creation and nurture of a desire to learn and to know must begin long before higher education comes upon the scene. They must come from the development of new teaching techniques used from techniques that tend to stimulate and foster the inquiring mind and that instill in youth the completion of the unfinished and continuing nature of their educational experience.

—SAMUEL B. GOULD, President,
Antioch College, *Antioch Notes*

916. The man who is too old to learn, was probably always too old to learn.

—HENRY HASKINS, *Champaign-Urbana
News Gazette*

917. Learning is like rowing upstream; not to advance is to drop back.

—Chinese proverb

Life

918. Let your life be like a snowflake which leaves a mark but not a stain.

919. One night while deep in starlight still, I dreamt that I received this bill:

Mr. You, in account with life:
5,000 breathless dawns, all new.
5,000 flowers fresh with dew.
5,000 sunsets wrapped in gold.
1,000,000 snowflakes served ice-cold.
100 music haunted drams of moon-drenched roads and
    hurrying streams, of prophesying winds and tower-
    ing trees, of silent stars and browsing bees.
One June night in fragrant wood.
One friend I loved and understood.

I wondered, when I waked that day, how in the world I could
ever pay.

—Calvary Messenger

920. You can't control the length of your life, but you can have
something to say about the width and depth.

—Defender, Defenders of the
Christian Faith

921.   A thing that makes life most distractive,
    Is a conscience that is retroactive.

922.   If you can keep your head when all around you others
  Are losing theirs on gambles left and right,
  But making gobs of money in the process;
  You start to wonder if you're very bright.
  If you had only bought that stock at twenty,
  Now selling at a cool two hundred five,
  You'd really be on easy street, forever,
  Instead of struggling just to keep alive.
  If you had kept that farm your father left you,
  Where now a fancy supermarket stands,
  You'd never have to skimp to buy the groceries;
  You'd have a good sized fortune on your hands.
  If you had bet that long shot at the races,
  Which came in paying thirty-five to one,
  You could have put an end to monthly payments
  And thumbed your nose at every nasty dun.

  If you had sought uranium in the mountains
  Instead of hunting hapless ducks and deer;
  Who knows, today you might have many millions
  And not be sobbing sadly in your beer.
  If you had married Bess, the boss's daughter,
  Instead of Mable bless her simple soul,
  Or better yet that rich but sickly widow,
  You'd now be starring in a playboy's role.
  If you had not been you, but Joe or Charlie,
  Whose ventures always turn to solid gold,
  While you are getting poorer by the minute;
  Your ulcers then at least would be consoled.
  If you can dream of all those missed bonanzas,
  The Might-Have-Beens that you will always flub,

Yet not completely lose your marbles, brother,
Then welcome to the Second Guessers Club.
—Courtesy *Arizona Progress,*
Southern Illinois Schools

923. A recent survey found that the average adult spends about one-third of his waking time bored!...Famed economist Stuart Chase once sat down to figure the calendar of his days. There is, he said, an ascending scale of human values and somewhere on it there is a line between living and mere existing. In how many hours of the week, he asked himself, had he truly and intensively lived? In how many had he just existed? Out of the 168 hours of the week, he found that he had been "alive" only 40, or about 25% of the total time!

—Ardis Whitman, *Woman's Day*

924. A curious fact about life is that when we just let ourselves go and do what we like when we like it, we cease before long to like what we do. William James said that a person should do one unpleasant duty every day just to keep himself in moral trim.

—Ralph W. Sockman,
Arkansas Methodist

925. If the sum of our unspoken admiration, love, and encouragement could find expression, nine-tenths of the world's woes would be healed as if by magic.

—Margery Wilson, *Sunshine Magazine*

926.   Question not, but live and labor
Till yon goal be won,
Helping every feeble neighbor,
Seeking help from none;
Life is mostly froth and bubble,
Two things stand like stone,
Kindness in another's trouble
Courage in your own.
—A. L. Gordon, *Ye Wearie Wayfarer*

927. The best way to cheer yourself up is to cheer everybody else up.

—Mark Twain

928. There are two days in every week about which we should not worry—two days which should be kept free from any fear and apprehension. One of these days is Yesterday, with its mistakes and cares, its aches and pains, its faults and blunders. Yesterday has passed forever beyond our control. All the money in the world cannot bring back Yesterday. We cannot undo a single act we performed; we cannot erase a single word we said; we cannot rectify a single mistake. Yesterday has passed forever beyond recall. Let it go.

The other day we should not worry about is Tomorrow, with its possible adversities, its burdens, its large promise and poor performance. Tomorrow also is beyond our immediate control. Tomorrow's sun will rise either in splendor or behind a mass of clouds—but it will rise. And until it does, we have no stake in tomorrow, because it is as yet unborn.

That leaves us but one day—Today! And man can fight the battles of just one day.

Yesterday and Tomorrow are futile worries. Let us, therefore, resolve to journey no more than one day at a time.

—ROBERT J. BURDETTE,
Sunshine Magazine

929. To the preacher life's a sermon, to the joker it's a jest; to the miser life is money, to the loafer life is rest. To the lawyer life's a trial, to the poet life's a song, to the doctor life's a patient that needs treatment right along.

To the soldier life's a battle, to the teacher life's a school; life's a good thing to the grafter, it's a failure to the fool. To the man upon the engine life's a long and heavy grade; it's a gamble to the gambler, to the merchant life is trade.

Life is but a long vacation to the man who loves his work; life's an everlasting effort to shun duty, to the shirk; to the earnest, sincere worker life's a story ever new; life is what we try to make it— brother, what is life to you?

—S. E. KISER, *Sunshine Magazine*

930. A maker of violins searched all his life for wood that would serve for making violins with a certain beautiful and haunting resonance. At last he succeeded when he came into possession of wood gathered from the timberline, the last stand of the trees of the Rockies, 12,000 feet above sea level. Up there where the winds blow so fiercely and steadily that the bark to windward has no chance to grow, where the branches all point one way, and where a tree to live must stay on its knees all through its life, that is where the world's most resonant wood for violins is born and lives and dies.

—W. HAYDEN AMBROSE,
Link

931. Many young people starting out in life believe that freedom means the right to do the things that they want to do, regardless of whether or not that right interferes with the rights and comforts of others. They mistake license for freedom; they are spiritually nearsighted. They want to be free to see life. This is a noble desire, but it is too often misunderstood and turned in the wrong direction. They should know that living does not consist in the dissipation of life but in the conservation of life.

—You Magazine

932. No man is so tall that he need never stretch, nor so small that he need never stoop.

933. "Life consists not simply in what heredity and environment do to us but in what we make out of what they do to us."

—Harry Emerson Fosdick

934. "What is life's heaviest burden?" asked a youth of a sad and lonely old man.

He answered: "To have nothing to carry."

—E. Scott O'Conner, *Ladies' Home Journal*

935. Man being unable to choose between two evils, often hunts up a third.

—Lebanon Reporter

936. "A man's life," sighed Joe, "is 20 years of having his mother asking him where he is going, 40 years of having his wife ask the same question; and at the end, the mourners are wondering, too."

—Weekly Animator

937. Life is partly what you make it and partly how you take it.

938. Living today is a game of robbing Peter to pay Paul to make it possible to stand Pat.

939. Wrinkles should merely show where the smiles have been.

—Mark Twain

940.
I do not mind my P's and Q's,
How careless I must B; nor
Do my actions always suit my
Neighbors to a T.
I think perhaps the greatest
Fault that I can now recall—

I make my I's a lot too large,
And all my U's too small.
—REGINOLD HOLMES in *Fireside Fancies*

941. Live in such a way that you would not be ashamed to sell your parrot to the town gossip.
—WILL ROGERS

942. Life isn't a bowl of cherries; it's a bunch of raisins—raisin' heck, raisin' kids, or raisin' money!

943. If all the people were clever, and all clever people were good, the world would be nicer than ever we thought that it possibly could. But, alas, it is seldom or never the two hit it off as they should—the good are so hard on the clever, the clever so rude to the good!
—WADSWORTH

944. You may bring to your office, and put in a frame, a motto as fine as its paint, but if you're a crook when you're playing the game, that motto won't make you a saint. You can stick up the placards all over the wall, but here is the word I announce: It is not the motto that hangs on the wall, but the motto you live that counts. If the motto says, "Smile," and you carry a frown; "Do it now," and you linger and wait; if the motto says "Help," and you trample men down; if the motto says "Love," and you hate—you won't get away with the mottoes you install, for truth will come forth with a bounce. It is not the motto that hangs on the wall, but the motto you live, that counts.
—*Kalends*

945. The ups and downs of life that one lives through and survives are the only things that give dimension and color and flavor to life.
—DR. GALEN STARR ROSS, president,
Capitol College of Oratory and Music,
Columbus, Ohio

946. One door may be shut, but there are many others that are open. He who allows his day to pass without practicing generosity and enjoying life's pleasures is like a blacksmith's bellows—he breathes but he does not live.

947. Last night I decided to count my blessings.
I didn't think it would take long.

But I certainly showed poor guessing,
For today I'm still going strong!

—Nicki Joy Doud, *Sunshine Magazine*

948. No one has any right to find life uninteresting or unrewarding who sees within the sphere of his own activity a wrong he can help to remedy, or within himself an evil he can hope to overcome, or within another a life he can assist to greater heights.

—*Odd Moments*, Sunshine Private Press

949. Fear less, hope more; eat less, chew more; whine less, breathe more; talk less, say more; hate less, love more; and all good things will be yours.

—Swedish Proverb, *Partners*

950. Business Card: As you slide down the banister of life—may the splinters never point the wrong way.

951. The world is a great book, of which they who never stir from home read only a page.

952.   Throughout life's journey,
            Be it ever so rough,
            Don't reach for the summit,
            By using the bluff.

—M. Dale Baughman

953.   Life may not begin at 40,
            but about then the hoof-prints
            of the bellowing herd begin
            to show on your trampled
            anatomy.

—*Nuggets*

954. "Take your needle, my child, and work at your pattern; it will work out a rose by-and-by. Life is like that. One stitch at a time taken patiently, and the pattern will come out all right, like the embroidery."

—Oliver Wendell Holmes

955. Life would be one delightful slide if we did not have to drag our sleds back up the hill.

—*Grit*

956. Life is divided into three terms—that which was, which is, and which will be. Let us learn from the past to profit by the present, and from the present to live better for the future.

957. Some people never put out anything but a chill, and then wonder why the world is sour.

—Dr. Galen Starr Ross, President,
Capitol College of Oratory and Music,
Columbus, Ohio

958. Have you ever watched a grower irrigate his grove, or a farmer his land? When he opens little gates to irrigation furrows there rushes in a life-giving flow of water which, in time, will result in beautiful trees and flourishing plants. Our lives are like that. Each of us is given a furrow into which flow power, wisdom, energy, and health from a divine source. Like the trees and plants, we thrive—or dry up—according to the degree to which our gates are opened. But there is this tremendous difference. God lets every man be the keeper of his own gate!

—R and R Magazine

959. The triumph song of life would lose its melody without its minor keys.

—Mary Clark Leeper, Sunshine Magazine

960. Every great song, story, painting, sculpture, invention or humanitarian work has come out of the "still place." The creators of the world's work and men of genius know how to be still. In that stillness a new idea comes to mind, and they work to bring it into visible form.

Thomas Edison lived and worked in the "still place" twenty hours out of the twenty-four. He slept little and talked seldom. He said he was glad to be deaf, for he did not have to listen to the chatter of people. He took no credit to himself for his electrical inventions and discoveries. "Had I not been there to get it," he said, "someone else would." He knew he was just an instrument for divine power and wisdom to work through, but he kept the dial of his mind tuned to the universal station.

George Washington Carver contacted that same creative power that is always ready and waiting to be used. It was a rule of this great scientist to rise at 4:00 a.m., and go out into the woods or fields. In the stillness of the dawn he asked what he was to do that day, and waited for God to tell him. He took the humble peanut to his laboratory and reverently asked God what a peanut was and why He made it, and it yielded more than three hundred more useful products and increased its yield 500 per cent.

—Friendly Chat

961. I remember once hearing a new golf game called "Drink and Smell." The rules were to have two players, two caddies, two bags of clubs, and one large bottle of whiskey. After the first hole the winner got a drink and the loser just a smell; the same procedure on the second and thereafter. If the same lost 3 or 4 holes in succession, he would be *bound* to win the next. So it is with life, even without the bottle and the golf game. Life is a game of alternate victories and defeats.

962. Admiral Byrd, the explorer, one day was passing through the lobby of a hotel when a large company of people commenced cheering him. Two men were joining in the salutation, when one was overheard remarking to the other: "He is the last of the explorers; there is nothing left for the rest of us to explore."

The companion replied: "This is the greatest age of adventure, perhaps, that the human race has ever seen. It is easier to conquer the unexplored seas, or forest, or aerial regions than to conquer the crowds that jostle at your elbow.

"One looks at the ever moving humanity, and it is just a mass. One looks at a profession or a trade, and it is just a mass. But now and then one, or two, or three out of the mass emerge, because in their own souls they have found the meaning of personality.

"The great adventure today is not to travel to Little America, on the edge of the southern pole, but to emerge from the crowd that is about to trample you, or to suffocate you, or to mold you as a part of it. You can emerge only by the strength of your personality—a personality that is independent in every temptation and supreme in every victory."

—A. E. Cory, *Sunshine Magazine*

Listening

963. More failures in academic and social growth can be traced to inability to listen than to any other single aspect of the language-arts.

—Mark A. Neville, Headmaster of the Latin School of Chicago, "Listening Is an Art: Practice It," *Elementary English*

964. Good listening has been described as an art; now it is a rapidly growing profession. The busy offices of social workers, our school counselors, personnel managers, and marriage consultants are filled with troubled people, in desperate need of listeners, talking out their problems.

Luck

965. Ill luck, in nine cases out of ten, is the result of practicing pleasure first and duty second, instead of duty first and pleasure second.

—Friendly Chat

966. Luck is efficiency's mistress.

—Persian Proverb

967.
You will find that luck
Is only pluck,
Trying things over and over;
Patience and skill,
Courage and will
Are the four leaves of luck's clover.

968. I am a great believer in luck and I find the harder I work, the more I have of it.

—STEPHEN LEACOCK

Memory

969. Be a Good Forgetter—Life is too short to remember that which prevents one from doing his best. "Forgetting the things that are behind, I press forward," said a brave old man in the first century. The successful man forgets. He knows the past is irrevocable. He is running a race. He cannot afford to look behind. His eye is on the winning post. The magnanimous man forgets. He is too big to let little things disturb him. He forgets easily. If anyone does him wrong, he considers the source and keeps sweet. It is only the small man who cherishes a low revenge. Be a good forgetter. Business dictates it, and success demands it.

—Lion Tales, Cumberland, Maryland

970. Dr. George A. Miller, conducting a study for the Office of Naval Research, discovered that the average person can remember accurately only 7 items on any list read to him . . . Dr. Miller offers this intriguing suggestion: Perhaps, since the human memory is limited to 7, this might explain why the number 7 crops up so often—the 7 wonders of the world, the 7 notes of the musical scale, the 7 seas, the 7 deadly sins, 7 ages of man.

971. We've often wondered how waitresses could remember the various orders for different meals that they receive day in and day out. And now we know, because while we were getting impatient at our table the other day, we called to the girl: "Waitress, have you forgotten me?"

And, to the amusement of everyone around, she answered pertly, "Oh, no, sir! Indeed not. You're the stuffed tomato!"

972. A retentive memory may be a good thing, but the ability to forget is the true token of greatness.

—ELBERT HUBBARD

973. The true art of memory is the art of attention.

—SAMUEL JOHNSON

974. A well-trained memory is one that permits you to forget everything that isn't worth remembering.

—O. A. BATTISTA

Mind

975.   Small minds discuss persons.
Average minds discuss events.
Great minds discuss ideas.

—SISTER MARY LAURETTA,
This Week Magazine

976. We all know and love the word "landscape." Someone has proposed a similar word, "Mindscape." That would mean a view of the mind, what a mind thinks about, what it desires most, the language it uses, the visions it has. It is a good word to think about.

—HALFORD LUCCOCK, *Christian Herald*

977. Broad-mindedness is the result of flattening high-mindedness out.

978. It wouldn't hurt so much to become angry, except that, for some reason, anger makes your mouth work faster than your mind.

979. In one of his most famous sermons, Harry Emerson Fosdick tells of a young invalid who wrote to her friend, "At first, I thought somehow to make the best of it, but now I am planning to make the most of it." Make the most of scrubbing a floor or ironing a basketful of laundry? Why not? While your hands are performing those routine tasks, your mind is free for excursions. It can go anywhere and do anything under the sun—mellow you with memories or intrigue you with plans for the future.

I have no glittering examples to set before you, but I will wager that more than one timesaving appliance now considered indispensable in your kitchen was invented by a woman with her hands in dishwater.

—HUGH B. CAVE

980. "The brain is a wonderful organ; it starts working the moment you get up in the morning, and does not stop until you get into the office."

—ROBERT FROST

981. Every mind is different; and the more it is unfolded the more pronounced is that difference.

—EMERSON, Essay on *Quotations and Originality*

Mistakes

982. To err is human, but when you wear out the eraser before the pencil, you're overdoing it.

—*Rotary Club News*

983. My friend R. B. Jones doesn't have a first or middle name— only the initials R. B. This unusual arrangement was never a problem until he went to work for a government agency. The government is not accustomed to initialed employees; so R. B. had a lot of explaining to do. On the official forms for the payroll and personnel departments, his name was carefully entered as R (Only) B (Only) Jones.

Sure enough, when R. B. got his pay check, it was made out to Ronly Bonly Jones.

—STEPHEN A. BOMER in *True, The Man's Magazine*

984. There are about three things a person can do when he makes a mistake. He can resolve that he will never make another, which is fine, but impracticable; he may let that mistake make a coward of him, which is foolish; or he can make up his mind that he will let it be his teacher, and so profit by the experience, that if the situation comes his way again, he will know just how to meet it.

—*Sunshine Magazine*

985. All men, no matter how big, make mistakes. But history teaches us that big men refuse to falter because of their mistakes. Henry Ford forgot to put a reverse gear in his first automobile. Edison once spent over two million dollars on an invention which proved of little value.

The man who makes no mistakes lacks boldness and the spirit of adventure. He is the one who never tries anything new; he is the brake on the wheels of progress. Remember, a mistake becomes an error only when nothing is done to correct it.

—*Gear-O-Gram*

986. Freedom from error isn't enough—a blank page can be free from errors.

987. Heard the other day about the Colorado mining town, just about on its last legs, which took on new life when uranium was discovered nearby and the government poured in a few millions to rejuvenate the local electric plant for a new operation. The town's editor, trying to do justice to the occasion with his hand-set paper, was all ready to print a special issue when his aged partner up and got married. Some front page type was hurriedly discarded and the wedding story inserted. The paper was on the streets the next day before the editor discovered he had neglected to revise the original headline on the space now recounting the wedding. The headline read, "Old Powerhouse Resumes Operation."

988. You'll find beyond the smallest doubt mistakes are bound to be found out.

989. *Definition:* Mark Twain was once asked the difference between a mistake and a blunder. He explained it this way. "If you walk into a restaurant and walk out with someone's silk umbrella and leave your own cotton one, that's a mistake. But if you pick up someone's cotton umbrella and leave your own silk one, that's a blunder."

990. Mistakes will happen but must you give them so much help?

Misunderstanding

991. A newspaper reporter phoned to ask the title of a speech to be given at the arts festival. Actually the speech title was "Moods in Water Colors," but in the newspaper it appeared "Nudes in Water Colors." There was an overflow crowd.

992. It is said that Phineas T. Barnum, the famed circus magnate, hung a large sign over one of the exits of his museum, which read, "This way to the egress." Many people in the crowds, eager to see what an egress looked like, passed through the door and found themselves out on the street.

993. *Carol:* "Daddy, who is Richard Stands?
Dad: "I never heard of him.
Carol: "He must be an important person."
Dad: "Why?"
Carol: "When we pledge allegiance to the flag in school we say, 'I pledge allegiance to the flag of the United States of America and to the republic for Richard Stands.'"

994. A clerk, checking over an applicant's papers, was amazed to note the figures 127 and 123 in the spaces reserved for "Age of father, if living," and "Age of mother, if living."
"Surely," said the surprised clerk, "Your parents aren't that old?"
"Nope," was the answer, "but they would be, if living.'

995. The large volume of newspaper space given to fast-developing missile news apparently confused two inebriated Washington sightseers recently. As they passed the Washington Monument, a small fire in the elevator sent billows of smoke out the Monument door. One leaned to the other: "I'll give you 8 to 5," he said, "it won't take off!"

996. A little girl took much too long returning from the store where she had been sent on an errand by her mother and she was asked, "What on earth took you so long?"
"I was watching the devil's funeral," she replied.
"What do you mean—the devil's funeral?" her astonished mother asked.
"Well, I was watching the cars of the funeral go by and counting

them, and a man next to me said the poor devil was only sick about a week."

— *Capper's Weekly*

997. Lecturing his teenage son on temperance, a father proclaimed, "There are at least 15 saloons in this town and I haven't been in one of them."

"Which one is that?" asked the son.

998. "When I applied for that job, the manager had the nerve to ask if my punctuation is good."

"What did you tell him?"

"I said I'd never been late for work in my life."

Motivation

999. It's a rare human being indeed who will not do his best when he feels that he will be rewarded as his work deserves.

— *Et Cetera*

1000. Excellent performance is a blend of talent and motive, of ability fused with zeal; aptitude without aspiration is lifeless and inert.

And that is only part of the story. When ability is brought to life by aspiration, there is the further question of the ends to which these gifts are applied. We do not wish to nurture the man of great talent and evil purpose. . . .

— *The Pursuit of Excellence*

1001. You won't see it on a balance sheet. But today, psychological momentum is a company great hope for making and increasing profits.

It can be seen at a store counter. For psychological momentum is the force that impels toward that counter not just people, but people with an impulse to buy. Yes, a company must move minds. And so must teachers move minds.

Music

1002. John D. Rockefeller III, president, New York Lincoln Center for the performing arts: "The most remarkable statistic of all; Americans now spend more money every year to attend concerts than to watch professional baseball. The American artistic scene has come alive."

1003. "Gee, Dad," asked the teenager, "did you ever hear anything like this rock 'n' roll?"

"Just once," replied the long-suffering father, "when a truck of live ducks hit a wagon loaded with empty milk cans."

—T. O. WHITE, *Champaign-Urbana*
News Gazette

1004. Good music? A bit too strait-laced;
We may use it later—no haste.
Our tunes may be trite,
But for kids that's all right;
They've not yet acquired a true taste!

—DAN HAYES, University of Illinois
Daily Illini

1005. Is there any music like that of a car starting on a cold morning?

—CARMAN FISH, *National Safety News*

1006. Music, once admitted to the soul, becomes a sort of spirit, and never dies. It wanders perturbedly through the halls and galleries of the memory, and is often heard again, distinct and living, as when it first displaced the wavelets of the air.

—EDWARD GEORGE BULWER-LYTTON

1007. The music teacher was proudly presenting her pupils in a recital. After the extended musical program, ice cream, cake, and fruit were served. One of the young musicians had brought her little brother along as a guest.

As the youngster was taking his departure, the teacher asked, "Well, Jimmie, did you enjoy the recital?"

"I sure did," Jimmie replied, "that is, all but the music."

Nature—Nature Study

1008. "Teacher training is the bottleneck in the movement toward universal education in nature appreciation, conservation and the wise use of our natural resources."

—*Annual Report of the Cook County*
Forest Preserve District in Illinois

1009. Most of the teachers who have grown up in cities know nothing at all about outdoor living. Many a city classroom teacher could do all right in an examination in geology and biology, but when it comes to firsthand contact with the outdoors, all she can recall are a few field trips in science classes and some wienie roasts on the beach. She can't call a dozen trees by name. She likes birds, but she can't get much beyond sparrows and robins in bird recognition. As for insects, they are either (a) the subject of a chapter in a textbook, or (b) something that gets into the cake at picnics.

—DOROTHEA KAHN JAFFE, "Preparing Teachers to Teach Outdoors," *The Nation's Schools*

1010. The children had been very attentive while the teacher told them about the animals. "Now," she said, "name some things that are very dangerous to get near to, and have horns."

"I know, Miss Teacher," exclaimed Mary, with hand raised.

"Well, Mary?" said the teacher.

"Motor cars, Miss Teacher."

1011. A teacher testing her class in nature study, asked: "Who can tell me the name of the male, the female, and the baby sheep?"

"I can," replied one youngster. "Ram the daddy, dam the mammy, and lam' the kid."

—JOSEPH FEDERICO, *Laugh Book*

1012. The first grade was having a lesson about birds. After some discussion the fact was established that birds eat fruit. One small girl, however, was unconvinced. "But, teacher," she asked, raising her hand, "how can the birds open the cans?"

1013. A rather stout schoolmistress was talking about birds and their habits. "Now," she said, "at home I have a canary, and it can do something that I cannot do. I wonder if any of you know just what that thing is?"

Little Eric raised his hand. "I know, teacher. Take a bath in a saucer."

—*Kablegram*, SAC Sidelights

Objective

1014. Forward-looking Charles F. Kettering contends too many of us conduct business by using the past as a guide. "If we drove an automobile like we try to run the world," he says, "we would have the steering wheel looking out the back window to see where we came from. The only thing that is important is where you are going."

—JACK KYTLE, *Partners*

1015. The poorest man is not he who is without a cent, but he who is without a dream.

—EUGENE P. BERTIN, *Pennsylvania School Journal*

1016. There is a fable about a dog that boasted of his ability to run faster than any other one. One day he gave chase to a rabbit, but failed to catch him. When the other dogs ridiculed him for his previous boasting and his failure in the chase, he replied: "The rabbit was running for his life, while I was running only for my dinner."

—*The King's Business*

1017. If you go duck hunting, you aim at the point where the winging bird is going to be rather than where he is when you fire. Is there a lesson here for education?

Too often, says Dr. Harold Rugg, former professor of education, Columbia Teachers College, we aim our education plans at the point where the children are now or even where they were in a generation ago.

We need to aim at the point where children will be when the education plans mature, Dr. Rugg told a recent conference on current educational issues at Goddard College, Plainfield, Vermont.

1018. The world steps aside to let any man pass who knows whither he is going.

—DAVID STARR JORDAN

1019. To do the right thing, at the right time, in the right way; to do some things better than they were ever done before; to eliminate errors, and to anticipate requirements; to act from reason rather than rule; to work for the love of work and to be satisfied with nothing short of perfection.

1020. For lowest marks he set his bow, and shot it. He asked for little here below—and got it!

—W. L. HUDSON

1021. "Before you go to sleep, say to yourself, 'I haven't reached my goal yet, whatever it is, and I'm going to be uncomfortable and in a degree unhappy until I do.'"

—CARL SANDBURG

1022. The man who aims at nothing is almost sure to hit it.

1023. Charles Schwab was once asked if a big businessman ever reached his objective. He replied that if a man ever reached his objective he was not a big businessman.

1024. It doesn't matter where you come from, but where you're headed for does.

Opportunity

1025. Some people never see an opportunity because it so often masquerades as a hard job.

1026. There is an opportunity in every obligation. When we begin to assume responsibility, we start to mature. Many a man has started his upward climb when he came to the realization that many things depended upon him. No one is indispensable but when one is cooperative, efficient, courageous, patient, self-reliant and dependable, he becomes almost irreplaceable.

—CARL HOLMES, *Friendly Chat*

1027. I wonder how many beginning college professors in large universities felt as I did when I joined the College of Education in a large midwest state university. I was a member of the team but it appeared that every time I shot at the basket, it shrank just enough to cause a miss. Furthermore, I was certain, at times, that that same basket expanded to insure a successful shot for certain other players on my team.

1028. Contact with an opportunity is like contact with a live wire; it is likely to knock a man silly unless he is prepared to handle it.

1029. Perhaps some of us miss opportunity because we are broadcasting when we should be tuning in.

—*Mutual Moments*

1030. He who gets up at dawn to see the sunrise couldn't have picked a better time.

Junior is getting higher marks now . . . His teacher must be doing better.

1031. Many grownups do with opportunities as children do at the seashore. They fill their hands with sand, and then let the grains fall through, till all are gone.

1032. There is a familiar proverb to the effect that "Opportunity knocks on every man's door once, but only once." Here are a few instances when her knock was not heard, as cited by Webb B. Garrison in *The Uplift:*

A Nottingham plumber submitted to the British War Office in 1911 a design for a tank—a then unknown military device. Across the drawing in red ink was written the official comment: "The man is mad."

Those who loaned Robert Fulton the money for his steamboat project were so fearful of ridicule that they stipulated that their names be withheld!

When George Westinghouse had perfected his airbrake in 1875, he offered it to Commodore Vanderbilt. The railroad magnate returned Westinghouse's letter, with these words scribbled across the bottom. "I have no time to waste on fools."

One day a stranger approached Mark Twain with a request for $500 for which he would sell half interest in his invention. Twain, "bit" several times before, refused flatly. But out of courtesy he asked the stranger his name. "Bell," the man replied, turning away, "Alexander Graham Bell."

—Friendly Chat

1033. Opportunity doesn't knock at the door . . . . She answers when you knock.

1034. Wanted: A man for hard work and rapid promotion: a man who can find things to be done without the help of a manager and three assistants.

A man who gets to work on time in the morning and does not imperil the lives of others in an attempt to be first out of the office at night.

A man who listens carefully when he is spoken to and asks only enough questions to insure the accurate carrying out of instructions.

A man who moves quickly and makes as little noise as possible about it.

A man who looks you straight in the eye and tells the truth every time.

A man who does not pity himself for having to work.

A man who is neat in appearance.

A man who does not sulk for an hour's over-time in emergencies.

A man who is cheerful, courteous to everyone, and determined to make good.

This man is wanted everywhere. Age or lack of experience does not count. There isn't any limit, except his own ambition, to the number or size of the jobs he can get. He is wanted in every business.

—Cheer, published by Walker Electric
Supply Company of Terre Haute

1035. *Harlow H. Curtice:* The young man who doesn't keep his eye on the clock but still knows what time it is will find unlimited opportunities in this growing country.

*—*WILLIAM T. NOBLE in Detroit *News*

1036. Next to knowing when to seize an opportunity, the most important thing in life is to know when to forego an advantage.

—DISRAELI

1037. Four things come not back—the spoken word, the sped arrow, the past life, and the neglected opportunity.

—*Survey Bulletin*

1038. It's an old story—the one about the sailing ship, blown off its course, lost, and in desperate need of fresh water. One day, when it seemed that the crew could hold out no longer, they sighted another ship.

"Water! Water!" they signalled frantically. "We are dying of thirst!"

"Lower your bucket where you are!" came back the surprising reply.

The bucket they lowered over the side of the ship came up filled with fresh, sweet water. They had been drifting in the current from the mouth of the mighty Amazon River, whose great flood of fresh water spreads far out of sight of land before it is conquered by the saltiness of the sea.

—*Sunshine Magazine*

Optimism—Optimist

1039. An optimist and a pessimist were defined by a speaker at a meeting as follows: "An optimist is a man who sees a light that is not there, and a pessimist is the fool who tries to blow it out."

1040. "Twixt optimist and pessimist
The difference is droll;
The optimist sees the donut
The pessimist the hole."

—McWILSON

1041. An optimist sees an opportunity in every calamity; a pessimist sees a calamity in every opportunity.

—Anon.

1042. Extreme optimists and extreme pessimists are usually wrong but the former have more fun being that way.

—T. O. WHITE, *Champaign-Urbana
News Gazette*

1043. Face the sun and all the shadows will fall behind you.

1044. A pessimist complains because rose bushes have thorns. An optimist rejoices because thorn bushes have roses.

1045. The Golden Age Club, an organization for persons over 60, has its phone number listed under "Youth Center."
—Fond Du Lac, Wisconsin, (*UPI*)

1046. I rather like this definition by Grace Downs, who runs an air hostess school: "An optimist is a guy who figures when his shoes wear out he'll be back on his feet."

Parents

1047. "Now, then, where's the fare for that boy?" asked the conductor in the crowded bus.
"He's only three years old," replied the child's father.
"Three years! Go on—look at him!" snorted the conductor. "He's six at least."
The father leaned over and gazed earnestly at the boy's face. Then he turned to the conductor: "Can I help it if he worries?" he asked.

1048. A scientist of great intellectual brilliance confided to a colleague that he had great hopes for his son, who had just won a scholarship to college. "It's amazing," the scientist said, "the way that boy progressed, once he got started. It's hard to believe, but it took him two years just to learn the alphabet."
The colleague looked stunned. "Why, I've never heard of such a thing," he said. "You must have been terribly depressed. How old was the poor lad when he finally did learn the alphabet?"
This time the scientist looked surprised. "I told you it took him two years," he said. "Obviously, he was two."
—*Wall Street Journal*

1049. There is no sure way to guarantee that your child will grow up to be the kind of person you would like him to be. The most likely way is for you to be the kind of person you would like him to be.
—*Phi Delta Kappan*

1050. After a day of complete harassment, the mother shook her finger at her small son. "All right, Junior," she shouted, "do anything you damn well please! Now let me see you disobey THAT!"

—LEE J. BORDEN

1051. "Daddy," said the small boy, "where did I come from?"

The father, who had been dreading the day the question would be asked, launched into a long contrived explanation on the facts of life. The boy listened attentively. At last the father concluded, "So now you know—but just as a matter of curiosity, how did you happen to ask?"

"Nothing special, Dad," said the son, "the new boy at our school said he came from Chicago and I was wondering where I came from."

—*Santa Fe Magazine*

1052. *Advice to parents:* Don't be hard on the children when they fight; they may be just playing house.

—*Laugh Book*

1053. Parents registering their children for the fall term at a Detroit kindergarten were asked pertinent questions about the children's background. In the blank marked "Language spoken in the home," one mother proudly replied, "Nice."

—MARJORIE GRACE BUCHANAN

1054. "How far is your daughter with the singing lessons she's getting at home?" someone asked Mr. Gray.

"Oh, doing all right," said Mr. Gray. "Today was the first time I took the cotton out of my ears."

—*PAL*

1055. Behind a teenager's "customized" car usually is found a pauperized Pop.

—J. W. PELKIE, *Quote*

1056. Yes sir, I took my boy a-fishin'. Sure, his mother told me to, but besides, I kind of done it 'cause it seemed the thing to do.

It's a heap more fun a-fishin' when I'm out there with my son, 'cause we really get acquainted through a little fishin' fun.

When my creel of life is empty, and my life's line sort of worn, I shall always keep rememberin' that first early summer morn when I took my boy a-fishin', and I really learned the joy that comes to every father when he really knows his boy.

—Outdoor Nebraska,
Friendly Chat

1057. Jimmy Johnson's daddy is an awful lot of fun; he's a peacherino pitcher and can hit a real home run. I know my dad could play as well, but when I ask him to, he's always awful busy and got something else to do.

Jimmy Johnson's daddy knows a lot of dandy games, and he plays 'em with us fellers, and he don't call Jimmy "James." I'll bet my dad knows things that's fun fer fellers, too, but he's always awful busy and got something else to do.

Some kids' dads seem glad to have a chance to play with boys, and even when they're readin', they don't mind a little noise. I'll bet my dad could beat 'em all, if he just only knew how I miss him when he's busy and got something else to do.

—Author Unknown, *Sunshine Magazine*

1058. *Friend:* "Has your son's education proved of any real value?"

Father: "Yes, indeed; it has entirely cured his mother of bragging about him."

—*The Lookout*

1059. "Why were you kept in after school?" the father asked his son.

"I didn't know where the Azores were."

"In the future, just remember where you put your things."

1060. The life history of parents: They bear children, bore teenagers and board newly-weds.

1061. Standard operating equipment for the parent of a junior high school age youngster *ought* to be *shockproof* constitution, *limitless* supply of patience, an understanding of *how* adolescents grow, and an ability to *roll* with the punches.

1062. Someone said it's just too bad that the hardest of all careers are entrusted to amateurs—parenthood and politics.

—LEO AIKMAN, *Laugh Book*

1063. A mother entered the supermarket with her four bouncing boys and pleaded: "Isn't there a cereal that will *sap* their energy?"

—EUGENE P. BERTIN, *Pennsylvania School Journal*

1064. "I wouldn't worry too much if your son makes mud pies," said the psychiatrist, "not even if he tries to eat them. That's quite normal."

Tag team . . .

"Well, I don't think it is," replied the woman, "and neither does his wife."

—Chicago Daily News

1065. One dad to another: "I'm no model father. All I'm trying to do is behave so that when people tell my son that he reminds them of me, he'll stick out his chest instead of his tongue."

—Manchester Oak Leaves

1066. Save your child from the possibility of making mistakes and you save him from the possibility of being right.

—Dick Snow, Pageant

1067. One big problem parents face is how much to give their son. If he has a Corvette at sixteen, what'll he want at twenty-one?

And with the daughter it's the same—how much to give your Sue? If hers is mink at fourteen, what'll satisfy at twenty-two?

"But others have it," they will say, and you know, of course, that's so; but if you want the best for them, you'll have to tell them, "No."

—Dorothy Smith

1068. The parent may not always be right but he is always necessary.

1069. The parents of a large brood of children deserve a lot of credit; in fact, they can't get along without it.

—Roy A. Brenner

Patience

1070. Remember, Noah—he was 486 years old before he knew enough to build an ark.

1071. The reason people confuse patience and interest is simple enough. The same thing that inspires the keenest interest in one person might completely bore another.

This is illustrated in a homely way. Of two neighbors, one found little boys and girls a definite annoyance at all times. He asked the other, who seemed to attract them, how he could be so patient with children.

"Me patient!" the man replied in complete surprise. "Why I'm not patient. I just like kids."

1072. Patience is a great thing; but it never helped a rooster lay an egg.

1073. For harmony of two, be they friends or teacher-pupil, the patience of one is necessary.

—M. Dale Baughman

1074. Patience: The ability to idle your motor when you feel like stripping your gears.

Perseverance—Persistence

1075. "Tommy, can you tell me the difference between perseverance and obstinacy?"

"One is a strong will and the other is a strong won't."

"Mister, I didn't get it to give up with—I got it to learn how with."

1076. The tough job that tests your mettle and spirit is like the grain of sand that gives an oyster a stomach ache. After a time it may become a pearl.

—*Eastern Sun*

1077. Keep pushing—'tis wiser than sitting aside
And dreaming and sighing and waiting the tide,
In life's earnest battle they only prevail
Who daily march onward and never say fail.

In life's rosy morning, in manhood's firm pride,
Let this be the motto your footsteps to guide:
In storm and in sunshine, whatever assail,
We'll onward and conquer, and never say fail.

—Anon.

1078. A small boy was learning to skate. His frequent mishaps awakened the pity of a bystander. "Sonny, you're getting all banged up," he said. "Why don't you stop for a while and just watch the others?" With tears still rolling down his cheeks from the last downfall, he looked from his adviser to the shining steel on his feet and answered: "Mister, I didn't get these skates to give up with; I got 'em to learn how with!"

—*Arkansas Baptist*

1079. The clever fellow does not always win. The plugger, aiming for a definite goal, often passes him in the race, says G. G. Barnard.

—*Friendly Chat*

1080. Fate can slam him and bang him around, and batter his frame till he's sore, but she never can say that he's really down, while he bobs up serenely once more. A fellow's not dead till he dies, nor beat till he no longer tries.

—*Sunshine Magazine*

1081. The mechanical engineer tells us that it takes six times as much power to start a flywheel from a dead stop as it does to keep it going once in motion, according to an item in *The Right Hand*. In other words, it takes only one sixth as much effort to keep going once you are on the way as it does to stop a bit, and then start again. When tempted to slacken just because things are coming your way, remember the flywheel.

1082. Engineers were called in to give their ideas on a possible railroad through the Andes Mountains. These men proclaimed the job an impossible one. Then American engineers were called in to give their opinions whether the railroad could follow along the side of the River Rimac.

Even these intrepid engineers claimed that it could not be done. As a last resort, a Polish engineer named Ernest Malinowski was called in. Malinowski's reputation as an engineer was well known, but he was at that time in sixtieth year, so the authorities feared to impose such a rigorous task on the man.

Malinowski assured the representatives of the various countries interested that the job could be done, and in his sixtieth year he started the highest railroad in the world.

The railway began to worm its way across the Andes from Peru with sixty-two tunnels and thirty bridges along its way. One tunnel ran 4,000 feet in length, 15,000 feet above the level of the sea. Twice, revolutions in some of the countries through which the railroad passed, held up construction. Once Malinowski had to flee Peru and remain in exile for a time—but nothing deterred this aging Pole in completing the engineering feat that became one of the wonders of the world in 1880.

—Future, *Friendly Chat*

1083. Americans are noted for their soft hearts and deep sympathies for the "underdog." Wouldn't it be better if somehow the underdog could be so taught that he would quit being an underdog?

We must believe it can be done and determine to do it—so must the underdog. First of all, he must be taught persistence. Salesmen do the impossible every day. So do most all successful people.

A survey made by the National Retail Dry Goods Association reveals the following results:

48% of the salesmen make one call and quit; 25% make two calls and quit; 15% make three calls and quit; that shows that 88% of the salesmen quit after making one, two, or three new calls.

But 12% keep on calling. They do 80% of the business.

The 88% who quit after the first, second, or third calls do 20% of the business.

The underdog must be imbued with a deep-down desire to achieve, to be somebody, to work and budget and dream. He must be content to start—and start in a small way, gradually working his way to responsibility and success. Perhaps he can be given the stories of successful families and groups to study. He can read the stories of people with all sorts of handicaps who have succeeded.

Education for everybody will never be a reality until, by educational processes, we teach the underdog to quit being an underdog.

1084. He was only twenty-three years old when a Gloucester youth saw this advertisement in a Boston newspaper: "Wanted, young man as an understudy to a financial statistician. P.O. Box 1720."

He answered the advertisement, according to an item in *The Red Barrel*, but received no reply. He wrote again—no reply. A third time—no reply. Then he went to the Boston post office and asked the name of the holder of Box 1720. The clerk refused to give it. He saw the postmaster. He, too, refused; it was against the rules.

Early one morning an idea came to the young man. He rose early, hurriedly prepared his own breakfast, took the first train to Boston, went to the post office, and stood sentinel near Box 1720.

After a long interval, a man appeared, opened Box 1720, and took out the mail. The young man trailed him to his destination, which was the office of a stock brokerage firm. The young man entered and asked for the manager.

The youth told the manager how he had applied for the position of understudy to a statistician—that he had written three times without receiving any response, and had been refused the box-holder's name at the post office.

"But," queried the manager, "how did you find out that I was the advertiser?"

"I stood in the lobby of the post office for several hours, watching Box 1720," answered the young man. "When a man came in and took the mail from the box, I followed him here."

The manager said, "Young man, you are just the kind of persistent fellow I want. You are employed!"

—Sunshine Magazine

1085. The man who would stand out among his fellows must have persistence. An assistant, once asked by Edison to perform an experiment, failed four or five times. When a friend suggested that he give up, the assistant replied, "Mr. Edison did not say to try the job four or five times. He said to do it."

1086. An ambitious young man asked a great merchant to reveal the secret of success. "Just jump at your opportunity," answered the merchant.

"But," queried the young man, "how can I tell when my opportunity is coming?"

"You can't," replied the merchant. "Just keep jumping."

—Friendly Chat

1087. When you get into a tight place and everything goes against you, till it seems that you cannot hold on a minute longer, never give up then, for that is just the place and time that the tide will turn.

—Harriet Beecher Stowe

1088. John Wanamaker, who made quite a success in retailing, urged persistency in advertising, which he harnessed to build a giant merchandising enterprise. Said he: "Advertising does not jerk—it pulls. It begins very gently at first, but the pull is steady —until it exerts an irresistible power."

—Houston Times

1089. When you feel that being persistent is a difficult task, think of the bee. A red clover blossom contains less than ⅛ of a grain of sugar; 7,000 grains are required to make a pound of honey. A bee, flitting here and there for sweetness, must visit 56,000 clover heads for each pound of honey; and there are about 60 flower tubes to each clover head. When a bee performs that operation 60 times 56,000, or 3,360,000 times, it secures enough sweetness for only one pound of honey.

—Sunshine Magazine

Persuasion

1090. The North Wind and the Sun disputed which was the most powerful, and agreed that he should be declared the victor who could first strip a wayfaring man of his clothes.

The North Wind first tried his power, and blew with all his might, but the keener became his blasts, the closer the traveler wrapped his cloak around him, till at last, resigning all hope of victory, he called upon the Sun to see what he could do.

The Sun suddenly shone out with all his warmth; the traveler no sooner felt his genial rays than he took off one garment after another, and at last, fairly overcome with heat, undressed and bathed in a stream that lay in his path.

Persuasion is better than force.

1091. There is a story about a man who sat in front of a fire talking with his minister. He said to him, "Parson, I don't think I'll come to church any more. Religion is a very personal thing, I think I'll just try to work it out by myself."

The parson said nothing, but took a pair of tongs and lifted a live coal out of the fire, and laid it on the hearth. They both watched it slowly go out.

Then the man said, "I see what you mean. I'll be back next Sunday."

—Sam Shoemaker, How to Become a Christian

1092. The really successful teacher is not one who preaches or tells, or admonishes or explains or orders, but the one who can effect in his pupils vivid imagined experiences. The secret is that strong feelings lead to doing. Concentration and actual practice in causing pupils to feel themselves actually in certain settings is one high road to persuasiveness.

—M. Dale Baughman

1093. A life insurance agent has been unsuccessful in persuading a farmer to provide an educational policy for his daughter. The conversation shifted to the subject of the farmer's garden, especially to some fine looking rows of beans which ran along the fence. The farmer spoke of the profit which he made on beans each year. "About how much do you make on each row?" asked the salesman. The farmer gave a rough estimate of the amount. "Mr. Williams," asked the salesman, "wouldn't you be willing to cultivate two more rows of beans to make sure that if anything happened to you, your daughter would have the education that a bright girl like yours should have? It would be an easy way of paying for that education, in any case, wouldn't it?" The sale was made.

Philosophy

1094. Lookin' fer the sunshine when the clouds are low, ain't such awful trouble, but some folks think it so. Sun is always shinin' tho' its face is hid; sweetest consolation just to lift the lid.

There are lots of humans who should have a heart, and be seekin' sunshine, but you can hear them start to weepin' and a pinin' "in this world o' woe," when just a ray o' sunshine would make their troubles go.

Sun is always shinin' fer you every day, if you'll only let it drive the clouds away. Quit yer sad complainin', life ain't sour and tart; someone will always help you if you will do yer part.

—*Friendly Chat*

1095. Practice the grace of giving up, the art of giving in and the virtue of holding in.

—O. G. Wilson

1096. My clouds bring **smiles** instead of tears because I
      will it so.
It eases life to laugh **at doubts** and let dark idols go.

There is no way to combat fate, for life's a game
    we play.
The clouds of day are only fears which smiles will
    drive away.
                —EVERETT WENTWORTH HILL,
                Sunshine Magazine

1097.   For every evil under the sun,
          There is a remedy or there is none.
          If there is one, try to find it,
          If there is none, never mind it.

1098. There are two ways of being rich. One is to have all you want, the other is to be satisfied with what you've got.
                —CARL SCHURZ, *Friendly Chat*

1099. If I keep a green bough in my heart, the singing bird will come.
                —Chinese saying, quoted in
                Ladies' Home Journal

1100. You can't change the past, but you can ruin the present by worrying about the future.
                —Johnson County (Greenwood, Indiana)
                News

1101. If you confer a benefit, never remember it; if you receive one, never forget it.
                —CHILON

1102. All philosophy lies in two words, sustain and abstain.
                —EPICTETUS

1103. There is no dead end. There is always a way out. What you learn in one failure, you utilize in your next success. This was Henry Ford's philosophy.

1104. It is what we give up, not what we lay up, that adds to our lasting store.
                —HOSEA BALLOU

1105. Keep searching for the other fellow's good points. Remember he has to hunt for yours, and maybe he'll be harder put than you are.
                —*Survey Bulletin*

1106. Billy Bray, when he heard someone telling a long story of troubles endured and sorrowings suffered, exclaimed: "I've had my trials and troubles. The Lord has given me both vinegar and honey, but He has given me the vinegar with a teaspoon and the honey with a ladle."

—Robert G. Lee, *Moody Monthly*

1107. There is no limit to the good a man can do if he doesn't care who gets the credit.

1108. Cheerful people, the doctors say, resist disease better than the glum ones. In other words, the surly bird catches the germ.

—*Nuggets*

1109. Ideals are like stars; you will not succeed in touching them with your hands; but like the seafaring man on the desert of waters, you choose them as your guides, and following them, you reach your destiny.

—Carl Schurz, *Friendly Chat*

1110. Most of us waste time and energy worrying over things we can't control. It is well to do the best we can with what we have and be happy, for conditions are never so bad they couldn't be a lot worse. Remember the colored gal whose old man left her with 10 kids because he did not love her. "Just think," she said happily, "what might have happened iffen he did!"

—*P-K Sideliner*

1111. I believe there is more satisfaction in patting a man on the back than in standing on his neck, observed Jerome P. Fleishman, the lamented advertising specialist.

I believe there is more fun in lifting a man up than in holding him down.

I believe happiness is bound up with helpfulness.

I believe our job is to reach out for bigger things, rather than to curl up in our own little shells and snarl at the world.

—*Sunshine Magazine*

1112. If the sunflower follows the sunshine, if birds in the winter fly south, tell me, why do not men optimistic, look up when they're down in the mouth?

For the flowers find life in the sunshine, and the birds find warmth in the south; and men will find blue sky above them, looking up when they're down in the mouth.

—James E. Wagner

Potential

1113. We ought to search for a man's future possibilities instead of digging for the decay in his past.

1114. "Democracy is based on the conviction that there are extraordinary possibilities in ordinary people.
—HARRY EMERSON FOSDICK,
Friendly Chat

Power

1115. Power is what everyone wants, few acquire and none have yet survived.
—*S F C Spotlight*

1116. A. H. Graenser sat in the lobby of a hotel in Omaha. Certainly no one was ever in much lowlier circumstances. He had been told he could not re-enter his hotel room until he paid his rent. His baggage and his much needed overcoat were in that room. And Mr. Graenser had just five cents. This was the last straw—he thought. But those mysterious resources of man, that work even when objective senses are deadened, were marshaling for action.

Mr. Graenser walked to a window to look into the street and see just how cold and cruel the outside world was. But he could not see it—the cold glass was steamed over from condensed moisture in the warm lobby air.

But the steamed glass was a blow that did something. It pressed a button, releasing a bit of information long imprisoned and forgotten in a cell of Mr. Graenser's brain. He recalled that an old German chemist once had told him how glycerin soap, rubbed on glass and wiped off with a clean cloth, would prevent steaming.

His last nickel went for a cake of glycerin soap at a near-by drugstore. In the cold, he sat on a park bench and cut the soap into twenty pieces. A name came to him—Miracle-Rub. Then he began a round of the city's filling stations. He demonstrated his Miracle-Rub on windshields. The price was fifteen cents a cube, $1.50 a dozen. He sold his complete stock on his first two calls. There followed a series of triple plays—drugstore to park benches to gas stations. Mr. Graenser ended the day with twenty-seven dollars.

From Omaha he worked east, meanwhile improving his product and wrapping it in tinfoil, packed a dozen cubes to a box. He arrived in Detroit three months later with an automobile and a thousand dollars cash.

Today the Presto Company is a prosperous firm, manufacturing cleaning and polishing products.

Many men can cite episodes which in large or small degree compare with that of Mr. Graenser.

—DALE ERWIN-LANG, *Healthways*

Praise

1117. I can live for two months on a good compliment.
—MARK TWAIN

1118. Sigmund Freud once refused to attend a festival in his honor, remarking, "When someone abuses me I can defend myself; against praise I am defenseless."

1119. Every person needs recognition. It is expressed cogently by the lad who says, "Mother, let's play darts. I'll throw the darts, and you say 'Wonderful!'"

Prejudice

1120. You can sway a thousand men by appealing to their prejudices quicker than you can convince one man by logic.
—ROBERT A. HEINLEIN, *Indianapolis Star Magazine*

1121. Addressing a PTA and admitting being a bit pro-federal aid, an educator said, "I might be compared to a Republican who, in 2000 A.D. had written a book entitled an Unbiased History of the 1960 Presidential Election from the Republican's Point of View.
—M. DALE BAUGHMAN

1122. The late Jerome P. Fleishman once wrote in *The Walker Log* that he liked the story about the little girl who could not dust the furniture to suit her grandmother, and grandmother made her do it again—once, twice, three times, and still was not satisfied.

Finally the child looked up and said, "Grandmother, that dust is not on the furniture; it must be on your glasses!"

1123. The world is full of people who have never, since childhood, met an open doorway with an open mind.

Preparation

1124. Every corporal carries a marshal's baton in his knapsack.

—Napoleon

1125. On the western prairies in the old frontier days fleetness of foot was a highly prized skill among the native Indians. Young boys, eager to attain speed and endurance, asked the older men of the tribe how best to achieve their goal. The old Sioux told them to go out every summer and cover their hearts with the colorful dust of butterfly wings. Each boy had to catch his own butterflies. Any man who ever spent part of his boyhood in the neighborhood where he, too, chased butterflies across the fields knows what that meant. Those who caught butterflies summer after summer became excellent runners.

—Nuggets

1126. The old inmate greeted his new cell partner with the question: "How long you in for?"

"Twenty-five years," the new prisoner replied.

"Then you take the bed nearest the door," said the old timer. "You will be getting out first."

—Arkansas Baptist

1127. Once, when a conference of ministers was held in a certain town, a certain preacher had sat quietly through it for a number of days until, toward the end of the conference, he was suddenly and unexpectedly called upon to speak. He arose thoughtfully and almost stumblingly fumbled for his words. Finally, his thoughts took form, his words fell in the rhythm of a marching column, and his impassioned oratory beat down upon the upturned faces of his audience until, as he arose to his peroration and reached his climax, the whole sedate conference broke into a spontaneous applause that shook the room, according to an item in *Printer's Ink*.

He had delivered the master oration of the conference. When finally the applause subsided, a cocky young doctor of divinity strolled up to him. "That was a masterly address you delivered extemporaneously. Yet you must have had some preparation to have done it so well. How long did it take you to prepare it?"

The older man looked gently for some time at the younger one before he answered. And then: "Sixty years, young man, sixty years!"

—Sunshine Magazine

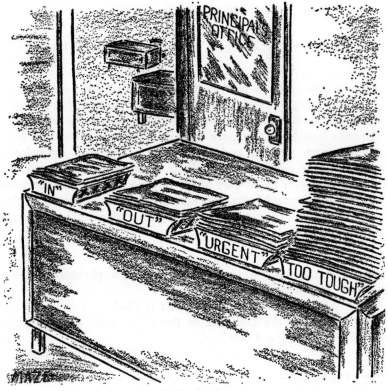

Coffee break.

Principal

1128. Did you hear about the principal who had a passion for order? On his desk were four baskets—one for "in," one for "out," one for "urgent" and a fourth marked "too tough."

1129. A school is often only the lengthened shadow of its principal.

1130. The outgoing principal was instructing his successor in human relations. "And remember, now, we have nothing but kind and cooperative patrons—until you try to change their reserved seats at basketball games."

1131. A portion of the nomination statement of 1959 Principal of the Year: "This is a young man (37 years of age), old enough

to be level headed, young enough to radiate the energies and
enthusiasms of youth. He has keen sense of humor, a frequent, full-
bodied laugh; yet serious, honest approach to the problems of his
profession. He possesses a knack of guiding factions to work har-
moniously together. He engenders proud supports from enthusiastic
patrons."

—*Principals Letter*, Arthur C. Crofts Publication

1132. *Teacher (to Principal):* "I understand you want to see me,
sir."

The scowling principal replied, "No, I *sent* for you. There's a
difference."

1133. What does a principal do about the short and tight skirt
situation. One secondary principals' group received board permission
to develop a code on dress standards based upon neatness, good
taste and economy. Principals will be empowered to make "emergency changes as deemed necessary."

The words "economy" and "emergency changes" leads one to
think about those triangular skirts for very young ladies.

1134. Schools there are of different kinds
For instance, "schools of fish"—
But if a school's to be not mere construction work of
  mortar, brick and wood in varying amounts
Let it be understood emphatically—It's the principal
  of the thing that counts.

—*Intercom*, Junior High Schools
of New York City

1135. The comic magician was in need of an assistant to aid him
in performing his mirth-provoking tricks, and was interviewing a
young man who had applied for the job.

"I need a man to help me," stated the magician, "a man who can
keep a straight face all through my performance, who will under
no circumstances allow a smile to show on his face, no matter what
silly things I might say or do. Now, what are your qualifications
for this job?"

"Well," replied the young man, "I used to run errands for my
high school principal."

1136. Wilbur D. Coon, retiring principal of Maple Heights High
School, Maple Heights, Ohio: "A good principal is like a human oil
can. He just goes around oiling the squeaks."

Problems

1137. So you have problems. Are they man made? Most are— and if men can create problems, surely they can solve them.

—Detroiter

1138. When a man says, "This is a difficult problem," he really says, "I am a soft drill on a hard piece of steel."

—CHARLES F. KETTERING, *The Lion*

1139. The important thing about a problem is not its solution, but the strength we gain in finding the solution.

—Friendly Chat

1140. Problem: Opportunity in work clothes.

—HENRY KAISER

1141. He stopped griping when his boss sent him this memo: "Be thankful for problems, for if we didn't have them you wouldn't be here and if they were less difficult someone with less ability would have your job."

—Service

Procrastination

1142. The greatest stumbling block in any man's path is not laziness or fear, but a low-necked, short-skirted, rose-scented, diamond-decked hussy named "Procrastination."

—Scandal Sheet, Graham, Texas
Rotary Club

1143. My friend, have you heard of the town of Yawn, on the banks of river Slow, where blooms the Waitawhile flower fair, where the Sometimerother scents the air, and the Softgoeasys grow?

It lies in the valley of Whatstheuse, in the province of Letherslide; that tired feeling is native there—it's the home of the listless Idon't-care, where the Putitoffs abide.

—Lockport, N. Y., *Baptist News*

Progress

1144. If we could have made as much progress these last 50 years with people as we have with things, what a world this would now be!

—WHEELER McMILLEN, *Farm Journal*

1145. Fear of change is always a brake on progress.

—Editorial, *Wisconsin Journal of
Education*

1146. Oscar Wilde said, "Discontent is the first step in the progress of a man or a nation." If you analyze the lives of great men, this appears to be the spirit they all have in common. No matter how much success they may have had, they always are looking ahead to the next goal. They always have new worlds to conquer. There are various degrees of greatness and success. But each of us, in our own way, can profit from this point of view.

—A. H. KULIKOWSKI, publisher in
editorial "Are You Satisfied?",
Salesman's Opportunity

1147. The art of wheelspinning is an activity without progress . . . and many of us do a lot of it.

—IRWIN COCHRAN, Director, Bureau
of Business Management, U. of I.

1148. "The millenium is at hand. Man has invented everything that can be invented. He has done all he can do."

These words were spoken by a bishop at a church gathering in 1870. They were challenged by the presiding officer, who suggested that a great invention would be made within the next fifty years.

The bishop asked him to name such an invention.

The reply: "I think man will learn to fly."

The bishop replied that this was blasphemy. "Don't you know that flight is reserved for angels?"

The bishop was Milton Wright, father of Orville and Wilbur.

—From address of the Reverend Walton
Cole at 26th Biennial Council,
Phi Delta Kappa

1149. On a dark night a very small boy was given a lantern by his father, who asked him to go out to the woodshed and bring to the house an armful of wood.

The boy said, "Daddy, I can't see."

The father then queried, "How far can you see?"

"Only three steps."

"Take them," said his father. "How far can you see now, son?"

"Three more steps."

Finally, by going forward three steps at a time, the boy reached the woodshed and brought in the wood.

—*Sunshine Magazine*

1150. The art of progress is to preserve order amid change and to preserve change amid order.

—ALFRED N. WHITEHEAD

1151. In a way, the Russians are quite helpful. If we didn't have them, how would we know whether we were ahead or behind?

1152. David Livingstone, great explorer and Christian pioneer, wrote in one magnificent sentence, "I will go anywhere—provided it be forward."

—*Houston Times*

1153. Don't look back; somethin' might be gainin' on you.

—SATCHELL PAIGE

1154. Emergencies have always been necessary to progress. It was the darkness which produced the lamp. It was the fog that produced the compass. It was hunger that drove us to exploration. And it took a depression to teach us the real value of a job.

—*Highways of Happiness*

1155. If you're doing something the same way you have been doing it for ten years, the chances are you are doing it wrong.

—CHARLES KETTERING

1156. Being satisfied with things the way they are is the quickest way to stop progress.

1157. A colleague boarded a Boston-to-Los Angeles jet airliner a day or so ago. After the plane took off, he overheard the stewardess approach a woman passenger and ask if she would like to remove her coat.

"No, thanks," the woman said. "I'm getting off at Chicago."

—Minneapolis Sunday *Tribune*

Psychology

1158. The sins I see in other folk are the only ones I mention—any mistake that I might make is justified by a good intention!

1159. They all sat around in friendly chat discussing mostly this and that, and a hat, until a neighbor's wayward lass was seen to act in ways quite bad. Oh, 'twas sad!

One thought she knew what must be done with every child beneath the sun—she had none. And ere her yarn had been quite spun, another's theory was begun—she had one. The third was not so sure she knew, but thus and so, she thought, she'd do—she had two. The next one added, "Let me see, these things work out so differently!" She had three.

The fifth drew on her wisdom's store, and said, "I'll have to think it o'er." She had four. Then one sighed, "I don't contrive fixed rules for boys, they're too alive!" She had five. "I know it leaves one in a fix—this straightening out of crooked sticks." She had six.

And one declared, "There's no rule given; just do your best and trust to Heaven." She had seven.

—Origin Unknown

1160. The dean of a girls' school was troubled because the girls insisted on crossing the street in front of the school without going to the corner. Warnings, penalties, and lectures did no good. Then the dean had a sign painted and set it up in the middle of the block. From that time on, the girls always walked to the corner to cross the street. What did the sign say? "Cattle Crossing!"

—*Pelican*

1161. Two psychologists were riding down on the elevator together. The young one was beat and drooping, his tie undone and his coat over his arm. The elder was neat and crisp.

"I don't see how you can do it," the young man said, "how you can listen to all those miserable people telling those heart-rending stories and come out at the end of the day looking fresh and neat?"

"Who listens?"

—*Pelican*

PTA

1162. At a PTA meeting in Hollywood the other night, one youngster was extremely proud—he had more parents there than any other child.

—*Laugh Book*

1163. Note on a PTA bulletin board: " 'Tis better to have loved and lost than to have to do homework for three kids."

1164. Small boy to father: "There's a special PTA meeting to night—just you, my teacher, and the principal."

—*The Amplifier*, Mansfield, Ohio

Dad, there's a special PTA meeting tonight . . . Just you, my teacher, and the principal.

1165. You'd like some fame to come your way?
You've only known rejection?
Well, just stay home from PTA
The night they hold election!
                    —KAY NELSON, *Better Homes and Gardens*

1166. Did you hear about the lady upon returning from a PTA meeting who was heard to remark, "That Mrs. Uppity thinks she knows so much. Over and over she referred to the 'intelligence quota' of the children; intelligence quota, imagine. Why everybody knows that IQ stands for 'Intelligence Quiz.'"

Publicity

1167. If you think advertising doesn't pay—we understand there are 25 mountains in Colorado higher than Pikes Peak. Can you name one?

                    —*P K Sideliner*

1168. A monkey (Aesop speaking) tried to take a handful of nuts from a small-necked jar, but he grabbed too large a handful and couldn't get his hand out, nor did he until he dropped some of the nuts. The attempt to grab too much of the public's attention often makes a monkey out of what might be a good advertisement.

. . . The neck of the jar is exactly as large as the public's interest— and no larger.

To get your hand out, to get the public to look at and absorb any of the advertisement, you must drop a few nuts.

—CALKINS AND HOLDEN, Advertising
Agents, New York

Public Relations

1169. The pressure of public opinion has been compared with the pressure of atmosphere; you can't see it, but it's there just the same; 14.7 pounds to the square inch.

—Speech by WILLIAM WERNER

1170. Too many school administrators use public relations techniques like a spare tire—only in emergencies.

—M. DALE BAUGHMAN

1171. We feel that a good Public Relations program is born of an appreciation of your public and a desire to serve and be a part of your community. Certainly techniques are used but they are only by-products. Techniques as ends in themselves serve no useful purpose . . . .

—F. H. MATTHIESEN, Principal,
Principal's Letter

1172. Public relations is a preventive medicine, not a deodorant to be sprayed around where it stinks.

—KENNETH HAAGENSEN, *Illinois
Education*

1173. If there is one enterprise in all "educationdom" that a "fritterer" should not touch, it is public relations. The public relations function must be handled by someone who can stick like a stamp to a letter. Returns do not come quickly nor in jerks but rather over an extended period of time in a steady pull.

—M. DALE BAUGHMAN

Pupil

1174. "You say Johnny is always sure of himself?"

"I'll say. He works crossword puzzles with a fountain pen."

The Lookout

1175. *Jenny:* "What would you do if a lion came after you at sixty miles an hour?"

Johnny: "I'd do seventy!"

1176. Alan, arriving home from school, beamed with such happiness that he almost forgot he was hungry.

"I didn't know my second-grade teacher liked me so well, Mommy," he confided. "I heard her talking to some of the other teachers, and she must be awfully fond of me! Do you know what she said?"

"What did she say, Alan?" queried his mother.

"She said that the happiest day of her life was the day little Alan Williams was promoted into the third grade."

—Woodmen of the World Magazine

1177. Schoolboy's definition of depth: Height turned upside down.

1178. He came home from school proudly exhibiting a book which he said he had won for accuracy in natural history.

"However did you do that?" asked his mother.

"The teacher asked how many legs an ostrich has, and I said three."

"But an ostrich has only two legs," his mother replied.

"Well, all the rest of the class said four."

1179. *Teacher:* "Can you give me Lincoln's Gettysburg address?"

Student: "Aren't you thinking of Eisenhower? Lincoln lived in Washington."

1180. A fifth-grade teacher in Ohio was giving the class a verbal test in word association. She singled out one youngster and asked: "Since pro means the opposite of con, can you give me an illustration of each?"

The youngster thought a moment then answered, "Progress and Congress."

—National Personnel Consultants

1181. While visiting a country school, the inspector from the Board of Education became angry because of the noise in the next room. He opened the door, grabbed one of the taller boys who seemed to be doing most of the talking, dragged him into the next room, stood him in a corner, and said, "Now be silent and stand there." A few minutes later a small boy stuck his head in the door and asked, "Please sir, may we have our teacher back?"
> —HAROLD BUCHANAN in *National Future Farmer*

1182. Asked to tell what caused the sinking of the *Titanic*, a high school sophomore replied "an iceberger."
> —HERRICK H. KESLER, *NEA Journal*

1183. A first-grade standardized reading test directed students to draw a line under the appropriate illustrations. When I checked over my pupils' answers, I found that one of them had drawn cat-like creatures complete with whiskers under several of the pictures.

Upon asking him to explain, I received this answer:

"That word (line) was new, but I sounded it out and drew a lion just like it said!"
> —IOLA SULLIVAN, Horace Mann School Harrisburg, Illinois, *NEA Journal*

1184. When I discovered that one of my ninth-graders was well stuck up with bubble gum, I removed him and sent him to the washroom to remedy the situation. As he left the class, came a voice from the rear, "Have gum, will travel."
> —CHARLES C. VORDERBERG, *NEA Journal*

1185. As school was letting out, a little boy went up to his teacher's desk. "Miss Smithson," he said, "could you please tell me what I learned in school today? My daddy always wants to know."
> —*Future*

1186. School has started again and everything is back to normal. In Whitefish Bay, Wisconsin, an eighth-grade English class was given an overnight assignment to write themes. One boy was given the topic "Five Ways to Develop a Good Memory." He wrote the theme but forgot to take it to school the next morning.
> —*Milwaukee Journal*

1187. A fourteen-year-old boy was considering the different girls he might ask to the next school dance. "I think I'll ask Marie," he decided at last.

"That surprises me," his mother said. "Last year you wouldn't even dance with her—you said she was too tall and skinny."

"Oh, but she's different now," her son assured her. "She's tops. Since last year she's mobilized her physique and brought up reinforcements."

—Laugh Book

1188. Little Bobby's mother had just presented the family with twins. The beaming father called Bobby aside and said:

"If you'll tell your teacher about it," he said, "I'm sure she'll give you a day's holiday."

That afternoon Bobby came home radiant.

"I don't have to go to school tomorrow," he announced happily.

"Did you tell your teacher Mother had twins?" father asked.

"No, I just told her I had a baby sister. I'm saving the other one for next week."

—Laugh Book

1189. Before Thanksgiving a Minnesota first-grade teacher asked her pupils to tell her what they had to be thankful for. "I am thankful," said one small boy, "that I am not a turkey."

—Minneapolis Tribune

1190. While the art class was setting up a Christmas scene on the school lawn, one of the boys asked uncertainly, "Where shall I put the three wise guys?"

—JAMES W. CORSON, NEA Journal

1191. "Now, boys," said the school master, "what is the axis of the earth?"

Johnny raised his hand and was asked to describe it. "The axis of the earth," he said, "is an imaginary line which passes from one pole to another and on which the earth revolves."

"Very good," said the teacher. "Now, could you hang clothes on that line?" to which Johnny replied, "Yes, sir."

"Indeed?" probed the teacher, disappointed. "And what sort of clothes?"

"Imaginary clothes, sir."

The Lookout

1192. A teacher was telling her second graders about various things on the farm, including the fact that chickens grow from tiny, fluffy chicks to full-grown roosters and hens with a full quota of feathers.

"That's strange," one little guy interrupted her, "our chickens don't have feathers—they have plastic bags on them!"

Capper's Weekly

1193. Joan completed the second grade with honors. Before entering the third grade she met her former teacher, whom she dearly loved. Said Joan, "I wish you knew enough to teach me next year."

1194. A teacher called in a group of small boys suspected of throwing rocks at little girls on their way home from school.

One indignantly denied the charge. "I'm not a rocker," he explained. "I'm a pincher."

HUGH PARK

1195. Daffy definitions from Sunkist School second graders:
"An island is a whole lot of water with a little dirt in it."
"Quiet is when there isn't 'enebode' saying 'enething.' "
"Washington is the last name of the first president of the U.S."
"A gem is a place where you play ball sometimes."

—*The Pointer*, Covina School District

1196. The teacher was checking her student's knowledge of proverbs.

"Cleanliness is next to what?" she asked.

A small boy replied with real feeling: "Impossible."

1197. The teacher asked her small pupils to tell about their acts of kindness to dumb animals. After several heartstirring stories, the teacher asked Tommy if he had anything to add. "Well," he replied rather proudly, "I once kicked a boy for kicking his dog."

—*The Rotary Call*, Winnetka, Illinois

1198. During a lesson on the functioning of the body a first-grade teacher for dramatic effect announced that there was a fire burning in the body all the time.

"Sure," enjoined one little tyke, "and on a cold day, I can see the smoke."

1199. The teacher was explaining to the class the meaning of the word "Recuperate." "Now, Tommy," she said to a small boy, "when your father has worked hard all day, he is tired and worn out, isn't he?"

"Yes, ma'am."

"Then, when night comes, and his work is over for the day, what does he do?"

"That's what Mother wants to know," Tommy explained.

1200. A teacher in Oswego, New York, was watching her second-graders happily building some out-of-this-world equipment. Suddenly, one youngster began to fret and he explained what was wrong: "The girls want to put up curtains in our space ship!"

—Michigan Education Journal

1201. *Teacher:* "This makes five times I have punished you this week. Now, Tommy, what have you to say?"

Tommy: "Well, I'm glad it's Friday."

1202. *Teacher:* "Yes, Jimmie, what is it?"

Jimmie: "I don't want to scare you, but Pop said that if I didn't get better grades somebody is going to get a licking."

1203. The pretty young teacher was explaining the difference between abstract and concrete. "Concrete means something you can see," she told the children, "and abstract means something you can't see. Now who will give me an illustration."

Little Jimmie in the second row quickly held up his hand. "My pants are concrete," he said. "Yours are abstract."

—Laugh Book

1204. Little Eldon, fretting at the teacher's assignment, asked skeptically, "Do you get paid for teaching us?"

The teacher smiled. "Yes."

Puzzled, the boy exclaimed, "That's funny! We do all the work!"

—Sunshine Magazine

1205. The teacher was trying to impress on the children how important had been the discovery of the law of gravitation.

"Sir Isaac Newton was sitting on the ground, looking at the tree," she said. "An apple fell on his head, and from that he discovered gravitation. Just think, children," she added, enthusiastically, "isn't that wonderful?"

The inevitable small boy replied, "Yes'm; an' if he had been settin' in school lookin' at his books, he wouldn't never have discovered nothin'!"

—Sunshine Magazine

1206. When one child reported that his mother had found lice in his hair, the principal started examining all the children's heads in school. That night David reported to his mother, "Mr. Stegall is examining our heads to see if we have lights in them."

—Oklahoma Teacher

1207. Some pupils are like sailboats. They both depend on an outside force to move them.

1208. Fourth grade teacher, in selecting the story of Samson to read to her class, said, "This story is about the strongest man who ever lived. Can you guess his name?" No one could. "His name begins with S," she hinted. The whole room spoke in one voice: "Superman."

—Joe Creason, *Louisville Courier-Journal*

1209. The teacher told the children to draw what each would like to be when he grew up. Bobby handed in a blank paper.

"Why, Bobby, isn't there something you'd like to be when you grow up?"

"Yes, teacher, I'd like to be married, but I don't know how to draw it."

—*Rex Top-ics*

1210. *Hungry schoolboy at lunch counter of school hangout:* "One hot dog!"

Waiter: "Will you eat it here or take it with you?"

Hungry schoolboy: "I hope to do both."

1211. Do you remember the episode in the life of Lewis Carroll's *Alice* when she found herself running with the Queen of Chess? Alice didn't quite know how it started but, somehow or other, they began to run.

The Queen kept crying "Faster! Faster!" until they went so fast that at last they seemed to skim through the air, hardly touching the ground with their feet.

Suddenly they stopped, and Alice found herself sitting on the ground, breathless and giddy. She looked around her in great surprise. "Why," she said, "I do believe we've been under the tree the whole time. Everything's just as it was." "Of course it is," said the Queen. "What would you have it?"

With regard to reading, how many students, do you suppose, are like Alice and the Queen? They realize they must "get over" a certain assignment, and therefore, with no thought to purpose or direction, they race along through meaningless words, sentences, paragraphs and chapters and wonder, when they are finished, why it is they are right where they started with no new facts collected and no new ideas for their trouble.

—SPACHE AND BERG, *The Art of Efficient Reading*

1212. Petey had just finished his first week of school. Older sister Willa asked, "What did you learn in school this week, Petey?"

The little lad answered like a flash, "I know the first letter of the alphabet."

"What is it?" asked Willa. "A," answered Petey. About this time Mom joined the conversation, "That's fine, Petey, and what comes after A?"

With much confidence Petey responded, "All the other letters. Don't you know that?"

1213. In a school essay on "Parents," one little girl wrote: "We get our parents when they are so old it is hard to change their habits."

—Sunshine Magazine

1214. The schoolboy's assignment was to illustrate the song, "America, the Beautiful."

The teacher recognized the flag, the map, the "purple" mountains, even the youthful artist's idea of "from sea to shining sea." But she couldn't understand the airplane in one corner, covered with red and yellow balls.

"That," explained the seven-year-old artist, "is the fruited plane."

1215. "Now, class," said the teacher, " I want you to be very still— so still that you can hear a pin drop."

For a minute all was still, and then a little boy yelled, "Let 'er drop!"

—EMILY LOTNEY

1216. *Teacher:* "Willie, correct this sentence: 'Girls is naturally better looking than boys.' "

Willie: "Girls is artificially better looking than boys."

1217. *Teacher:* "We will have only half a day of school this morning."

Class: "Hurrah!"

Teacher: "We'll have the other half this afternoon."

1218. "Well, Susie, do you like going to school?"

"Oh, very much. And I like coming back. But I just hate what happens between going and coming."

1219. A noted Canadian entomologist was delivering a lecture on the danger of rat infestation. The sixth grade class listened with apparent attention and after the lecture, one of them wrote the lecturer a note of thanks. It concluded by saying:

"We didn't even know what a rat looked like until you came."
—F. G. KERNAN, *Quote*

1220. The children were called upon to write a school essay, and at the appointed time little Hugh submitted one on the ark, in which he made the statement that Noah fished for about five minutes one day.

The teacher looked over the composition, and, puzzled, asked, "Hugh, why do you say that Noah fished only five minutes?"

"Because," was the prompt explanation, "he had only two worms."

The Lookout

1221. *Teacher:* "Can anyone give me an example of poor economy?"

Harry: "I know a man who took such large steps to save wear on his $10 shoes that he split his $20 trousers."

1222. The first-graders were visiting the airport. As the roaring planes landed and took off the teacher remarked to the class, "Isn't it wonderful that we have so many airplanes, and just think, a few years ago we didn't even have automobiles." One curious youngster piped up, "How did people get to the airports?"

1223. Billy's teacher was a plump and pleasant lady of 210 pounds. One day she lectured the class on the value of sufficient sleep. Billy protested, "Why, I don't see anything wrong with staying up late once in a while."

"Why, Billie," said the teacher, "I'm much older than you, and I go to bed with the chickens every night."

Billie looked her over in silence for a few moments and then said in a voice full of wonder, "I don't see how you ever make it up to the roost."

1224. Mrs. Orvold, first-grade teacher in the McFarland, Wisconsin public schools, was arranging her class for dismissal at noon and liked to have each group know exactly where they were going.

"Will all the boys and girls who are going to eat in the hot lunch room program stand over here," said Mrs. Orvold, as she pointed to an area in the room. "Now will the boys and girls who have their lunch in pails stand over here."

Johnny, who was patiently waiting for her to notice him finally raised his hand. "Yes, Johnny, what is it?" said Mrs. Orvold.

Asked Johnny, "Mrs. Orvold, where do the bags go?"

—Wisconsin Journal of Education

1225. A student defined a parable as follows: "A parable is a heavenly story with no earthly meaning."

1226. A teacher asked her class the difference between results and the consequences.

One pupil replied, "Results are what you expect; consequences are what you get."

1227. *Teacher:* "How old were you on your last birthday?"
Junior: "Seven, ma'am."
Teacher: "How old will you be on your next birthday?"
Junior: "Nine, ma'am."
Teacher: "Nonsense. If you were seven on your last birthday, how can you be nine on your next birthday?"
Junior: "I'm eight today."

—Sunshine Magazine

1228. *Emma Lou:* "Don't you think an awful lot of rough stuff goes on before the footlights in our senior play?"
Ruth: "Yes, but I think more goes on after rehearsal behind the headlights."

1229. The third-grade teacher wrote this sentence on the blackboard: "I ain't never had no fun at the seashore."

She then turned to her pupils, singled out one of them and asked, "How can I correct that?"

Little Tommy at once responded, "Get a boyfriend!"

—Cook County Education Digest

1230. The fifth grade teacher, who had always had her picture taken with her class, noticed a pupil looking through the pictures. "Are you looking for a friend?" she asked. "No," he replied, "I'm trying to see which of your classes aged you the most."

—Dixie Roto Magazine

1231. Two second-grade boys were sitting on the school steps at recess, absorbed in a serious debate. As their teacher passed by, she overheard one of the boys say, "The principal does not have an electric paddle!"

—*NEA Journal*

1232. Recently a youngster returned from school and told his mother he had put a stick of dynamite under the teacher's chair.

"Why, that's terrible," his mother cried. "You march yourself right back to school immediately!"

To which the boy of course replied: "What school?"

—Hugh Scott, *Today*

1233. When a first grader was asked why the ugly troll wouldn't let the goats across the bridge, he replied, "You have to pay money to cross a troll bridge."

Quality

1234. The bitterness of poor quality lingers long after the sweetness of cheap price is forgotten.

—*Woodmen of the World Magazine*

1235. Man is by nature an inquiring being, yet all too often our educational system seems to work counter to this tendency in him. The desire to know seems to have been effectively stifled except in rare cases. Furthermore, the discipline of intellectual labor is far too infrequently applied and emphasized. All this combines to form a major stumbling block in the way of educational quality. For unless there is a predilection for learning on the part of the student there is little likelihood of his attaining high quality work.

—Samuel B. Gould

1236. A farmer brought his gawky, 18-year-old son to a Danish Folk High School.

"My boy wants to spend five months at your school," the farmer said to Professor Grundtvig, founder of the famous Folk schools in Denmark.

"However, I have looked over your course of studies, and I see only such courses as history, literature, civics, geography, and science. Nothing about farming.

"Tell me, will my son be a better farmer after he takes this program with you?"

Professor Grundtvig was silent for a moment, then replied quietly,

"No, your son won't learn how to make better butter at our Folk school. But all his life he will be ashamed to make bad butter."

1237. Do small things well; and great things, half begun, will crowd your doorway begging to be done.

1238. Very few do their best. That is why there is always so much room for improvement.

—MARTIN VANBEE

1239. Three young men, arguing heatedly about the merits of their respective churches, turned to a white-haired old-timer, and asked, "What's your denomination, Mr. Crawford?"

"Well, boys," he answered slowly, "somehow it seems to go sorta like this: There's three roads to the city—the long road, the short road, and the road through the swamps—but when I get to town with my load of corn the man doesn't say 'Mr. Crawford, which road you come by?' But instead he asks, 'Mr. Crawford, how good is your corn?'"

—ANNA ZACHARIAS, *Together*

Reading

1240. Some forty years ago, a United States Senator, who was respected and admired for his knowledge, wisdom and understanding was asked, "Senator, you never spent much time in college, if any. How have you acquired your understanding of national and international affairs? Where have you learned so much about so many things?"

His answer was simple and to the point. "I made a rule when I was eighteen years old that I would read for two hours every day; that sometimes in every twenty-four hour period I would thoughtfully and carefully read for at least two hours. On trains, in hotels, in waiting rooms, I have read: magazines, news digests, political reports, good books, poetry, and the Bible." And then he added, "Try it, young fellow. You will be an educated man in spite of yourself."

SAY

1241. Travel opens the mind, but so does print, and print is the cheapest mind opener there is, and the best.

—JOHN COTTON DANA, quoted in *Community Teamwork*, Adult Education Newsletter, Purdue University, Indiana

1242. Read something every day. Discipline yourself to a regular schedule of reading. In fifteen minutes a day you can read twenty books a year.

—WILFRED A. PETERSON, *Jaqua Way*

Report Card

1243. Father, looking over his son's report card: "One thing in your favor—with these grades, you couldn't possibly be cheating."

1244. From the report of a committee of teachers, in a junior high school in Queens, appointed by the principal to find ways of saying things more tactfully on report cards.

How shall we say it on report cards and record cards?

SOMEWHAT HARSH EXPRESSIONS	EUPHEMISMS
Awkward and clumsy	Appears to have difficulty with motor control and muscular coordination
Does all right if pushed	Accomplishes tasks when interest is frequently stimulated
Too free with fists	Resorts to physical means of winning his point or attracting attention
Dirty; has bad odor	Needs guidance in development of good habits of hygiene
Lies	Shows difficulty in distinguishing between imaginary and factual material
Cheats	Needs help in learning to adhere to rules and standards of fair play
Steals	Needs help in learning to respect the property rights of others
Insolent	Needs guidance in learning to express himself respectfully
Lazy	Needs ample supervision in order to work well
Rude	Needs to develop a respectful attitude toward others
Dishonest	See either Lies or Steals, depending on what is meant

SOMEWHAT HARSH EXPRESSIONS	EUPHEMISMS
Selfish	Needs help in learning to enjoy sharing with others
Coarse	Needs assistance in developing social refinement
Noisy	Needs to develop quieter habits of communication
Has disgusting eating habits	Needs help in improving table manners
Is a bully	Has qualities of leadership but needs help in learning to use them democratically
Babyish	Shows lack of maturity in relationships with others
Associates with "gangs"	Seems to feel secure only in group situations; needs to develop a sense of independence
Disliked by other children	Needs help in learning to form lasting friendships
Often late	Needs guidance in developing habits of punctuality
Is truant	Needs to develop sense of responsibility in regard to attendance

1245. A year ago, a girl brought home a second-grade report card bearing this comment from her teacher: "It is a real pleasure to have your daughter in my class because she adds so much zest to it."

This year's card also has a comment—but from a different teacher with a different outlook. It says: "Your daughter talks too much."

—Laugh Book

1246. The current system of school grading is designed not to discourage any parent or student. Even though Junior may be dumber than an ox, the idea is to hold out some encouragement. The ultimate in strained encouragement came when one teacher added this note to what was otherwise a very poor report: "He contributes nicely to the group singing by helping listening."

—Toastmaster

1247. *Hygiene Teacher:* "Do you think paper can be used efficiently to keep people warm?"

Joe: "I should say so! The last report card I took home kept the family hot for a week."

1248. A teenager with his own car said to his girl friend, "My Dad wants me to have all the things he didn't get when he was my age—and that includes a straight 'A' report card."

1249. *Bob:* "What grade did you get on your final exam?"
Bill: "I believe that grades should be kept a secret; they are personal and should not be revealed under any circumstances."
Bob: "Too bad! I failed, too."

1250. *Mother:* "John, sit down and tell me what your grades are."
John: "I can't sit down. I just told pop what they are."
—BONNIE FRAZIER

1251. *Junior:* "Dad, why did you sign my report card with an X instead of your name?"
Dad: "I didn't want your teacher to think that anyone with your marks has parents who can read and write."

1252. *Pa:* "Tommy, I am not at all pleased with the report your teacher sent me about your conduct in school."
Tommy: "I knew you wouldn't be, and I told her so. But she went right on and made it out that way—just like a woman!"

1253. *Mother:* "Johnny, this isn't a very good report card. Are you trying?"
Johnny: "Yes, my teacher said I am the most trying boy in the class."
—The Lookout

1254. The father was reading the school report which had just been handed to him by his hopeful son. His brow was wrathful as he read: English, poor; history, weak; mathematics, fair; and he gave a glance of disgust at the quaking lad. "Well, Dad," said the son, "it is not as good as it might be, but have you seen that?" And he pointed to the next line, which read: "Health, excellent."

Research

1255. Dr. Albert von Szent-Gyoryl, 1937 Nobel prize winner in medicine and physiology, once gave this perceptive description:

"Research is to see what everybody else has seen, and to think what nobody else has thought."

—Wheeler McMillen, *Chemurgic Digest*

Resourcefulness

1256. Early in the eighteenth century, Leningrad was laid out. A number of large rocks, brought by a glacier from Finland, had to be removed. A particularly large piece of granite was lying in the way of the principal avenue, and bids were advertised for its removal. All of the proposals submitted by contractors were exorbitantly high because there were no mechanical means for removal, no hard steel for drilling or cracking the stone, and no explosives except inferior black powder.

Before the contract was awarded to the lowest bidder, an insignificant-looking peasant appeared and offered to remove the boulder for a small fraction of the sum quoted by the other bidders. Since the government ran no risks, the moujik was authorized to try his luck.

He got together a lot of other peasants with spades and timbers, and they began digging a deep hole next to the rock. The rock was propped up to prevent its rolling into the hole. When the hole was deep enough, the props were knocked out and the boulder peacefully dropped into its grave, where it rests to this day, below the street level. The rock was covered with dirt, and the rest of the earth was carted away.

Moral to the story: The contractors thought in two dimensions, planning to remove the rock to some other place on the surface of the earth. The peasant thought of the third dimension as well, namely, up and down. Since he could not remove the rock upward, he put it underground.

—Adapted from Vladimir Karapetoff in
The Clarkson Letter, Sunshine Magazine

1257. According to one story Chinese ingenuity makes up for any lack of technical know-how. One oriental engineer described the building of a tunnel this way: Put 10,000 Chinese on one side of a mountain and 10,000 on the other. Then start digging—if they meet, there is a tunnel—if they don't meet, there are two tunnels.

1258. Little Mary insisted that she be allowed to serve the tea when her mother was entertaining one afternoon. Mother, with crossed fingers, consented. However, she became annoyed by the long day and asked, "Why did you take so long, child?"

"I couldn't find the tea strainer," answered Mary.

"Then, how did you strain it so well?"

"I used the fly-swatter."

—*Iowa State Green Gander*

1259. Damon Runyon used to tell this story of how he got his first newspaper job. It happened in Denver. He sat in the outer office patiently waiting while an office boy carried in his request to be seen to the busy editor.

In about ten minutes the boy came back and said, "He wants you to send in a card." Runyon had no card, but being resourceful, he reached into his pocket and pulled out a deck of cards. From the deck he carefully extracted an ace and said, "Give him this."

He got in and he got the job.

—*Journal of the American Medical Association*

1260. My grandmother used to remark about one of her sons: "I kind of admire Wayne. He's hard to squelch—just like a gopher. If you stop his usual exits, he digs another tunnel and goes out of another hole."

—Maureen Applegate, *Childhood Education*

Retirement

1261. There are a lot of good books available telling how to manage when you retire. How about one that tells how to manage *until?*

1262. At the Playbill they told of the guy who retired after 30 years. Instead of a gold watch the boss gave him the water cooler.

Salesmanship

1263. Dr. Lee H. Stoner, School of Education, Indiana University, likes to tell the story of the fellow who, according to all school records, was rated very low mentally. Despite his inability to cope with the fundamental tools of learning, he was always the top salesman in the school. He sold the most popcorn at the ball games, led in the sales of candy, magazines and other items his class sold to raise money for the class trip to Washington.

Returning to this community several years later, it was noted that there was a large appliance store in town with this fellow's name in neon letters across the building. Stepping inside, the teacher found his former pupil busily selling electrical appliances in the store which looked prosperous and well stocked. After exchanging the usual amenities, the former teacher asked the appliance store owner about his bookkeeping and tax problems. "Oh, that's easy," said the former pupil. "It doesn't cost me very much to hire a good bookkeeper." Tapping his forehead, he added, "You know it takes something up here to be a good salesman."

—Marie Fraser, *Indiana Teacher*

1264. The best "top salesman" we ever heard of was the one who sold two milking machines to a farmer with only one cow and then took the cow as a down payment.

—*Speed Queen News*

1265. After all a salesman is nothing but a burglar with social charm.

1266. Representative Brooks Hays (D-Ark) tells of an insurance man back home who used an effective introduction:

"I'm just an ignorant fellow," the salesman would begin. "I don't know much about insurance, but I'm interested in your children and how they're going to get along in later years." Then he'd proceed to wade into an enthusiastic and high-powered sales talk.

On one occasion he was interrupted by a prospect:

"You say you dont know much, brother," said the listener, "but I declare you sure do believe what little you do know!"

—Quote in *Washington Bureau*

School

1267. After the first week of school, officials required teachers to fill out forms about their new classes. One question was: "Have you any abnormal children in your class?"

"Yes," wrote the teacher. And in the blank space for explanation, she wrote: "Two of them have good manners."

—*Sunshine Magazine*

1268.   There's a crisis in the household,
Getting Johnny off to school
For the books must be assembled

During breakfast's fast refuel.
At the meal he has to hurry
And not linger at his plate
Since all the time his mother fears
That the kid will check in late.
Then amid the sound and fury
He's dispatched with tearful care,
And his mother sighs: "Thank heavens
He's now in the teacher's hair!"
—VIRGIL MAYBERRY, Trumpet, Harrisburg
Junior High School, Illinois

1269. What makes Johnny's inability to read so shocking is the universal delusion that his parents could.
—American Mercury

1270. The way things are going, it won't be long until you will need a college degree to get into high school.

1271. Extract from a schoolgirl's letter home: "We all have to have a dictionary here so I have asked for one to be ordered for me. I hope you don't mind. Apparently Miss Foster thinks they are essensual."
—Peterborough, Daily Telegraph

1272. 'Twas the day before Christmas and all through
    the school,
Kids were preparing to celebrate yule.
The first grade made reindeer to paste on their
    chairs,
When someone discovered that glue tastes like
    pears.
The second grade served the yule lunch it had
    made—
Doughnuts and bubble gum, cake and Kool-
    Aid.
The third grade popped popcorn to make into
    balls,
And left sticky fingermarks all down the halls.
The fourth and fifth graders were giving a
    drama
When a voice from the manger yelped "I want
    my mama."

The sixth grade went caroling 'til the chief of
  police
Hinted that they were disturbing the peace.
And our dear stalwart teacher—now what was
  she doing
To welcome the season of cutting and gluing?

ANSWER:

Blowing noses, wiping feet, guiding children to
  their seat,
Feeding turtles, mending books, hanging coats
  on proper hooks,
Sketching babies in the manger (one more
  carol will derange her).
Climbing ladders, trimming trees, nursing cuts
  and scuffled knees,
Hanging wreaths upon the door, sweeping pop-
  corn off the floor,
Teaching children how to add, going abso-
  lutely mad.
Sorting through the coats again, pulling boots
  on little men
Buttoning sweaters, drying tears, tying scarves
  around little ears;
Wishing all the little heathens many joyous
  happy seasons—
Close the door and turn the lock,
Joy to the world; it's four o'clock.

1273. Alonzo Banks, principal of the Baltimore intermediate
school, listed ten commandments for parents and children. Speaking at the 13th annual summer conference of Seventh-day Ad-
ventists, he listed:

FOR PARENTS:

1. Thou shalt not become an Army sergeant, barking orders
to thy children, but shalt guide them by thine own perfect examples.
2. Thou shall not treat thine erring son or daughter as a crimi-
nal, but shalt remember he or she is but a chip off the old block.
3. Thou shalt not chase the almighty dollar so furiously that

thou become a bear instead of a father, or a workhorse instead of a mother.

4. Thou shalt not let thine appearance go to pot, nor conduct thyself in such a way that thy children become ashamed of thee.

5. Thou shalt pray with and for thy children morning, noon and night.

FOR CHILDREN:

6: Thou shalt not look upon thy parents as policemen.

7. Thou shalt not use thy home merely as a base of operations from which thou goeth forth for pleasure, but shalt wash a dish and mow the lawn now and then.

8. Thou shalt remember that someday thou wilt become a parent and consider how thou wouldn't like a child who puts furrows in thine brow and gray hairs in thine head.

9. Thou shalt take counsel from thy parents, for it may be possible thou hast not yet found all the answers.

10. Thou shalt honor thy father and thy mother that the days may be long and happy in the home thy parents giveth thee.

—*UPI*, Pine Forge, Pennsylvania

1274. "What do you have in school now?" we asked a beginner, after a few weeks of it, "reading yet or writing?"

"All we have is line-up," he said grimly. "Line-up for cookies, line-up for milk, line-up for the bathroom, line-up for rubbers, line-up to go out, line-up to come in."

—*Food Marketing in New England*

1275. Abraham Lincoln told this story of Daniel Webster's boyhood:

Young Daniel was not noted for tidiness. One day in the district school the teacher told him if he appeared in school again with such dirty hands, she would thrash him. But the next day Daniel appeared with his hands in the same condition.

"Daniel," the teacher said in desperation, "hold out your hand!"

Daniel spat on his palm, rubbed it on the seat of his trousers, and held it out. The teacher surveyed it in disgust. "Daniel," she exclaimed, "if you can find me a hand in this school that is dirtier than this one here, I will let you off."

Daniel promptly held out his other hand. The teacher had to keep her word.

—*Sunshine Magazine*

1276. The schools are not in business to teach everything to everyone. They are not to be confused with shopping centers. We do not, I hope, put signs in our school corridors saying, "What you don't see, ask for."

—WILLIAM CORNOG, *Education Digest*

1277. The schools must never neglect the creative arts. Through the arts, life becomes much more reasonable and understandable.

—VAN CLIBURN, Annual Convention of
AASA, *Teachers Letter*

1278. Some of our schools are getting so crowded that any place that's hollow they have a class in it.

—Midland Schools

Gadsl

1279. One day a teacher friend of mine asked each of the pupils in her kindergarten class how near he lived to the school and how long it took him to get home. She couldn't help smiling at one little boy's answer: "I must live pretty close because when I get home, my mother always says, 'Good grief, are you home already?'"
—Dixie Roto

1280. At a school the following letter was received from a parent, following a hygiene lesson on the digestive system:
Dear Miss,
Please don't let my Lily learn that there Hygiene. There is no need for her to know nothing below the waist; moreover, it puts her off her meals.
—Mrs. L. Swan, *Laugh Book*

1281. Tom Phillips, of the Pana, Illinois News Palladium tells of a fellow who folded a blank sheet of paper, placed it in an envelope, and addressed it carefully. Asked what was the idea, he explained, "I'm taking a correspondence course and I'm cutting class."

1282. The school should be a place where all kinds of pupils— book-minded and hand-minded, sociable and shy—are rewarded for doing well the desirable things they can do best.

1283. In a certain school in New York there was a teacher, an energetic advocate of "Safety First," who opened her class each morning by rising and asking: "Children, what would you do if fire were to break out in this building?"
The children would reply in chorus: "We would rise in our places, step into the aisle, and march quietly out of the building."
One morning when the children arrived at school they found themselves honored by the presence of Dr. Henry Van Dyke. The teacher stepped before the class and, instead of the usual fire drill questions, said, "Children, what would you say if I were to tell you that Dr. Van Dyke is to speak to you this morning?"
Instantly from the class came the resounding chorus: "We would rise in our places, step into the aisle, and march quietly out of the building."
—The Lookout

1284. "Mary, where did you learn to sing?"
"I graduated from a correspondence school."
"You must have missed a lot of mail."
—The Lookout

1285. Do you know anyone who ever left his more-beautiful-than-ever home and drove his bigger-than-ever-hardtop down the wider-than-ever freeway through the more-modern-than-ever shopping center to pick up children who attend bleaker-than-ever P.S. 39?

1286. The teenager down the street says it was his misfortune to go to grade school when the aim was to make every pupil happy and to hit high school when the aim is to make every pupil smarter than the Russians.

—BILL VAUGHN, *VFW Magazine*

1287. Modern Street Sign: "School Zone, Drive Carefully—Acute shortage of teachers."

—JACK HERBERT

1288. Attendance records are like clinical thermometers. Truancy is a symptom like fever.

1289. A school is a shop, in which young sits are fashioned to virtue, and it is distinguished into Forms. The Master sitteth in a chair, the Scholars in Forms; he teacheth, they learn.

1290. School seeks to get you ready for examination; Life gives the finals.

—SAY

1291. Little Dennis, while playing on his way to school, had torn the seat of his trousers. A playmate attempted to mend them with safety pins, but had only one pin.

As Dennis marched into school a few minutes late the teacher remarked, "I see you're a little behind this morning, Dennis."

"Well, you wouldn't," Dennis explained apologetically, "if we'd had more pins."

—JAY MOON, *Laugh Book*

1292. Our high school plans classes for exceptionally bright students this fall. Principal Hanson says he'll need one to four extra teachers, depending on whether school officials or parents decide who'll take the courses.

—BURTON HILLIS, *Better Homes and Gardens*

1293. One thing today's student learns is that it's the early bird who gets a parking place close to the school.

1294. "Chewing gum" was a luxury for school children in the old days. They used wax from nearby trees. Usually there was not enough to supply the demand, so the older boys loaned theirs to the younger ones or to the best girl friend after they got tired of chewing it. One instance is reported of a youngster crying because he had swallowed his gum. "It won't hurt you," consoled his teacher. "But," wailed the boy, "I borrowed it from Bill and I'll get a lickin' at recess."

—RAYMOND L. FOSTER, Lecturer, Southern Illinois University

1295. A father was telling a neighbor how he stopped his son from being late to high school. "I bought him a car," he said.

"How did that stop him from being late?" the neighbor asked.

"Why, he's got to get there early to find a parking place."

—*Concrete Citizen*

1296. Teacher was making a pitch to her junior high class for the students' purchase of the class Yearbook.

"Think of it," she spouted.

"How wonderful to own this book with all the class history and individual photos in it! Why, 20 years from now you can look through this class annual and say, 'There's Bobby Ames, he's that famous judge. And there's Jessie Williams, she's that well-known author. And . . .'"

. . . she rambled on, citing various members of the class and her predictions of their future. Until, finally, from the rear of the room, a frank stage whisper: "And there's Teacher, still single."

—HERB SMITH, *Laugh Book*

1297. The good old summertime apparently ended none too soon for the mothers of children in Seattle's Broadview elementary school. On the opening day of school, this telegram was read over the public-address system:

"TO ALL BROADVIEW TEACHERS—HALLELUJAH! WE'RE GLAD YOU'RE BACK. HURRAH!" It was signed, "BROADVIEW MOMS."

—"Strolling Around" in *Seattle Times*

1298. I'm not a penpoint, nor a brush, neither typewriter nor a stencil. I'm just a piece of rubber on the end of a lead pencil.

I never get to write a line, nor even to improve it; but each time a mistake is made I'm called on to remove it.

The dawn brings me but little hope; the night portends but terrors. All that I ever get to see of people is their errors.

—CLARENCE FLYNN in *The Uplift*

1299. Don't expect the school to give you anything unless you bring something to put it in.

1300. All right, so maybe the Russian children are ahead of ours in algebra. How are they at selling peanut brittle, cookies or chocolate mints door-to-door?

—*Hartford Courant*

1301. As a visiting consultant I was exploring the junior high school plant in Ottawa with Principal George Kindle as my host and guide. As we neared the end of the tour around lunch time and approached the cafeteria, we saw that the lunch period had just ended. Two attractive, bright-eyed girls approached the two of us, one of them addressing Mr. Kindle as she extended a small cardboard container. "Won't you and your guest have a cupcake?" she suggested. Mr. Kindle refused courteously, explaining, "We'd like to, but we're both on diets." Although he said it in jest, each of us is the kind of physical specimen who ought to say "no" to cupcakes.

The girl didn't give up. "Oh, come on, Mr. Kindle, there's only two left. Please take them!" It was plain to see. She *wanted* us to have them. I said, "Come on, George, let's have one. We'll need dessert after our lunch, anyway." So we did take the remaining cupcakes. Then the laughing girl made me so glad that I had accepted her offer. It made Mr. Kindle glad, too. Buoyantly, she announced, "It's my birthday," and with a twinkle in her eye, she went on her way.

—M. DALE BAUGHMAN

1302. A teacher called on the mother of a boy who came to school in a dirty condition.

"Can you explain," she asked, "how he gets his nails so dirty?"

"I expect that's because he's always scratching 'imself," replied the fond mother.

—*Laugh Book*

1303. *Police:* "Can you give me a description of your missing school treasurer?"

Superintendent: "He was nearly six feet tall and nearly $1,000 short."

1304. We must teach mathematics—for we dare not face the lack—of kids who need to know the tricks—to feed a Univac.

We ought to teach the art of verse—with more hyperbole—so that our offspring may coerce—with jingles on TV.

Our science teaching needs to grow—until our kids excel—or else we won't have folks to blow—the rest of us to hell.

—Frederick J. Moffitt, *Nation's Schools*

1305. When the chronic critic complains that schools do not teach children to think, he really means: "Schools do not teach children to think—as he does."

—*Nation's Schools*

1306. Schools were never intended to be tranquilizers; they should be agitators.

—Henry Steele Commager, author of *The American Mind*

1307. When the great Teacher walked the earth, He had many troublesome pupils. They were sometimes inattentive. They misquoted their Teacher and misunderstood Him. One day in the Master's class things got so crowded that a hole was cut in the roof and a sick man lowered thru the hole. This Teacher did not thunder out "Not in MY class, you don't!"

1308. Famed Eton public school has opened its own pub where boys over 16 can get a drink of beer between or after classes.

It is believed to be the only licensed bar in any secondary school in the world.

For many years senior boys were allowed to drink at the Christopher Tap Inn, which recently closed after the death of its landlord.

Eton authorities then decided to take over the inn and turn it into a club for teachers and students.

Most of the boys prefer cider, but several take their share of beer.

—*Chicago Herald American*

1309. A little girl returned from her first day in school and proudly exclaimed, "Mother, I was the brightest one in my class?"

"That's fine, Janie," her mother said, "but tell how it happened."

"Well," Janie replied, "the teacher told each of us to draw a picture on the blackboard, and then the others were to guess what the picture was. Mine was the only one no one could guess—but I knew exactly what it was all the time."

—*Sunshine Magazine*

1310. The teacher can light the lantern and put it in your hand, but you must walk into the dark.

—WILLIAM H. ARMSTRONG, *Study Is Hard Work*

1311. Latin has taken on a new look in our modern schools. A London high school teacher writes ghost stories in Latin to hold his students' interest in the language of the ancient Romans.

But an American teacher has devised a popular way to get students to learn the many endings of Latin nouns and verbs. A typical sample of first declension nouns runs this way: coca cola, coca colas, coca colam, coca colas, coca colae.

1312. After attending a rural school for six years a country girl came home from her first day at school in the town's junior high school. "Mother," she exclaimed, "I'm going to learn domestic silence."

"You must mean domestic science," explained her mother.

Father chimed in, "Shh! there's a bare hope that she really means it."

1313. Today's student rules for success in school: 1. Have a car; 2. Be a pleasant conversationalist; 3. Have a car; 4. Be congenial; 5. Have a car; 6. Be a good listener; 7. Have a car. (Numbers 2, 4 and 6 can be omitted if the car is a red convertible.)

1314.   A hasty snack of bread or bun,
      Gulped down while you're on the run,
      Can't serve as breakfast for the lass
      Who wants top grades in every class!

1315.   O there she stands so great and grand;
      I love her more than any in the land.
      O there she lies against the skies,
      To make a wonder for my eyes.
        I love her doors so wide and tall;
        I love her long and winding halls.
        Oh she's stood there through fire and rain;
        And she'll be there when I come again.
      I love my school more than any other;

I would not go to another.
In one or two years we'll graduate,
To another school, to a faster gait.
  So while we're here, let's be proud,
  Let's shout her praises good and loud.
  Of all the schools in all the land,
  O there she stands so great and grand.
                    —David Deputy, *Trumpet*, Harrisburg
                    Junior High School, Harrisburg,
                    Illinois

1316. The couple was married last Saturday, thus ending a friendship which began in school days.
                    —Sea Island City, New Jersey,
                    Seven Mile Beach Reporter

1317. "My sister is older than me," said the new girl at school, answering the teacher's inquiries.
  Teacher: "And who comes after her?"
  New Girl: "Nobody. If anybody did they could have her."

1318. The pastor of a Methodist church observes in his bulletin that it will be a welcome change for a lot of kids to get back to school, where the first words they hear probably will be from the school nurse: "Open your mouth."

1319. Oddities in school management: At one school in southern Illinois a successful search located a man who could drive the bus in the morning, serve as the hot lunch cook at noon and then bus the pupils home after school. A few years ago in a trustee-dominated high school in southern Indiana, two educators more or less took turns serving as the principal. If a Democrat Trustee were elected, the Democratic principal took over while the other man, a Republican, assumed the role of custodian. The pay was about the same.
                    —M. Dale Baughman

1320. A school inspector, to get an idea of the standard of teaching, entered a classroom while the lesson was in progress and decided to ask the children some questions.
  Calling on one small boy he asked, "Who broke down the walls of Jericho?" The boy answered, "Not me, sir." The inspector turned to the teacher and asked, "Is this the usual standard in this class?" The teacher replied, "The boy is usually quite honest so I believe him."

Leaving the room in disgust the inspector sought out the head-master and explained what had transpired.

The headmaster said, "I've known both the teacher and boy concerned for several years and I'm sure that neither of them would do a thing like that."

By this time the inspector was furious and reported the incident to the director of education.

The director said, "I feel, you know, we are making a mountain out of a molehill in this case. I suggest we pay the bill and write the sum off."

—Woolery Digest

1321. This item was found in the old files of an Officer in Charge who recently cleared the base. List included the rules governing the first weather students at Chanute, around the turn of the century.

1. Students each day will fill lamps, clean chimneys and trim wicks. Wash windows once a week.

2. Each student will bring a bucket of water and a scuttle of coal for the day's classes.

3. Make your pens carefully. You may not whittle nibs to your individual taste. Follow Pen Trimming S.O.P. #4.

4. Male students will be given an evening off each week for courting purposes, or two evenings a week if they go regularly to church. There will be no inter-class courting during school hours.

5. After 13 hours of labor in the classroom, the student should spend the remaining time reading the Bible and other good books.

6. Every student should lay aside each payday a goodly sum of his earnings for his benefit during his declining years so he will not become a burden on society.

7. Any student who smokes Spanish cigars, uses liquor in any form, or frequents pool and public halls, or gets shaves in a barber shop, gives good reason for us to suspect his worth, intentions, integrity and honesty.

8. The student who has performed his studies faithfully and without fault for the year will be given increases of five cents per day in his pay, providing Congress increases budget.

9. Neckgear may be loosened when temperature in classroom exceeds 90 degrees.

Today all we require is:

INDIVIDUALS:

Keep desk top reasonably clean
Place chair on table for cleanup
Store extra and/or old charts in drawers
Replace manuals in the bookcases when not in use

DAILY CLEAN UP DETAILS:

Pull light table and fan plugs from all outlets
Pull up all shades
Lock all windows
Dust erasers
Wipe chalkboard and clean chalkboard tray
Sweep floor
Empty waste basket
Put chairs on floor after clean up
Shut off lights

Above action is recommended if you care to join the "first" students as alumni of this institution.

—The 330 Management

1322. A Scottish farmer, being elected to the school board, visited the village school and tested the intelligence of the class by the question:

"Now, boys, can any of you tell me what nothing is?"

After a moment's silence a small boy in a back seat rose and answered:

"It's what ye paid me the other day for holding yer horse."

1323. Evan Evans, former superintendent of schools in Nebraska told me how he paid his bus drivers 15 years ago. Drivers were paid according to the type of road driven: 15¢ per mile on hard-surfaced roads, 20¢ a mile on gravel and 25¢ a mile in mud.

—M. DALE BAUGHMAN

1324.   Oh, give me a schedule, a wide open
                     schedule, a flexible schedule for all
          Where seldom is heard
          A bell or a bird
          While kids create activity all day.

          School, school time today
          We're all for a full longer day

Where grouping is done
Not only for fun
But to initiate structure all day.

1325. *Robert:* "Daddy, what would you do if I got a 100 in Math?"

Dad: "Boy, I'd faint!"

Robert: "That's what I was afraid of, so to be on the safe side I got only 50."

School Administration

1326. Questions and answers on a regular form for job searchers used by our administrative placement office.

What was the starting salary of your present position?—$5,000

What is your present salary?—$5,000

What is your reason for leaving?—$5,000

I swore to help him find a new administrative post.

—M. DALE BAUGHMAN

1327. Nowadays most school boards are looking only for alert young men between the ages of 30 and 40 with Doctor's degrees and 20 years of experience.

—M. DALE BAUGHMAN

1328. This is a reaffirmation of the protest of my youth, when I wanted to teach and was constantly pushed toward administration because the pay was higher. Then, as now, I think that administrators can be trained, and with a smart secretary, the mediocre administrator can fool quite a few of the people for a long time.

—KERMIT EBY

1329. Deposed administrators are urged to remember the old proverb, "When one door shuts, another opens."

—M. DALE BAUGHMAN

1330. The executive type school administrator is one who can take a two-hour lunch break without anyone missing him.

1331. Problems are to a school administrator like dandelions in the spring lawn—they keep coming back.

1332. A campaign for a new bond issue without adequate preparation and publicity is like a rocket without a nose cone. It isn't going anywhere.

1333. You cannot give wings to the weak by using a tight rein on the strong.

You cannot promote harmony among the staff by inciting distrust and skepticism.

You cannot raise the performance level by taking away a teacher's initiative and independence.

You cannot be a crutch and help teachers permanently; you *can* be a cane and help them learn to do what they should for themselves.

—M. DALE BAUGHMAN

1334. Excerpt of a note from a new staff member to the American Association of School Administrators:

"The opportunity to join the official A.A.S.A. family has caused as much talk around our home as a new rooster in the hen house."

—WILLIAM J. ELLENA

1335. Notes from an outdoor notebook: Because the sloth spends most of its time upside down, its fur lies in the opposite direction to that of other animals, toward its back instead of down from it. When torrential rains fall, the moisture merely drops off instead of soaking in.

Mr. Administrator, don't you wish you had such built-in equipment to prevent your torrential rains from soaking in?

—M. DALE BAUGHMAN

1336. A successful school administrator is a person who can delegate all the responsibility, shift all the blame and take all the credit.

1337.   Out of thirty-one pieces of mail
Only one has a genuine claim—
Of the rest of the postal parade,
Two-thirds are evangels of trade;
Full twenty go on to regale
The teacher with items for sale
From peanuts, to jackets, to fame,
To trips with expenses delayed,
(Not to trips with expenses defrayed!)

Of the ten morning pieces of mail
That are left, let these comments suffice;
At least one will fondly abuse
You for not having sent in your dues;

At least one will gravely detail
The ways that a teacher can fail
(Unless one accepts this advice!)
Some catalogues come through in two's
You may get some rare items thrice!
And what of the one lonely note
That plugs neither products nor stunts?
A character reference blank,
It seeks a "completion at once."

—WILLIAM J. MURPHY, Principal
Minersville Area Joint High School
Minersville, Pennsylvania

1338. The albatross has the widest wing span of all birds in relation to body-size. It occurs to me that some school administrators have large wing spreads, in relation to body size, which enables them to fly on and on.

—M. DALE BAUGHMAN

1339. When placement offices failed to help Homer Schroughams, he put an ad in the paper which read, "Exhausted, bored, frustrated superintendent resigning from present position. Incompetent, thinks too little and talks too much, seeks new position, not too much work. Age 50, looks 65." He was swamped with offers.

1340. Poker isn't the only game played with chips. In the game of school administration chips are here and there, mostly on shoulders and too often the chips are down for many school superintendents.

—M. DALE BAUGHMAN

1341. About fifteen years ago Grover G. Brown, then county superintendent of schools in Brown County, Indiana, was hired by the Columbia Press to call on county, city and town superintendents and high school principals in the southern half of Indiana to tell them about the new writing books which had just been adopted for state-wide use.

As a rule school people are very courteous to all agents, but it sometimes happens that when two or three call on the same day, it may become a trifle annoying to school administrators. About 11:00 o'clock one summer day when schools were not in session superintendent Brown went into the office of the city superintendent of schools in New Albany, Indiana.

The city superintendent's expression and manner seemed to say "another confounded agent!" Brown sensed this feeling and asked,

"Will you give me about four minutes of your time to explain this writing material?"

The school man looked him straight in the eye and said, "You know it will take you more than four minutes." Brown retorted, "I know when to shut up." "Shoot" replied the city administrator. Brown shot and in four minutes FLAT picked up his briefcase and started out. The city superintendent announced, "Hold on a minute, my boy. Sit down."

The two visited together most congenially for a full hour.

1342. Curiously it's the hard job not done that tires us out more than the difficult task over and done with. The housewife taking mental inventory of the day's chores will sometimes slump into an armchair more exhausted than if she had just completed a grueling day. The writer gazes vacantly at the blank page in his typewriter, sighing so heavily you would think he had just finished a novel. And often the mere sight of the morning mail, memoranda, and stack of reports, will paralyze the executive into virtual immobility.

Why is this so? One school administrator, taking stock of the many problems looming ahead for schoolmen, supplies an answer. Says Clara E. Cockerville, Assistant Superintendent, Armstrong County, Kittaning, Pennsylvania: "It's what Dorothy Canfield Fisher calls 'anticipatory fatigue.' We look at the gigantic task and as we think of all that must be done we are tired before we begin. This is a dangerous tiredness; to give in to it, to say all this talk about school changes will pass, to stand still, to do nothing is to be a traitor to the position we occupy—that of educational leader of a community. One of the best antidotes to anticipatory fatigue comes from an ancient sage. Said Confucius: 'He who walks a thousand miles must take the first step.'"

—Educator's Dispatch

1343. The handwriting isn't on the wall any more. The superintendent has had his back to the wall for so long that the handwriting is on his back.

1344. One of the topics for discussion at a state school administrator's workshop at the University of Illinois was "The Role of the Superintendent in School Plant Planning." I had written this topic along with four others on the blackboard at the opening session.

On the second morning of the workshop one of the participants called my attention to an apparent misspelled word. Now the topic reads, "The Roll of the Superintendent in School Plant Planning." Someone with a sense of humor plus experience in school building problems had changed one letter and the group agreed that perhaps the word "roll" *was* more appropriate.

—M. Dale Baughman

1345. Above all run a functional office. Know the definition of functional. It looks like H—— but it's handy.

1346. In baseball the shortstop who gets one "too hot to handle" is not credited with an error but the school administrator who can't handle the hot ones is always credited with errors.

—M. Dale Baughman

School Board

1347. A wife's lament: Monday, hubby said, "I'll be late. I've got a school committee date."

Tuesday, he vanished in his den, with two other committee men.

Wednesday, he had to miss a play. He spoke before the PTA.

Thursday, he skipped a fine dessert. Late for a meeting and had to spurt.

Friday, at bridge he forgot to play, thinking about the teachers' pay.

Saturday was no fun at all. An irate parent came to call.

Sunday, we sat beneath a tree. I thought and thought, and tried to see how different life for us could be. Free from chores of the committee. But here's the truth, so help me Lord. I would not have him off that Board.

—Erma Reynolds, *Illinois School Board Journal*

1348. Did you hear about the school board's letter of thanks to a lady who donated a cake for the post-meeting snack. It read, "Thanks for your cooperative attitude of which your cake is concrete evidence."

1349. Around school board election time each year, it is too often true that the man with the hoe doesn't always get as far as the man with the hokum.

1350. More than likely a school board sets out to find the best man available. Once they find him, they set out to prove the opposite.

1351. The young daughter of a school board member was heard calling her new born kittens "citizens." Sometime later she changed their names to "School Board." A neighbor asked for an explanation. "Well, they were little then—now they have their eyes open."

—M. Dale Baughman

School Buildings

1352. We shape our buildings and thereafter they shape us.

—Winston Churchill

1353. The architecture of schools has seemed to complete a cycle. Now, modern school buildings, like the early one-room structure, are built mostly on one floor. The experience of fire hazard and noise in the vertical buildings, popular about the turn of the century, prompted this return to tradition.

—*Sunshine Magazine*

1354. As the new educational plant probably will serve the area for several generations—you can figure on from 75 to 100 years— it is a long-term investment for the taxpayers. The campus, therefore, must be selected with even more care than an intelligent citizen would give to the choosing of his own homesite.

—As told to Vernon MacPherson, in
"Where Shall We Build" by Arol
Burns, Director of Real Estate, Los
Angeles City Schools

1355. It is unquestionably safer in the long run and cheaper to build school rooms and not use them than it is to need rooms and not have them.

—M. Dale Baughman

1356. Buildings have personalities; some by their immense dignity speak almost as music speaks, and change anxiety to trust.

1357. *Ventilation:* "In every schoolhouse without proper means of ventilation, there is a slow and subtile (sic) poison which enters the blood and brains of the pupils, and saps the very foundation of life. There can be no escape from its deleterious influences, for exposure to it is violation of one of the laws of Gad!"

Sex: "In most cases, it will be observed, a double porch, with separate entrances for boys and girls, has been provided, and this arrangement is regarded as highly important. It prevents the possi-

But our gym will seat several thousand.

bility of improper communication between the two sexes, while passing in and out of the schoolroom."

—Architecture, Ventilation and
Furnishing of School Houses

1358. Some low cost school buildings are like a courthouse restroom—they serve a purpose but aesthetic values are lacking.

—M. Dale Baughman

School Bus Driver

1359. *Definition of a school bus driver:* A man who thought he liked children.

1360. An iron worker was nonchalantly walking the beams high above the street on a new skyscraper, while the pneumatic hammers made a nerve-jangling racket, and the compressor below shook the whole steel structure. When he came down, a man who'd been watching him tapped his shoulder. "I was amazed at your calmness up there; how did you happen to go to work on a job like this?"

"Well," said the other, "I used to drive a school bus, but my nerves gave out."

—Wisconsin Journal of Education

School Custodian

1361. The time had come when the faithful old school janitor needed to be replaced by a newer model. With considerable embarrassment, the superintendent undertook to break the news to the old man. In tactful terms he extolled the glories of social security, retirement, pension and a testimonial dinner. The janitor registered surprise, disbelief and indignation. "Durn it all," he said, "when I took the job in 1890, they promised me it would be permanent."

—FREDERICK J. MOFFITT, "Chalk Dust," *Nation's Schools*

1362. Some aeronautic students designed a model of a new plane: Th tryout of the model was a failure since the wings broke off at the fuselage. Later on a discussion was going on where the students were trying to learn just what caused the structural failure. The custodian happened by, listened to the seminar, and asked if he might make a suggestion. He was allowed to and he explained that they should drill some holes or perforations along the wing and fuselage where they met. This was done and another model was made which performed admirably. The amazed students asked the custodian how he got the idea. He replied, "I've been a custodian for 30 years and I've never known even paper towels to break at the perforated line."

1363. In the educational world a school administrator knows something about everything, a specialist knows everything about something—and the custodian knows everything.

1364. School superintendent to applicant for the position of custodian: "Most of all we need a thoroughly responsible man."

Applicant: "I'm sure qualified—every place I've worked, when things went haywire, they never failed to tell me I was responsible."

School Secretary

1365. A filing cabinet is a repository where papers are lost alphabetically.

1366. Placement Director to shapely secretary: "Take the afternoon off, Miss Hall, I want to think."

1367. Superintendent to Secretary: "You're very versatile, Miss Smith; I didn't know anyone could be so inefficient in so many different ways."

—Southern California Water Company Bulletin

1368. "Miss Bliss," said the perplexed superintendent, "I don't see how you do it. You've been here one month and you're already two months behind."

1369. While diplomats jockey for position in the world, political candidates jockey for position in the nation, and business and professional people jockey for position in their fields of endeavor, I sit smugly by and watch, perfectly content in the knowledge that my job is the "greatest."

What job is this? I am a secretary. Surely, then, I must be secretary to the major or the president or some executive who holds the future of the world in his hands. Or is it a famous author or a movie star whose life is filled with glamour and excitement? No, none of these. True, those I work with do indeed have lives filled with glamour and excitement. They do, without a doubt, hold the future of the world in their hands. They are the teenagers of our community. I am a secretary in a high school.

Where is the glamour? Where is the excitement? What is so thrilling? Have you ever noticed how the room lights up and the air becomes alive when several children or teenagers come in? You can feel the vitality and youth in the air like a charge of electricity. Imagine, then, how much life, vitality, and youth there must be in a building with over 1500 teenagers. When you walk into the building you can fairly feel it soaking into your system, no matter how tired or dejected you might have been before entering.

Being secretary in a high school gives me definite advantage. I am not a teacher, with powers of "passing" or "flunking," nor an administrator charged with the duties of discipline or maintaining order. I'm just someone to say "Hi" to when you come through the office—who tries to be friendly and help a bewildered or scared student find the right person to take care of his or her problem.

No serious problems come to me. We have trained personnel to handle these. But students do come with news of an exciting weekend visit to a boy friend's college homecoming or to show me a newly acquired "going steady" ring. They let me give them a pat on the back when they make the honor roll, pitch a good game, win a medal, or in some cases, when they finally make a passing grade. I have previewed their reports and term papers, loaned them safety pins, laughed at their jokes, fixed sagging hems and obstinate zippers, consoled them in their disappointments, been shocked at their frankness and constantly amazed at their knowledge and thoughtfulness or lack of them.

Where in books or movies could you get the thrill to be had in watching a shy, frightened freshman develop progressively into a straightforward sophomore, a jaunty junior and finally a sincere, skilled and somewhat sophisticated senior?

These kids are real. They are America. They are the world. Anytime I begin to worry a little about rockets or bombs or to wonder about the future, I need only look up and see young America passing by in the hall, confident and assured, giving me a smile or a wave. These are the boys and girls who will be captains of industry, captains of airliners, captains of armies, captains of their homes, and, please God, captains of their souls.

Glamour and excitement? My job is filled up and running over ... and I love it.

—HELENE KOPP, Guidance Department
Secretary, Oak Lawn Community
High School

Science

1370. We know something should be done about our science education when a small son confuses quicksilver with a fast buck.

—BERT KRUSE, *Quote*

1371. In the lab school at the University of Illinois a very bright eleven-year-old junior high pupil asked for the key to the physics lab.

"It can't be!" thought the principal, "an eleven-year-old wanting to work in the physics lab."

"Why," asked the principal, "do you want in?"

"I left my yo-yo in there."

—DAVID JACKSON, Principal
University High School,
University of Illinois

1372. "Now," said the teacher, "give me a definition of space."

Junior stood up, flustered and red. "Space," he began, "is where there is nothing. I can't explain it exactly, but I have it in my head all right."

—*American Mercury*

1373. *Teacher:* "When water becomes ice, what is the greatest change that takes place?"
Bright boy: "The price, ma'am."

1374. Three methods used to transfer heat, one pupil wrote, are: oil trucks, coal trucks, and fire trucks.

—*Science Review*

1375. Science deals in the truth, not its implications.

—IRVING COX, JR.

1376. Science is resourceful. It couldn't open a day coach window, so it air-conditioned the train.

—*Phi Delta Kappan*

1377. An old Indian was standing on the top of a hill with his son, looking over the beautiful valley below them. Said the old Indian, "Some day, my son, all this land will belong to the Indians again. Paleface all go to the moon."

—*Capper's Weekly*

1378. The teacher was lecturing to a class in science. "Now, then, Bill," he said, "name me a poisonous substance."

Bill Smith, who was not gifted with an oversupply of intelligence, thought deeply. "Aviation," he said.

The class tittered with amusement, and the teacher looked sternly at the embarrassed pupil.

"Explain yourself, Bill," he demanded.

"One drop will kill, sir," responded Bill.

—*Sunshine Magazine*

1379. Fifty percent of scientific literature is in languages which more than half the world's scientists cannot read.

—*Scientific and Technical Translating*

1380. Definition of "uranium" found in a quarter-century-old dictionary still being used by George M. Ober in his law office:

"Uranium—A white, lustrous, radioactive metallic element . . . used in photography and coloring glass."

There have been some changes made since then.

Self

1381. One time the newspaper cartoonist H. T. Webster amused himself by sending telegrams to twenty of his acquaintances, selected at random. Each message contained the one word, "Congratulations."

So far as Webster knew, not one of them had done anything in particular on which he might be congratulated. But each of the twenty took the message as a matter of course, and wrote him a letter of thanks. Each had assumed he had done something worthy of a congratulatory telegram.

—*Sunshine Magazine*

1382.
Sometime when you're feeling important
Sometimes when your ego's in bloom
Sometime when you take it for granted
You're the best qualified in the room.

Sometime when you feel your going
Would leave an unfillable hole
Just follow this simple instruction
And see how it humbles your soul.

Take a bucket and fill it with water
Put your hand in—up to your wrist
Take it out—and the hole that's remaining
Is a measure of how you'll be missed.

You can splash all you please as you enter
You can stir up the water galore
But STOP—and you'll find in a minute
That it looks quite the same as before.

There's a moral in this quaint example
Just do the best that you can
Be proud of yourself but remember
There is no indispensable man.

—GIC Salesman, The Ranch House,
Central Pier, Atlantic City, New Jersey

1383. Glass blowers will never produce anything as fragile as the human ego.

—ARNOLD H. GLASGOW

Self-Analysis

1384. Man has now made his first step to the stars, yet we know little more about ourselves than we did 1,000 years ago.

—HELEN GAHAGAN DOUGLAS

1385. The spider spins his own reel from within, and when a man has come to the point where he wishes to determine the kind of employment in which he will best succeed, he must take thought of the spider, for only out of himself can he produce the web with which he is to snare fortune.

—*Sunshine Magazine*

1386. Very few people know themselves. You may have created an image which you strive to present to the world as your true self. But it is a false image. In a secret corner of your mind you are aware that it is false—but you run away from that awareness because you really do not understand yourself or know how to be yourself.

—*Chicago Herald American*

1387. If you use the head with which you reprove others to reprove yourself, there will be fewer faults; if you use the heart with which you forgive yourself to forgive others, there will be perfect friendship.

—S. C. CHAMPION, *Houston Times*

1388. I'm sure that I've got lots of faults—you know, that's only human. Why, just last week a friend of ours got my cool temper fumin'. Of course, I knew that I was right, and she was wrong as sin, but convincing her, I'm telling you, was something else ag'in!
My smug and patient husband says I've got a lot to learn. Well, I could teach him worlds of things, and still have brains to burn! Oh, yes, I must have lots of faults—my friends possess so many! I'm sure that I have three or four—but I just can't think of any.

—MARGY KIRKHART, *Sunshine Magazine*

1389. Oren Arnold, writing in the *Kiwanis* magazine, offers this lively philosophy: "It wouldn't help much for me to see myself as others see me. I simply wouldn't believe it."

Self-Confidence

1390. Do not attempt to do a thing unless you are sure of yourself; but do not relinquish it simply because someone else is not sure of you.

—STEWARD E. WHITE

1391. A jet airliner captain was about to take off on a flight to London. "Good evening, ladies and gentlemen," he said over the loud speaker system. "This is your captain speaking. We'll be crossing the Atlantic this evening at an altitude of 37,000 feet. Our estimated speed is 730 mph. We should reach London in approximately 5 hours." After a moment of silence, the captain continued, "We will take off as soon as I get up enough nerve."

—PAUL LIGHT, *St. Paul Pioneer Press*

Self-Improvement

1392. Within us all there are wells of thought and dynamos of energy which are not suspected until emergencies arise. Then oftentimes we find that it is comparatively simple to double or treble our former capacities and to amaze ourselves by the results achieved. Quotas, when set up for us by others, are challenges which goad us on to surpass ourselves. The outstanding leaders of every age are those who set up their own quotas and constantly exceed them.

—THOMAS J. WATSON, *Forbes*

1393. There is one knob to the door of a man's life, and that is on the inside. That door never opens except as the man inside opens it.

—*Megiddo Message*

Self-Reliance

1394. No bird soars too high, if he soars with his own wings.

—*The Lion*

1395. To do the thing I think is right is always my intention. No matter what the world may say, I'll disregard convention. My friends say, "Oh, you can't do that! It simply isn't done!" But does that stop me? No, siree! And I have lots of fun!

Do you think that those who lived before should regulate your actions? And if you don't obey their rules you'll suffer for infractions? Take my advice: Think for yourself. Do right, then don't explain. God meant for you to think for you—that's why you have a brain!

—LYLA MYERS, *Keystone Butler*

Self-Respect

1396. I have no right, by anything I do or say, to demean a human being in his own eyes. What matters is not what I think of him; it is what he thinks of himself. To undermine a man's self-respect is a sin.

—ANTOINE DE SAINT-EXUPERY

1397. When you get what you want in your struggle for pelf and the world makes you king for a day, just go to the mirror and look at yourself, and see what that man has to say.

For it isn't your father, or mother, or wife, whose judgment upon you must pass; the fellow whose verdict counts most in your life is the one staring back from the glass.

You may be like Jack Horner and chisel a plum, and think you're a wonderful guy, but the man in the glass says you're only a bum, if you can't look him straight in the eye.

—ROY H. PHILLIPS, *The Anagram*

Service

1398.
Do all the good you can,
By all the means you can,
In all the ways you can,
In all the places you can,
At all the times you can,
To all the people you can,
As long as ever you can.

—JOHN WESLEY

1399. A chapel speaker was preaching to our school on the lack of Good Samaritan spirit in the world today. To illustrate, he recited an episode that had happened in New York: "During the lunch hour I walked with a friend toward a nearby restaurant when we saw lying on the street a helpless fellow human who had collapsed." After a solemn pause he added, "Not only had nobody

bothered to stop and help this poor fellow, but on our way back after lunch we saw him still lying in the same spot."
—Contributor's note: *For goodness' sake with-hold my name if this ever gets printed.*

1400. Genius and strength are worth nothing if we do not put them to the service of our fellow beings. The most sacred duty of youth lies in the relation to the community in which it lives.
—Carlos Contreras, *Partners*

1401. The greatest thing in the world is a human life; the greatest work in the world is the helpful touch upon that life.
—Charles Lamoureux, *The Lion*

1402. Leadership and service belong together: They spiral in unison. Each involves the dynamic relationships which exist in social situations. However, there are significant differences, for leadership is always a group phenomenon. Consideration of the ideal of leadership thus invites a good look at human relations.
—D. Willard Zahn, *Dean, College of Education, Temple University, Phi Delta Kappan*

1403.　　In my poor uncertain way
I try to use each given day
As though it were but loaned to me . . .
A priceless cup from which to sip
But once, a precious stewardship
To serve with love and dignity.
—Lloyd C. Lewis, *Sunshine Magazine*

1404. In this world it is not what we take up, but what we give up, that makes us rich.

1405. Three Boy Scouts were at a Scouts' meeting and told the scoutmaster they had done their "good deed" that day.

"Well, boys, what did you do?" asked the scoutmaster.

"We helped an old lady across the street a little while ago," claimed the boys in unison.

"And did it take all three of you to do that?" asked the master suspiciously.

"Oh, yes, it did!" again chimed the boys. Then the smallest added, "She didn't want to go."
—*Sunshine Magazine*

1406. Serve that you may own; own that you may serve.
—SAY

1407. No one is useless in this world who lightens the burden of anyone else.

—CHARLES DICKENS

1408. It was Albert Einstein, outstanding scientist, who said: "It is high time the ideal of success should be replaced with the ideal of service." And it was E. Stanley Jones, a missionary who has dedicated his life to service, who said: "The man is not greatest who has the greatest number of servants, but the man is greatest who serves the greatest number of people."

—Ross M. WILLIS, "The House On Straight Street," *Pulpit Digest*

1409. All useful service is raised to the plane of art, when love for the task is fused with the effort.

1410. Our chief want in life is somebody who shall make us do what we can; this is the service of a friend.

—EMERSON

1411.
"Who is my neighbor?
He who needs my care!
Where is my neighbor?
Everywhere!
When my neighbor's eyes are weary,
And his heart is sad,
Help me, Lord, to help my neighbor
To be glad."

Special Education

1412.
We stood,
The Principal and I,
Watching them go
And chatted about
Inane things for a minute or so,
Then Carl, vacant of eye,
Cap on, sauntered by
Alone. . . . .
So awfully alone
That I wanted to reach out,
Take his hand,
And walk with him.

"Poor Carl," the Principal said,
"Uneducable."
And shook his head.

"Oh, no!"
But protest lay unuttered
On my lips
As if suspended
By the futility of defense;
Rather I chose to remember
A morning in December
Sleet sharp with windy snowing,
And Carl, tardy, eyes glowing,
Unbuttoned and stumbling
Offering me, oh so carefully
In his red, unmittened hands,
A perfect autumn maple leaf!
The blued circle of his lips mumbling
Painfully, slowly,
As if rehearsed,

"Is booful!"
"Is booful!"
O'er and o'er.
　　　　　—ANTHONY TOVATT, Burris Laboratory School
　　　　　　Ball State Teachers College
　　　　　　Indiana Teacher

Specialist

1413. In the court of Judge William K. Thomas, over in Cleveland last week, a damage suit was in trial. In the course of testimony a witness, asked for an interpretation of the term "specialist" came up with a definition which we have a feeling may stand unchallenged for quite some time: "A specialist," he said, "is one step above a man who gets paid overtime."

1414. A teacher being interviewed for a job in a modern junior high school with a dynamic curriculum was asked if she had taught previously at the secondary level.
　"Certainly."
　"In junior high school?"

"Yes."

"In grade eight?"

"Yes."

"Block-of-time method?"

"Yes."

"Integration of subject matter in the block-of-time in grade eight?"

"No, no integration of subject matter."

"Sorry, we need a specialist."

Speakers—Speaking—General

1415. Raconteur Brooks Hays, former congressman from Little Rock, moved back to Washington to be an assistant secretary of state. Testifying before the Foreign Relations Committee, Hays told members: "I'm so flustered I feel like the preacher whose congregation gave him a large, expensive automobile. He got mixed up and said: 'I don't appreciate this, but I sure do deserve it.'"

Quote

1416. An after-dinner speaker is one who blows in, blows off and blows out.

1417. He makes a great splash; it's like holding a narrow-necked bottle under the tap and turning the water on full force. There is a lot of display and excitement but very little water runs into the bottle.

1418. Some learned speakers have a habit of mentioning unusual things they have done or famous places they have visited as one did recently at a University of Illinois forum. He remarked in a worldly way, "I walked in and out of that old ———— (name) Cathedral a dozen times as you have." Now, I had never walked in and out of that old ———— cathedral even once; as a matter of fact that's the first time I ever heard of it.

—M. DALE BAUGHMAN

1419. Two women were preparing to board an air liner. One of them turned to the pilot and said, "Please don't go faster than sound; we want to talk."

—*The Lookout*

1420. Did you hear about the master of ceremonies who was down on his luck? After floundering around for a long time, he finally had to settle for a job at Union Station announcing incoming and outgoing trains.

"All rightie, folks," he called over the public address system his first day on the job. "Now coming in on track number 3 from Chicago, the El Capitan—exactly ten minutes ahead of schedule. Let's give it a great big hand!"

—BARRY ATWATER, *Journal of the American Medical Association*

1421. When the audience is talkative, the toastmaster might first utter, "Let me say something, too, will you?"

1422. Through a national survey it has been determined that, among those who choose the engineering profession and fail to make good, the majority fail, not because they lack training and cannot cooperate or adjust themselves to industrial conditions, but because they lack the ability of self-expression.

1423. The woman had a speech impediment . . . she had to stop to breathe once in a while.

1424. When I was just getting started in public speaking I often needed a drink of water to moisten my dry and tense throat, but I was usually so nervous I couldn't get the glass to my lips without spilling some.

Now, I'm more relaxed and can pick up a glass with a sure hand, but I don't need the water now.

—M. DALE BAUGHMAN

1425. It has been estimated that from the first "good morning" to the last "good night," the average man engages in approximately 30 conversations a day.

1426. Jack Waldron recalls he used to practice speaking with pebbles in his mouth: "It worked fine till I got the hiccups one day. I broke two mirrors and a picture window."

1427. If a speaker rehearses his speeches, can you say that he practices what he preaches?

—*Inspiration*

1428. To tell a story is to distill a human experience and recreate it in a form understandable and enjoyable to others. Note that this is more than simple narration or mere technique. This is as true of a Joe Miller joke as of a Joseph Conrad story. A good spinner of yarns can excite and interest by exact description, by a fine sense of the poignant, the humorous, the human.

—ROBERT WAGNER, Bureau of Education
Research and Service, Ohio State
University, Columbus, Ohio
The Newsletter

1429. "I don't know what happened," said H. Gordon Burroughs, attending a spiritualist meeting, "but I became unconscious. When I came to, people were applauding. I had been talking to them for a half-hour but I had no idea what I said." What's the man waiting for? Why doesn't he run for office?

—THOMAS MORROW, *Tribune*

1430. A speech expert forecasts that everybody, sooner or later, will get tired of talking and stop. Not as long as we have politicians and news commentators, doctors . . . and women.

—*Phoenix Flame*

1431. Master of ceremonies at banquet where there was no principal speaker: "Let's have a round of applause for the wonderful job the program committee did in not being able to obtain a speaker."

1432. (*After major speaker finishes*): There is an ageless custom by which the audience expresses its appreciation for a significant and appropriate contribution. (applause) . . . ., you have just witnessed a sample of this custom. Is that ample remuneration or will you still insist on your honorarium?

—M. DALE BAUGHMAN

1433. Slips of the tongue are made far more frequently than slips of the pen, and although many wise words have fallen from foolish lips far more foolish speeches have come from the mouths of the wise. As our speech is so are we, for it is by the spoken word that we show the degree of our culture or betray the depth of our ignorance. It may take a wise man to make a fool, but that is not reason enough for us to encourage the belief that every time we talk nonsense we become humorists.

—FUNK AND WAGNALLS, Introduction to
Slips of Speech

1434. Good manners and good speech are the magic master keys to the good life.

—DR. GALEN STARR ROSS, president, Capitol
College of Oratory and Music, Columbus,
Ohio, *Sunshine Magazine*

1435. Toastmaster remarks acknowledging the address: Your remarks were refreshingly different and appropriately relevant. These were exactly the two criteria set up by this group for speakers.

1436. Speaking straight from the shoulder is okay, but be sure it originates a little higher up.

—*Laugh Book*

1437. A film actor was disappointed at not being asked to make a speech on the occasion of his retirement from films. As he said to a friend, "What makes it worse is that I spent three hours in the makeup department having a lump put in my throat."

—*Indianapolis Star*

1438. Freedom of speech too often seems to mean "free to say what you please as long as you please enough people."

—FRANK J. PIPPIN, *Ethical Outlook*

1439.

When called on to utter
Don't panic or flee 'em;
Don't mutter or stutter,
Just dalecarnegiem.

—FREDERICK J. MOFFITT, *Nation's Schools*

1440. Chief Rain-in-the-Face was persuaded to attend a lecture. When it was all over, someone asked him what he thought of it. "Uh!" he grunted. "Big wind, lotta dust, no rain."

—*Sunshine Magazine*

1441. Most speakers have just one speech. Sometimes they holler louder in some places than in others. Usually they start at the front but occasionally one will start at the back and work toward the front. It's not too uncommon for a speaker to now and then start in the middle and work both ways.

1442. A top Army communications expert has said if you want people to remember what you say, illustrate your talk. If you use audio only, listeners will recall 70% of what you say in three hours, only 10% in three days. If you use visuals only, viewers will recall 72% in three hours, 20% in three days. If you use audio-visual presentations, your audience will recall 85% of the message in three hours, 65% in three days.

—*Survey Bulletin*

1443. A speaker of some renown once during a lecture startled his hearers when he suggested a 10-minute intermission. The audience sat there bewildered for a few moments. The speaker gazed over the listeners briefly and then relieved their perplexity by saying, "Meanwhile in order to pass the time, we will proceed with the address."

1444. For solid comfort and general satisfaction, you can't beat an old time-worn story. Then the audience is a step ahead of you. They know precisely when to laugh.

1445. An effective speech ought to gall the orthodox and annoy the complacent.

1446. The speaker on farm management had given much good advice, but finally sat down. The chairman rose to summarize. "Our speaker has made our situation very plain. If our outgo exceeds our income, the upkeep will be our downfall."

—Toastmaster

1447. I was amused at the toastmaster's statement that "what he says, goes." He is somewhat like the man who was riding on a railway train beside a certain stranger. After five minutes of silence, the stranger became confidential.

"I," he said, impressively, "am a starter of elevators in a city skyscraper. When I signal them to go up, they go up. And your line is—?"

"I," said the other, "am an undertaker. When I signal them to go down, they go down."

—Bright Bits

1448. (*Hints for the educator lecturer at school institutes and workshops*):

One of the prime purposes of a professional meeting of teachers is to make each of them a student for the duration of the meeting. The successful lecturer fits himself to do just that. No man earns his pay at such an event unless he feels a strong desire, much as the skilled actor on the stage, to communicate something of value.

If he is to help the teachers present, he must know something of their status, their training, their knowledge, their school system, their state and their country. If the lecturer doesn't have some idea of these things, he runs the risk of flying, as Icarus did, too high or too low. The educational history of Indiana does not prepare for institute work in Illinois any better than the agricultural history of the tomato growing region of Indiana prepares one to lecture to the bean growers of Brown County. Of course the Indiana tomato grower may give a bundle of accurate knowledge, perhaps even interesting, but how well does it satisfy the needs of the man eager to learn more about raising beans in Illinois?

—M. Dale Baughman

1449. On one occasion at one of those farmer's institutes a young man had come down to talk soil analysis to the farmers. He was a very young man and had carefully prepared his address. He read it and it abounded in chemical formulas and technical terms, and one after another the farmers got up and went out. He had a very long address, because he wanted to cover the subject completely. When he got through, he noticed that he had just one man left in the audience. He called to the man after he had finished and was taking up his hat to leave and said, "My friend, I appreciate very much your interest in this subject. What was there about the discourse of this evening that interested you most?" To which the man replied, "Interested me nothing. I am the next speaker."

W. K. Tate

1450. One day in the House of Commons, British Prime Minister Benjamin Disraeli made a brilliant speech on the spur of the moment. That night, at a party, his hostess said to him:

"I must tell you how much I enjoyed your extemporaneous talk. It's been on my mind all day."

"Madam," confessed Disraeli, "that extemporaneous talk has been on my mind for 20 years."

—*Milwaukee Journal*

1451. Joe Garagiola was showing his announcing partner, Harry Caray, around his recreation room. Noticing a mounted deer's head above the fireplace, Caray remarked, "I didn't know you were a big game hunter, Joe."

The former big league catcher explained that he had not shot the deer, that it had been presented to him by a civic group for whom he had made an after-dinner speech.

"You know," said Caray, "you're probably the first guy who ever shot the bull and got a deer."

—*Scholastic Coach*

1452. A little word said and remembered is better than any amount of weary, casual talk which men endure and gladly forget.

—*The War Cry*

1453. Among Americans, 15,000,000 have impaired hearing, but for every one who can't hear there are at least five who won't listen.

That, according to Atlanta *Constitution* columnist Leo Aikman, is why history repeats. Nobody listens.

1454. An ancient king once commanded his wise court jester to prepare him the finest dish in the world. He was served a dish of tongue.

Then the king demanded the worst dish in the world, and again was served a dish of tongue.

The king asked the reason and the wise man said: "The tongue is the greatest of blessings when wisely and lovingly used, but becomes the greatest curse when it is unkindly and dishonestly used."

—REVEREND A. PURNELL BAILEY, *Grit*

1455. A politician of quite ordinary intellect once amazed his hearers with a flowery, but brilliant, speech.

As he sat down amidst tumultuous applause, a voice at the rear of the audience, obviously a member of the opposition party, implored: "Author! Author!"

1456. The president of Ohio State University tells this story on himself: He had just completed his address before a certain civic organization and was receiving the usual commendations when presently a young lad approached and said, "That was lousy." Rather nonplussed, the speaker turned to the man next to him, who hurriedly explained that the boy wasn't quite bright and only repeated what he heard other folks say.

—*Rotarian*

1457. Don't worry about tension (in speechmaking); it's natural and useful. "A course in speaking should not put emphasis on making you feel at ease," asserts David C. Phillips, American Management Association speech teacher. "Nervousness makes your brain sharp and alert. Any time I'm not keyed up before a speech, I take it as a bad sign."

—MAX GUNTHER, *Popular Science*

Speech Openers

1458. I was just about halfway through my speech to the elementary teachers of Bay City, Michigan when a terrific thunderstorm hit. Thunder and the torrent of rain on the metal roof of the gymnasium caused temporary cessation in my talking. We waited for the storm to abate, but it continued. Finally, a public address system was quickly set up so that I could finish my speech.

Next day the Bay City News carried this account of my talk: "The fury of the storm forced the speaker to cease talking but the relief was short-lived as a public address system was quickly put into use."

—M. DALE BAUGHMAN

1459. No doubt you were under the impression that the last course of this banquet had been served. I assure you that the impression is erroneous, for I am about to serve to you a conglomeration of nonsense which I choose to call, "hash."

1460. The speaker was addressing a large group, and had been talking for some time when the microphone ceased to function. Raising his voice, he asked a man in the back row if he could hear.

"No, I can't," said the man.

Whereupon a man in the front row stood up. "I can hear," he shouted to the man in back. "And I'll change places with you."

1461. A few months ago I heard an after-dinner speech by a gentleman who had some trepidation in making it. He said he had consulted a friend of his who was highly skilled in making after-dinner speeches. The friend advised him that the best kind of audience to address, as an after-dinner speaker, was an audience, intelligent and well-educated, but half-tight.

Now all I can say is that this audience is one of the best audiences I ever saw for an after-dinner speaker. Something has made up for the absence of that element that the remark implied, and I must think it is the spirit of the .... (appropriate group).

—WILLIAM HOWARD TAFT

1462. I was speaking at an assembly in the Arkansas Ozarks one summer when a sudden shower held my audience captive beyond the hour of adjournment. Since no one could leave without getting soaked, I attempted to time my conclusion with the end of the shower. The presiding officer sat on the edge of his seat, nervously watching the rain and the speaker. The rain and I finished simultaneously and the presiding officer rushed to the podium. His first words were: "Now that the drip has stopped..."

—W. L. HOWSE, of the Sunday School Board, *Southern Baptist Brotherhood Journal*

1463. (*On the occasion of a return engagement*): I spoke here last year and you provided for me an appreciative audience and a generous honorarium. I understand 1,000 letters were written asking that I be allowed to come back. I think you'll agree that a man who will write 1,000 letters deserves to come back.

1464. We will now observe a ten-second period of sympathy for (1) those who have heard this speech before and are too courteous to walk out and (2) those who deplore nonsense but don't have enough nerve to leave.

1465. When I count three, will you all stamp your feet in unison? That is a precaution I sometimes take to guarantee that at least you won't be asleep when I start my speech.

1466. It was a women's meeting and a prominent authoress rose and went to the mike. As she began, she was aware of hissing from the wings. A man in overalls, obviously an engineer, stood there with a screwdriver. The lady chairman went to investigate. She returned, rather flustered, and brushing past the speaker, said: "Before we continue I have a very unhappy piece of news to communicate. Word has been given to me from the wings that there is a screw loose in our speaker."

—Illustrated Weekly of India

1467. A speech is like a wheel—the longer the spoke, the greater the tire.

—Telegram, Worcester, Massachusetts

1468. You may not agree but I have observed that far too many speakers when they have occupied the rostrum become dealers in dry goods and notions.

1469. I was once giving my speech on humor to a group of teenagers. Communication wasn't well established, it seemed. At least there was little laughter as I finished each story or anecdote. Finally, in desperation, I announced, "I am inclined to believe that it would take a surgical instrument to put a joke into the heads of some of you frozen faces."

One teenager, bolder than the rest, replied, "Yeah, man, but it would have to have a finer point than your stories."

—M. Dale Baughman

1470. I remarked to my wife that I did very well until I had spoken for about 30 minutes; after that I didn't seem to know just

what to do with my hands. In her wisdom, she suggested, "Why
don't you try clamping them over your mouth?"

—M. Dale Baughman

1471. Tonight my job is to talk; yours is to listen; if you finish
your job before I finish mine, please don't disturb the others as you
go out.

1472. I make no pretensions to oratorical ability. This being my
first attempt to make an after-dinner speech, I believe I rank as the
amateur of amateurs. I believe I am about as green at orating as
my friend, Bob Kennedy, is at fishing. You know I took Bob on his
first fishing expedition. He did not have any tackle, so I volunteered
to let him use mine. We went out to Bass Lake, picked out a nice
shady nook, and threw in our lines. After a few minutes, Bob said
calmly:

"Say, George, how much do these green and red bobber things
cost?"

"Oh, about ten cents," I replied.

"Well, then," he said, "I owe you a dime. Mine's just gone under."

1473. (*Opener for the substitute speaker*): I have never traveled
with a circus, so I don't know just exactly how it feels when the
sideshow has arrived but the big tent has been held up; but that
is pretty nearly the situation tonight. All of you doubtless came
here to listen to a great scholar and a great lecturer but for reasons
unknown, he has not made it here. Only the sideshow is here.

1474. It is a great privilege to be with the teachers of this enlightened (city, state, etc.). I mean exactly what I say. . . . .
is the most enlightened (city, state, etc.) of any I know. (Hesita-
tion) I am glad you admit it.

1475. For you who are over 39 I have some jokes; for you who
are under 39, I have some jokes; for you who are just 39, "Happy
Birthday."

1476. Speakers will confuse the seating capacity of the hall with
the sitting capacity of the audience.

—Noel Wical

1477. At a recent convention a sign had been erected near the
speakers' platform. It read: "Do not photograph the speakers when

they are addressing the audience. Shoot them as they approach the platform."

—*Seng Fellowship News*

1478. I agreed to make a speech at the club this month, mainly because Fred Randolph is the program chairman. After I told him I'd do it, though, I wish he hadn't said, "Thanks, boy, I was really getting desperate."

1479. In all my addresses before nearly all kinds of groups, I always relate some anecdotes, stories or illustrations. Tonight, I've had several requests, but I'm gonna' tell some anyhow.

—M. Dale Baughman

1480. Every time I look out over an audience the question comes to my mind: Is there anyone out there who could do a better job of saying what I have to say? I may add, however, that I never wait for an answer.

—W. I. Price

1481. A good speech helps people in different ways. Some rise from it greatly strengthened. Others wake from it refreshed.

1482. Many mothers have not had their ears pierced—but many have had them bored by PTA speakers.

—M. Dale Baughman

1483. A farmer bought a pig in June for $10, spent $30 for feed and sold it for $40 in the fall.
  Another farmer commented, "But you didn't make any money."
  Said the first, "But I had the company of the pig all summer."
You may not make any money as a result of hearing this speech but you will have my company for the evening.

1484. William E. Gladstone, distinguished English statesman, was an eloquent and moving speaker. When a friend asked him the secret of his power as a speaker he replied that he drew from his audience in vapor what he poured back upon them in a flood.

—Reverend Walter L. Lingle,
Christian Observer

Speech Brevity

1485. A carpenter once said: "Best rule I know for talkin' is the same as the one for measurin'—measure twice and then saw once."

1486. One prospective buyer, about to succumb to some high-powered direct mail publicity, took a second look and tore up his order.

The book was entitled *How to Say a Few Words Effectively* and it had 348 pages!

1487. I arrived late at Muncie Central High School in Indiana to make an address on "The Nature of Young Adolescents." The chorus was singing two or three additional numbers when I finally walked into the auditorium. Chairman Omer Mitchell, whom I had not met before, sensed that I was the speaker and approached me. He announced in a whisper, "You're on in a few minutes and you're through when your time's up."

—M. Dale Baughman

1488. I'll be brief this morning. It's chiefly because of my throat. (Pause) I don't want to get it cut.

1489. Eddie Cantor was telling about the entertaining he does as toastmaster and MC, and the practical solution he has to holding down after-dinner speakers. "I ask the speakers in advance how much time they want. If a man insists he needs an hour to get his message across, I take a slip of paper out of my pocket and give it to him: 'This one can be read in a minute and 50 seconds.' Immediately the speeches get shorter and surer. On the slip of paper: the Gettysburg Address."

—*Ladies' Home Journal*

1490.
  To those who talk and talk
  This adage doth appeal;
  The steam that blows the whistle
  Will never turn a wheel.

—*Keynote*

1491. There was a commencement speaker named Zore,
  Whose speeches were always a bore.
  One night in May,
  He had his full say,
  And collected his fee but no more.

—M. Dale Baughman

1492. After the death of the Roman emperor, Marcus Aurelius, legend has it that the Olympian gods gave a banquet in his honor. During the evening Jupiter announced a contest to determine which of the great Roman emperors had been the greatest. All of them were present, and each in turn stood up to make an address in his own behalf. Most of the emperors boasted of their conquests, or of their wealth and power, but when Marcus Aurelius was called on to speak, he modestly exclaimed, "I, a humble philosopher, have cherished the ambition never to give pain to another." Thereupon, amid resounding acclamation, he was crowned the greatest of the Romans.

—Sunshine Magazine

Speech—Relief Devices—Transition

1493. Am I going too fast for those of you who are taking notes?

1494. (*When jokes don't go over*): I'm feeling just like the weatherman so often in error in his predictions that he was laughed at so much he sought transfer to another station.

"Why do you wish to be transferred?" asked the boss. "Because," the forecaster answered, "the climate doesn't agree with me."

—M. DALE BAUGHMAN

1495. That joke was equally unsuccessful the last time I told it.

1496. (*When they laugh*): "Not too much laughter, please, you're going to kill my timing!"

1497. (*When they laugh*): "I wonder who fixed the audience?"

1498. To the audience: When I count three, everybody stamp their feet. Thanks! .... always sleeps when I talk and I told him I would wake him up at ...... o'clock.

1499. All right, don't laugh! I *know* it wasn't funny. I only told it to make a point! Who wants to tell the next one?

1500. (*After quoting poetry*): That's the only poem I've memorized. I thought I'd throw it in there, whether it fits or not.

1501. Now, listen—this is something like an auction sale. Somebody has to open the bidding—here somebody has to start the laughter.

—M. DALE BAUGHMAN

1502. It's quite obvious this audience isn't fixed—at least, not in my favor—you're going to make me work hard tonight.

1503. When I count three, will you all look up and blow toward the ceiling? Thank you—this joint isn't air-conditioned and we all know that hot air rises.

Speech Introductions

1504. If I were to ask one of you what is the outstanding quality of . . . ., you would no doubt say it is her extreme quietness. I believe the only alibi we need to give for this pecularity is that on a large tree, the smallest twigs usually do the most rustling.

—Bright Bits

1505. When Dr. Pierce Harris of First Methodist Church, Atlanta, Georgia, spoke recently at a prison work camp, the prisoner introducing him recalled earlier days of association with the minister.

"Many years ago," he said, "two boys lived in the same community in north Georgia and attended the same school, played with the same bunch of fellows, and went to the same Sunday School.

"One of them dropped out of Sunday School because he felt he had outgrown it, and that it was sissy stuff. The other boy kept on going because he felt that it really meant something in his life.

"The boy who dropped out is the one who is making this introduction today. The boy who kept going to Sunday School is the famous preacher who will preach to us this morning."

—Wesleyan Methodist

1506. At our club's Ladies Night, President Bill Norman introduced Jack Morgan's bride. "Better known—and better off—as Helen Hughes," he added.

1507. The chairman in introducing the principal speaker who happened to be a good friend of his, was making an analogy between the program and a train. He concluded with "Trains start on time—we do. Trains always start with a jerk. Here is . . . .

1508. It's always a pleasure to welcome and introduce to you a a man who always makes such expiring speeches.

1509. Dave Howell, World Service Y.M.C.A. Secretary who spent a number of years in Liberia, described the following introduction he once received prior to a speech.

It seems that there was sort of a three-way chairmanship at this meeting and the first who opened the meeting briefly mentioned that Howell was from Libya. Howell whispered to the man nearby who was to speak next and asked him to correct the party about Libya. But this man when he rose to speak, after making some routine remarks referred to Howell as the man from Nigeria. Now by this time Howell said he was a little confused himself, but he nudged the man who was to introduce him officially and reminded him that to set the record straight, he was from Liberia. This gentleman nodded his head and said he would straighten out matters. He concluded his introductory remarks with these words: "And now it is my pleasure to introduce Dave Howell from Siberia."

1510. When introducing someone you know well at a less than ultraformal gathering, try this: "I am told that as a speaker he is a whirlwind. He will now whirl wind."

1511. Introducing a speaker you know intimately you can say, "The speaker's name is .... and before tonight I never heard of him."

1512. I'll just launch him—to use space age terminology, get him off the pad.

1513. There is so much to be said about our speaker this evening that one encounters grave difficulty in choosing a beginning. However, as the Frenchman explained in answer to the question why he always kissed the ladies' hands, "One has to start somewhere."
—M. Dale Baughman

1514. At one interdenominational meeting, a minister from the same denomination as the speaker made the introduction. Eager to impress the audience with the speaker's qualifications, he said, "Our speaker is known in the churches of our denomination throughout the world—and probably in regions beyond!"
—New Christian Advocate

1515. (*Someone you know well*): And now, ladies and gentlemen, here is one of the greatest educators of our time—our time is 7:30 to 9:30.

Speech Response to Introduction

1516. For months I have been looking for a competent publicity agent. At last, I've found him. Thanks, ... for that generous introduction.

1517. I think I'll leave now; after such a glowing introduction what can I do but give my usual thrilling speech. I'm not conceited —just challenged.

1518. Thank you for that kind introduction. My cup of appreciation runneth over: I have only one regret, and here's why. I have three children—Mrs. Baughman has the same number—and I do wish all of them could have heard what a great man I am. At home they think I'm so unimportant.

—M. DALE BAUGHMAN

1519. Introducing the guest speaker, the MC listed his virtues in glowing terms.

"That introduction," grinned the guest, "reminds me of the man who on judgment day stuck his head out of the grave and read the epitaph on his headstone. "Either somebody is a terrible liar, or I'm in the wrong hole!"

—EDWARD C. O'CONNOR, *Quote*

Speech Closers

1520. Speakers at the weekly luncheon meeting of a particular organization are always informed that they must finish by 1:30 and a huge clock hangs on the wall to remind them. On one occasion the speaker of the day glanced at the clock when it indicated 1:20 and remarked, "Now in closing I have ten points to emphasize; if I'm on number nine when the hand reaches 1:30, I'll finish anyway."

1521. I'm finished but my speech isn't—it goes on and on.

1522. You probably think I'm like the little girl who said she knew how to spell banana but she didn't know when to stop.

1523. As the fat man said when he crawled through the barbed wire fence, "One more point and I'm through."

1524. We had occasion recently to address an editorial colleague here in the middle western area and concluded our missive, "See you Sunday, G, w, a, t, c, d, r."

We were surprised when he came back and asked for decoding. For generations this has been the departing observation of the rural Midwest. As two wagons pulled away from the Sabbath meeting-house, one householder would call to another, "See you Sunday!"

And the other would respond, "Sure, see you Sunday, God willin' and the creeks don't rise!"

Spelling

1525. When a small girl filled out a registration card at a girls' club recently she listed her church membership as "Babtist."

"Honey," said Mrs. Ila Huff, the director, "you're not a Babtist, are you?"

"No'm, I'm Episcopalian," she said, "but I can't spell it."

1526. When the air conditioning at an Omaha theater fails to function, it must really get hot inside.

A sign near the box office of the establishment pleads:

"Our air conditioning is out of order. Will you please bare with us?"

1527. Sign on a student bulletin board at a large university: "Expert typing, 25 cents a page. Good speler."

1528. Student: "Is waterworks all one word, or do you spell it with a hydrant in the middle?"

1529. *Teacher*: "Tommy, can you spell 'fur'?"
Tommy: "Yes, f-u-r."
Teacher: "Correct. Now tell me what fur is?"
Tommy: "Fur is an awful long way off."

—The Lookout

1530. "F-e-e-t," the teacher exclaimed, "what does that spell, Mary?" "I dunno."

"Well, what is it that a cow has four of and I have only two?" So Mary told her.

—Typo Graphic

Sports

1531. Tommy Stewart is a fine football coach. He has done an excellent job with Champaign's Maroons.

But now he is trying to be a comedian.

In season, you know, he coaches the swimming team, and the other day he was being questioned about the chances of winning the Big 12 title.

"I don't believe we can win it," he said. "Not enough depth."
—T. O. WHITE, *Champaign-Urbana*
News Gazette

1532. Duffie Daugherty, coach at Michigan State, recently described the qualities he looks for in his athletes at the University. "Of course, we like them big," he said, "but we'll settle for players with 3 kinds of bones—a funny bone, a wishbone and a backbone. The funny bone is to enjoy a laugh, even at one's own expense. The wishbone is to think big, set one's goals high and to have dreams and ambitions. And the backbone—well, that's so a boy will have the gumption to get up and go to work and make all those dreams come true."
—ROLAND F. MEISSNER, JR., *Nylic Review*

1533. "Dora is the dumbest girl I've ever seen."
"Why?"
"She wants to know how many quarters in a baseball game."
"That's nothing. Margy wanted to know if a football coach has wheels."

1534. A champion track man was once asked his recipe for winning races. "Well, it's simple," he said, "the thing to do is take the lead at the start and improve your position throughout the race."

1535. Two women were returning from their first attempt at bowling.
The husband of one, an inveterate golfer, asked with a raised eyebrow: "How'd you make out?"
"Well," she said, "at least we didn't lose any balls."

Student Masterpieces

1536. A grammar schoolboy handed in his composition on "Cats": "Cats that's meant for little boys to maul and tease is called Maultease cats. Some cats is rekernized by how quiet their pur is and these is Pursian cats. Cats what has bad tempers is named Angora cats. And cats with deep feelings is called Felines. I don't like cats."

1537. When a certain schoolboy was asked to write an essay about a goose, he wrote the following:
"The goose is a low heavy set bird, composed mostly of meat

and feathers. His head sets on one end and he sets on the other. He cannot sing much on account of the dampness in the moisture in which he lives. There ain't no space between his toes, and he carries a balloon in his stomach to keep from sinking.

"A goose has two legs on his running gear, but they came pretty near missing his body. Some geese when they get big are called ganders. Ganders don't have to set or hatch, but jest loaf, eat, and go swimming. If I was a goose, I'd rather be a gander."

1538. A class in English was assigned the task of writing four lines of dramatic poetry. The results were variegated, and, selecting the verse of a bright boy, the teacher read: "A boy was walking down the track; the train was coming fast; the boy stepped off the railroad track to let the train go past." "This verse is very well done," commented the teacher, "but it lacks the dramatic. Try again, Johnny, and make it more dramatic."

Whereupon, in a short time, Johnny produced the following: "A boy was walking down the track; the train was coming fast; the train jumped off the railroad track to let the boy go past."

—Sunshine Magazine

1539. Excerpt from a book review written by an Ohio ninth-grader: "The story takes place throughout the life of a young girl of today. Her mother tells the story and the problems that arise in bringing up an addle essence."

1540. The identity of the young lady is withheld, but the memory of her answers lingers on with the instructor conducting a science course at high school. One of the requirements in the written quiz was "Define a bolt and nut, and explain the difference." The girl wrote "A bolt is a thing like a stick of hard metal, such as iron, with a square bunch on one end and a lot of scratching wound around the other end. A nut is similar to the bolt only just the opposite, being a hole in a little chunk of iron sawed off short, with wrinkles around the inside of the hole."

The startled professor marked that one with an "A."

—Sunshine Magazine

1541. In writing about the changes the fall season brings, one of my fourth-graders came up with the following: "Today, brides fly away for the winter."

—BERNARD SCHNEIDER, Public School 165, Queens, New York, NEA Journal

1542. The bird that I am going to write about is the owl. The owl cannot see at all by day and at night it is blind as a bat.

I do not know much about the owl so I will go on to the beast which I am going to choose. It is the cow. The cow is a mammal. It has six sides—right, left, an upper and below. At the back it has a tail on which hangs a brush. With this it sends the flies away so that they do not fall into the milk. The head is for the purpose of growing horns, and so that the mouth can be somewhere. The horns are to butt with and the mouth is to moo with. Under the cow hangs the milk. It is arranged for milking. When people milk the milk comes and there is never an end to the supply. How the cow does it I have not yet realized but it makes more and more. The cow has a fine sense of smell—one can smell it far away. This is the reason for the fresh air in the country. The man cow is called an ox. It is not a mammal. The cow does not eat much but what it eats it eats twice so that it gets enough. When it is hungry it moos and when it says nothing it is because its inside is all full up with grass.

—The Atlantic Monthly

1543. Mr. Krebs is my teacher; I shall not pass. He maketh me to sit in a classroom. He leadeth me to the blackboard. He handeth me the chalk. He guideth me in a straight path for my class's sake.

Yea, though I walk through the valley of knowledge, I learneth not, for I am dumb. My notebook and pencil accompany me.

He maketh me to show my ignorance in the presence of my fellow students. He anointeth my head with a ruler. My fountain pen runneth over.

Surely English and social studies will follow me all the days of my life, and I shall dwell in the eighth grade forever! Amen.

*—*JAMES EVANS, *The Hanley Acorn*
University City, Missouri

1544. During our study of the Revolutionary War and Paul Revere's ride, one of my fifth-graders quoted, "Ready to ride and spread the alarm to every insect, village and farm."

*—*EVA CLAGUE, Tampa Florida,
NEA Journal

1545. English common law gave us the "Writ of Hideous Corpus."

—NEA Journal, reprinted in *Education Digest*

1546. Rain is a form of participation.

—Metropolitan Detroit Science Review,
reprinted in *Education Digest*

1547. Asked to write an essay, one little girl submitted the following: "My subjeck is Ants. Ants is two kinds, insects and lady uncles. Sometimes they live in holes and sometimes they crawl into the sugar bole, and sometimes they live with their married sisters. That is all I know about ants."

—Kentucky School Journal

1548. Paul Nathan writes (in "Rights and Permissions," *Publishers' Weekly,* June 30, 1958) that while judging a sixth-grade essay contest, he found the following entry, which, though not a winner, was his favorite. The topic? "Courtesy, the Art of Being Nice."

Courtesy can help us mentally, for it leaves us with a free conchonce & a happy soul. Courtesy has helped us win wars. Suppose the U.S. is being beaten in the war of missiles by Russia. Briton chimes in & we soon beat Russia. They did this kind deed for they knew we could help them too.

Courtesy can save money & lives too. Imagine that Ichabod is driving in the suburbs of a large establishment. Having smoked a cigar, he flicks it out the window. Ichabod's cigar started a gigantic fire which claimed 3,000,000 lives & just as many dollars damage. By the way, Ichabod's children were killed. He could have stopped this disaster by simply putting the cigar in the ashtray. . . . . . Courtesy Pays!!

—NEA Journal

1549. Creative Expression! . . . After the children at the Fiedler Elementary School in Merrillville returned from a field trip to Chicago to see the Egyptian mummies, each child wrote an essay, based on what he had learned. One elementary school child submitted a picture with three figures: a modest, unwrapped mummy, a mummy swathed in a cartonnage, and a mummy case—all the work of careful observation while on the field trip. Here's his essay:

"Mummies is a way for being dead. In Egypt they used mummies in many wayes. In this picture you see a unwraped mummy. This mummy has bin dead thousands of years ago. He did not rot because the people of Egupt put the bodies in a sulaon of salt, water and spíes, and then they wrap them up in long strips of wide cloth as a mummy. The boal like on top of his head is so they can glue the end of the tape on it. After they wrap the body up they put it in a mummy case. A mummy case is usly made of wood and then panted up as a person."

Stunts

1550. Ask a friend to read this sentence slowly: FINISHED FILES ARE THE RESULT OF YEARS OF SCIENTIFIC STUDY COMBINED WITH THE EXPERIENCE OF YEARS.

Then tell him to count aloud the F's in that sentence. Let him count them only once. How many?

One of average intelligence finds three F's. If you spotted four, you're above average. If you got five, you can turn up your nose at almost anybody. If you caught all six, you're probably a genius, and its a question whether you should spend time taking tests like this.

—The Correspondent

1551. Think of a number, then double it. Add 4 and multiply by 5. Add 12 and multiply by 10. Subtract 320. Strike off the last two ciphers and you will again have the original number.

1552. You wouldn't think this is possible, but it works every time! Try it and see for yourself!

Take your house number or box number and double it. Add five. Multiply by 50. Add your age. Add 365. Subtract 615. The last two figures of the total will be your age; the others will be your house or box number, whichever you used in the beginning.

1553. How does Jo Harris win her coffee? As follows: She asks a friend to stand and press his left ankle, left knee, left hip, left shoulder and left cheek against a wall. Then she bets that he can't lift his right leg an inch off the floor.

She wins every time. It can't be done.

1554. Professor Robert Tannenbaum of the University of California stumped all but a few of 100 executives when he wrote "IX" (Roman numerals) on a blackboard during a business management lecture and asked them to "add one more symbol which will transform that into 6." Add an 'S'—is that right, Prof?

—Daily News Wire Services

Success

1555. If you wish to gain success, do not stare up the steps—step on the stairs.

Working 100% of the time to be on top . . . Not just wishing you were there.

1556. People who achieve happiness and success are those who refuse to accept the idea of defeat. They know it is the thought of defeat that causes defeat, so they go to work and organize victory out of mistakes.

—"Blunders," *Megiddo Message*

1557. You won't find many success rules that will work, unless you do.

—*Friendly Chat*

1558. Success is the fine art of making mistakes when nobody is looking.

1559. The Father of Shakespeare was a wool merchant.
The Emperor Diocletian was the son of a slave.
Abraham Lincoln's father was a poor farmer and laborer.
Cardinal Antonelli's father was an Italian bandit.
The father of Adrian, the ascetic pontiff, was a beggar.

Virgil's father was a porter and for years a slave.
Demosthenes' father, a blacksmith and swordmaker.
Ben Franklin was the son of a soapboiler.
Daniel Webster was the son of a poor farmer.
Christopher Columbus was the son of a weaver.
Sophocles, the Greek poet, was the son of a blacksmith.

—Sunshine Magazine

1560. Conspicuous successes are comparatively few because most people think of success as acquired; it is more correctly contributed.

People who try to break in by the gate of acquisition are knocking at the wrong door. The entrance to success is by the gate of contribution. Everything that is taken out, someone has put in. How much have you put in?

—Friendly Chat

1561. Young man, if you're going to keep ahead of the cost of living these days you've got to find the secret of perpetual promotion.

—Oren Arnold, Kiwanis Magazine

1562. The secret of success: Never let down! Never let up!

—T. Harry Thompson, Sales Management

1563. Success is full of promise till you get it; and then it is a last year's nest from which the bird has flown.

—Henry Ward Beecher, Lutheran Digest

1564. The hard part of making good is that you have to do it again every day.

—Survey Bulletin

1565. The successful man was asked the secret of his accomplishments. His reply was:

"Good judgment."

"Where do you learn good judgment," he was asked.

"From experience."

"From where do you get experience?"

"From poor judgment."

1566. In 1869 H. J. Heinz planted a small plot of horseradish. He and two women and a boy grated and bottled the root.

J. L. Kraft was a grocery clerk who started with a capital of 65 dollars to peddle cheese from a one-horse wagon.

Coca-Cola was first made in the kitchen of an old home adjoining Mr. Pemberton's Drug Store.

Charles W. Post made the first Postum in a barn.

1567. Success is the ability to get along with some people, and ahead of others.

1568. Nine ships in the fleet "Success" are: Sportsmanship, Citizenship, Leadership, Statesmanship, Ownership, Craftsmanship, Scholarship and Stewardship.

1569. When the students of several nations voted on the greatest man in history, Louis Pasteur headed the list. The four outstanding qualities of this "greatest man in history," according to a psychologist, were: enthusiasm, courage, work, and ability to learn from his mistakes.

1570. A man must win general success to get the word "private" on his office door.

1571. If you are set on making good somewhere, why not make good where you are?

—*Try Square*

1572. If I cannot do great things, I can do small things in a great way.

—Author Unknown

1573. Webster's dictionary says a "prodder" is "that which incites, as to activity." A prodder may appear in many forms—a set of circumstances, or a particular person—and often we are not aware of the prodding. Many successes in the world can be traced to a "prodder," somewhere along the line.

1574. The persistent exercise of a little extra effort is one of the most powerful forces contributing to success.

—*American Mercury*

1575. Never you mind the crowd, lad,
Or fancy your life won't tell;
There's always work for a' that
To him that doeth it well.
Fancy the world a hill, lad,
Look where the millions stop;
You'll find the crowd at the base, lad—
There's always room at the top.

—*Success Nuggets*

1576. Flash powder makes a more brilliant light than the arc lamp, but you can't use it to light your street corner because it doesn't last long enough. Stability is more essential to success than brilliancy.

—RICHARD LLOYD JONES, American
newspaper editor, Tulsa, Oklahoma

1577. It takes a little courage and a little self-control
And some grim determination, if you want to reach the goal.
It takes a deal of striving and a firm and stern-set chin,
No matter what the battle, if you really want to win.
There's no easy path to glory; there's no rosy road to fame.
Life, however we may view it, is no simple parlor game.
You must take a blow or give one; you must risk
  and you must lose
And expect that in the struggle you will suffer from the
  bruise.
But you mustn't wince or falter, if a fight you once begin
Be a man and face the battle—that's the only way to win.

—*Anonymous*

1578. One day in huckleberry time, when little Johnny Flails and half a dozen other boys were starting with their pails to gather berries, Johnny's Pa, in talking with him, said that he could tell him how to pick so he'd come out ahead.

"First find your bush," said Johnny's Pa, "and then stick to it till you've picked it clean. Let those go chasing all about who will, in search of better bushes, but it's picking tells, my son. To look at fifty bushes does not count like picking one."

—*Sunshine Magazine*

1579. The successful man is the one who does what he has to do at the time he hates to do it most.

1580. "I think I can" are four magic words that create success; four magic words that when woven into the fiber of our human thoughts can make all the difference in the world as to whether we succeed or fail.

—GERTRUDE CRAMER WILLIAMS,
You

1581. Patient meditation plus information equals triumph.

1582. Happiness and success include the seven absolutes of life: health, beauty, wisdom, love, friendship, goodness and God.

—REVEREND BOB RICHARDS

1583. Successful men are all good "mixers"—of high-grade intelligence with unremitting energy.

—*Facts and Fancies*

1584. To attain greatness a man must excel. And to hold his position he must keep right on excelling. When a man does a job superbly well, he sets a standard for himself that people expect him to live up to. They expect a Babe Ruth to knock home runs, a Joe Louis to score knockouts, a Red Grange to make touchdowns, a Hemingway to write masterpieces, a Caruso to sing his heart out.

1585. There is a four word recipe for success that applies equally well to organizations or individuals—make yourself more useful.

—*Megiddo Message*

1586. To succeed in this modern age of the atom, the jet, and the satellite, you need also a big charge of gumption, guts and go. Even then, the only way you can avoid losing your shirt is to keep your sleeves rolled up.

—Eugene Bertin, *Pennsylvania School Journal*

1587. 75 years ago a young grocery clerk had $372 and an idea. He founded a little store on the Cincinnati riverfront. Today that one store has grown into a system operating some 2,000 stores in 19 midwestern and southern states. His name was Bernard H. Kroger.

He helped foster a merchandising revolution based on the premise that if a large enough volume of goods could be sold at a very small unit profit, a satisfactory total profit would be earned.

We bet there were plenty of folks standing around telling him it couldn't be done.

1588. 56 years ago a courageous man and a not-very-dashing horse became partners—and started what was to grow into one of America's largest food processing companies. The man was a young grocery clerk who had conceived the idea of selling cheese from store to store by horse and wagon. This combination of man with an idea and a horse with plenty of endurance was the genesis of one of the most fascinating modern day sales stories. J. L. Kraft started with Paddy the horse and $65 capital.

1589. When things go wrong, as they sometimes will,
When the road you're trudging seems uphill,

When funds are low and the debts are high
And you want to smile, but you have to sigh;
When care is pressing you down a bit,
Rest! if you must—but never quit.

Life is queer, with its twists and turns,
As every one of us sometimes learns;
And many a failure turns about
When he might have won if he'd stuck it out.
Stick to your task, though the pace seems slow,
You may succeed with another blow.

Often the goal is nearer than
It seems to a faint and faltering man
Often the struggler has given up
When he might have captured the victor's cup;
And he learned too late, when the night slipped
　　down,
How close he was to the golden crown.

Success is failure turned inside out,
The silver tints of the clouds of doubt,
And you never can tell how close you are—
It may be near when it seems afar—
So stick to the fight when you're hardest hit;
It's when things seem worst that you mustn't quit.

　　　　　　　　　—Author Unknown, *The Lookout*

1590. If you wish success in life, make perseverance your bosom friend, experience your wise counselor, caution your elder brother, and hope your guardian genius.

　　　　　　　　　　　　　　—*Sunshine Magazine*

1591. A youth entered the University of Wisconsin in 1953 with $5,000. He put money as down payment on a rooming house, bought 47 acres of land with profit from rooming house; the land he cut into three plots and sold separately. He made enough money from the first two plots to buy another rooming house. By 1956 he had accumulated $30,000, enough to buy a farm and home for his bride. The only sour note in his career was a near-failing D in a real estate course.

1592. This is an age of specialization. The secret of success is to make an extraordinary use of the talent that sets you apart as an expert. *Work and personality* are the two priceless ingredients in happy living; *Dedication* to some honorable task that *serves other people*. Then nothing can hurt you, except your own folly or laziness.

—DR. GALEN STARR ROSS, president, Capitol
College of Oratory and Music, Columbus,
Ohio

1593. Those at the top have reached their positions by tackling uphill jobs.

—*Friendly Chat*

1594. Make good! Don't complain! Do the things you are expected to do—and more. Don't waste time in giving reasons why you didn't, or couldn't, or wouldn't, or shouldn't. The less you do, the more you complain. Efficiency—keep that word in your heart. Get to saying that word in your sleep. Do your work a little better than anyone else does it. That is the margin of success.

—*The Craftsman*

1595. This is success: To be able to carry money without spending it; to be able to bear an injustice without retaliating; to be able to keep on the job until it is finished; to be able to do one's duty even when one is not watched; to be able to accept criticism without letting it whip you.

—*The Uplift*, Stonewall Jackson Manual
Training School, Concord, N. C.

1596. One of the most important lessons of life is that success must continually be won and is never finally achieved.

—CHARLES EVANS HUGHES

1597. The road to success is dotted with many tempting parking places.

1598. We do not know, in most cases, how far social failure and success are due to heredity, and how far to environment. But environment is the easier of the two to improve.

—J. B. S. HALDAN, *Illinois Medical Journal*

Sunday School

1599. *Sunday school Teacher:* "The man named Lot was warned to take his wife and flee out of the city, but his wife looked back and was turned to salt."

Little Willie: "What happened to the flea?"

1600. A fifth-grade Sunday school teacher reports that one of her students who had been absent for several Sundays returned to the classroom. She walked up to the teacher, asked, "Do you know where I've been? I've been on vacation, had measles, and two enemas!"

1601. A Sunday school teacher was relating to his class the incident in the Garden of Gethsemane, when one of Jesus' disciples drew a sword and cut off the ear of a servant of the high priest. Thinking of Matthew 26:52, where Jesus said, "They that take the sword shall perish by the sword," the teacher asked, "And what did Jesus say then?"

There was a silence, finally broken by a timid voice, "How're you fixed for blades?"

—Lois F. Pasley, *Quote*

1602. Some years ago at our Sunday school the teachers took turns addressing the pupils. Usually they rounded off a fine, well-told story with, "Now, children, the moral of this story is. . . ."

Came the day when one teacher did an extra-fine job. The youngsters were delighted—so much so that one asked if that particular teacher might talk more often. "We like Miss Brown very much," explained the boy, "because she hasn't any morals."

—Mrs. M. O. Lakeman, *Together*

1603. A ten-year-old Sunday schooler was the only one in his class who responded when the teacher asked who knew the story of Jonah.

After his accurate summary, the teacher complimented him on being the only student who had read the Bible lesson that week.

Painfully honest, the boy corrected the teacher: "I didn't read it in the Bible," he explained, "it was on a bubble gum wrapper."

—*Laugh Book*

1604. *Not guilty:* The Sunday school teacher was reviewing a lesson. "Who led the children of Israel out of Egypt?" she asked the class.

There was no answer, but a little boy in the back row raised his hand.

"Do you know, Jimmy?" the teacher asked.

"It wasn't me," Jimmy said timidly. "We just moved here last week. We're from Missouri."

1605. A doctor, who was superintendent of the Sunday school, asked one of the boys this question: "William, what must we do in order to get to heaven?"

"We must die," said Willie.

"Very true," replied the doctor, "but what must we do before we die?"

"We must get sick and send for you."

Superintendent

1606. Alex Jardine, superintendent, South Bend, Indiana schools: "A school superintendent, these days, is just a custodian—cussed by half the community, toadyin' to the other half."

1607. Under a sagging courthouse roof—
The superintendent sits:
The soup—a martyred man is he—
With temperamental fits:
The brain cells of his meager mind
Can never call it quits.

His hair gets thinner through the years—
His face a puzzled pan:
His eyes are wet—he thinks of debt:
He earns what'er he can:
But looks the world not in the face—
He owes most every man.

Week in week out from morn till night
They hear his bellows roar:
And teachers coming home from school
Peek in the open door:
They love to see him rant and rave
And stomp upon the floor—

Boiling—recoiling—despoiling—
While on his duties soar!
Each morning sees ten tasks begun—

Each evening sees ten more;
Plenty attempted—little done—
Night has no sleep in store.

He goes on Sunday to the church and sits
Far in the back;
He does not hear the parson preach,
His thoughts are off the track;
They leap from tests to taxes
And span the Zodiac!
Fie— fie on thee— relentless fate—

For lessons too late learned;
It's at this flaming forge of life—
That fingers soon get burned;
And by the smoke and sweat and tears—
The mind of man is turned.
So for such jobs as village smith—
The soup for long has yearned.

—WINSTON BROWN

1608. Have you ever stood at the seashore and watched the surf rushing up on the shore and then going out again? And do you remember how the ebb and flow of water washed the grains of sand from underneath your feet? Well, then, it may have occurred to you that being a superintendent is like that. Increasing enrollments, building programs, heightened citizen interest in school problems can wash away the ground you stand on.

Unless you stay alert to new developments in economics, sociology, and education, you may find yourself on the toboggan—and you can't leave your footprints on the sands of time sitting down.

—M. DALE BAUGHMAN

1609. I cannot say that I was one of the popular men in my community, but I enjoyed a measure of respect from those whom I served. This is my story at the mid-century point of my life, after bearing the burden of chief school administrator at Carmel Ridge, three years, Fruitdale, six years, Jackson Central, six years, and Lake Park, four years. Actually, I was rather well liked in all of those communities, especially by my fellow members of Rotary, Lions and Kiwanis.

For one thing there were always one or two Board Members who wouldn't seem to agree with my ideas about education. Oh, yes, the majority usually went along with me, that is until I fought the battle of Lake Park. It was there that my followers on the Board were finally outnumbered by younger men with fresh, new ideas. They seemed to think that Lake Park needed a younger man, one with more imagination and a more experimental attitude.

With a few exceptions, most of my teachers usually liked me and tried to cooperate with my policies and projects; but there was always sure to be a few with influence on key community members and certain board members who stalled my progress and thwarted my plans. One time a custodian wrote my swan song. It's hard to believe, as I think back, that I failed so many times to make the proper decisions. I can talk well, I write clearly and forcefully— yes, I was no loafer. My work days were long and well planned.

In my first two jobs I was eager and optimistic. My job was my life, almost. Confidence and hope filled me. During study for my Master's Degree I had taken two course in school administration and they provided a basis for a start in school administration. Somehow, as I progressed to better and bigger schools, my task became more complex and more overwhelming.

I don't seem to be very good in community sociology. Around every corner there seemed to be problems which I couldn't solve— problems involving power structure and pressure groups. My administration courses didn't tell me how to handle these. They didn't tell me how to study community organizations and groups. OH! Yes, they talked about leadership behavior but I never was able to tell when to use that principle.

I'm not good in economics or finance either. Of course I bluffed a little here and there and picked up some knowledge about such things. It was at Lake Park that we had to build and build and build . . . I struggled through the whole mess somehow with help from the State University and the State Department and my name is on the recognition plate in the foyer of the new high school building.

Well, what next? Who wants a superintendent of two score and ten years? I've always had the reputation of "running a pretty smooth school" but nowadays that isn't a complimentary statement. Today, it seems that everybody's slogan is "there's always a better way." Maybe I can land a smaller superintendency something like Fruitdale, my second job. For that matter I'm tired, and teaching jobs are plentiful. I have 30 hours in math and I taught it at Carmel

Ridge while serving as superintendent. Perhaps I would be wise to withdraw from the firing line to the relative safety and calm of the classroom.

—M. DALE BAUGHMAN, *The Clearing House*

1610. The short and unhappy life of many superintendents—or they only have "ize" for you:

First year: EUGOLIZED
Second year: CRITICIZED
Third year: OSTRACIZED
Fourth year: RUBBERIZED (bounced)

—EARL WILTSE, *Educator's Dispatch*

1611. When we read *Alice in Wonderland* to our children and recite the queen's dramatic words, "Off with their heads!" we know we are in the land of make-believe. But do we know that in almost every state of our fair land some boards of education are saying "Off with his head!" in a reckless use of power to fire superintendents.

—*The School Administrator*, American Association of School Administrators

1612. As good old Superintendent McGillicuddy used to remark after an exhausting session with his school board: "A schoolteacher is one who makes education happen; a college professor is one who watches education happen; but a school superintendent is the one to whom education happens whether he is watching or not."

—FREDERICK J. MOFFITT, *Nation's Schools*

1613. Don't be surprised if some extrovertive superintendent doesn't go down in history as the most persevering administrator of all time by willing that his ashes be scattered from one end of his school district to the other.

—M. DALE BAUGHMAN

1614. *Doctor to superintendent:* "Tell your wife to forget that slight deafness—it's merely an indication of growing older."
Superintendent: "You tell her!"

1615. The new superintendent soon gets measured. One inquisitive teacher asked the secretary, "How is our new superintendent on dictating?" "Well," replied his aide, "you just have to take some things for grunted."

1616. The superintendent of a school in a neighboring town was unexpectedly called upon to address a group of youngsters in the schoolroom. To gain time, he asked, "Well, what shall I speak about?"

A young one in the front seat, who had committed to memory a number of declamations, held up his hand, and in a shrill voice asked, "What do you know?"

1617. The school administrator who does the hiring of teachers might well heed the same advice the old Quaker gave to his son: "When thee went acourting, I told thee to keep thy eyes open; now that thou art married, I tell thee to keep them half shut."

For the administrator this would read, "When thee goes a-recruiting, keep thy eyes open; but when thou hast married the teacher to the school, keep them half shut."

—M. Dale Baughman

1618. A superintendent visited kindergarten one day and while observing the children playing outside, he noticed that one little lad fell and skinned his knee. The superintendent picked him up and asked, "Are you hurt, son?"

"Hurt, hell," he answered, "Somebody's gonna' get sued!"

1619. When the superintendent of a large school learned that one of his recruiters had been found dead in a hotel room, he immediately wired the hotel: "Search body for signed contracts and return same by special delivery."

1620. A congressman had a hard time explaining his vote on a measure objectionable to the right-minded members of his constituency. At last he said: "But, gentlemen, you simply do not understand the outside pressure brought to bear on a man in my position!" In reply to that an old sea captain in the audience cried out: "But where are your inside braces for that outside pressure?" The inside braces in a vessel are made of the strongest material. Set firmly in place, they are able to withstand the greatest outside pressure of storms and waves. A school superintendent needs inside braces to withstand the assaults of his critics.

1621. "Wanted, an administrator! Not a bookkeeper, not an accountant, not a business manager, not a mechanic, not a public relations expert, not a communications consultant, not merely the friend of the teacher, the student, and Mr. Citizen; but a superintendent or a principal who is a combination of all these and more, who is willing to endure all things if only education may progress and the future of the American nation is served wisely and well."

—DR. LLOYD N. MORRISETT, Professor of
Educational Administration, University
of California, Los Angeles, California,
NITPA Newsletter

1622. Two teachers were discussing their new superintendent. "You can't help liking the guy," said one. "If you don't, he fires you."

1623. Years ago when I was a young, beginning teacher I frequently found myself standing in a long, long applicant's line winding around the corridors waiting to be grilled by some superintendent who had just one vacancy.

Now, I stand in those same long lines but they're made up of superintendents waiting to interview just one applicant.

1624. You may have heard about the canary sucked into the vacuum cleaner as the lady of the house attempted to clean the cage. Yes, the bird was retrieved alive but much the worse for wear with tail feathers missing and otherwise in disarray.

Superintendents too are often sucked into a wind funnel of public pressure. Safety experts and animal lovers suggest a precaution in the case of the bird—take him out of the cage before using the vacuum. Unfortunately, the superintendent is always on display and it is difficult for him to remove himself when the pressure pulls him toward danger and possible professional destruction.

—M. DALE BAUGHMAN

Supervision-Supervisor

1625. The supervisor's prayer: Lord when I am wrong, make me willing to change; when I am right, make me easy to live with. So strengthen me that the power of my example will far exceed the authority of my rank.

—PAULINE H. PETERS, *Secretary*

1626.   There was a young teacher from Purvis
Whom supervision made nervous;

She faltered and tensioned
When the matter was mentioned,
Wanted: democratic supervisory service.

—M. Dale Baughman

Tact

1627. Tact is the business of handling porcupines without disturbing the quills.

1628. "One of the most tactful men I ever knew," says a Florida manufacturer, "was a man who fired me from my first job. He called me in and said:

"'Son, I don't know how we're ever going to get along without you, but starting Monday, we're going to try.'"

—*Rotarian Magazine*

1629. Tact is the ability to get the fleece off the flock without a flinch.

—O. A. Battista

1630. Tact: Getting your point across without stabbing someone with it.

—Richard Gordon in *Boys' Life*

1631. Tact is hard to define, but as I get it, it's a combination of flattery, lying, and wisdom.

—*Farm Journal*

Talent

1632. Talent is wanting something bad enough to work for it.

1633. Use what talents you possess; the woods would indeed be very silent if no birds sang there except those that sang best.

—*Odd Moments*, Sunshine Private Press

1634. Many a genius has been slow of growth. Oaks that flourish for a thousand years do not spring up into beauty like a reed.

—George Henry Lewes

1635.   Some talents that we little guess
     Our humblest neighbors may possess.

Talk

1636. Be a good listener first, a good talker second, and you will not "wish I hadn't said that." Think twice and speak once, and you won't always be "shooting off."
—ELMER WHEELER, *Kiwanis Magazine*

1637. The biggest talker is usually the littlest doer.

1638.
You can always tell when a man's
A fool by his chatter and his way.
You can always know when a man is
Wise by the things he does not say.
—*Sunshine Magazine*

1639. Quiet people aren't the only ones who don't say much.

1640. Curtis Bok once said, "In the whole history of law and order the longest step forward was taken by primitive man when, as if by common consent, the tribe sat down in a circle and allowed one man to speak at a time."
—*New Outlook*

1641. *Barber*: "I believe in free speech."
Customer: "That's good. I'd hate to have to pay to hear you."
—*The Lookout*

1642. Thomas Carlyle, the sage of the 19th century Scotland once said, "Talk that does not end in any kind of action is better suppressed altogether."

1643. The trouble with the fast talker is that he may say something he hasn't even thought of yet.

1644. The less a man knows, the more he wants to tell it.

Teacher—Teachers—Teaching

1645. Public schools need teachers brimming with the enthusiasm of football coaches.
Teachers should induce the lazy student to "play over his head intellectually," just as the football coach encourages his players to play to the limit of their ability.
—VERNON NICKELL, Former Superintendent
of Public Instruction, Illinois

It's not real expensive . . . We get the nails wholesale.

1646. There are as many kinds of good teaching as there are good apples, good times, or good women. Appreciating one kind of good apple, good time or good woman does not make all other kinds bad.

—Don Robinson, *Phi Delta Kappan*

1647. The great teacher is rarely popular. He is interested in something more important than winning the affections of an unending anonymous procession of young people . . . I have long maintained that any college can raise its standards simply by firing annually whichever professor is voted "Best Liked" by the graduating class.

—Clifton Fadiman, *Holiday*

1648. Four ninth-grade classes in a Philadelphia junior high school were asked to describe the qualifications of an ideal teacher . . . came this solitary gem, an unintentional proverb from Tom: "An old grouch discourages learning even more than a grouch."

—Harry H. Matlock, *Clearing House*

1649. In the U.S. the average college and university instructor now gets less pay than the average wageworker; the average full professor gets only 55% more than the wageworker despite his large investment of time and funds in obtaining a license to practice his profession. In Russia, by contrast, the average full professor gets 700% more than the average wageworker.

—DR. F. A. HARPER, *Freeman*

1650. As a teacher he was a firebug; he had the ability to light a lot of fuel.

1651. *Teacher to small boy*: "No matter what your father said, money is not considered one of this country's major exports."

—LARRY HARRIS, *The Christian Science Monitor*

1652. A teacher should always be determined to make it tough for his students, and by tough we do not mean unpleasant. We mean make the work tough enough to challenge them. "Challenge-stimulated learning" is a tired but everlasting truism.

—DON ROBINSON, *Phi Delta Kappan*

1653. Unless teachers catch the new "drive and enthusiasm" in education, something new may be added to the handbook prepared by the principal.

It might read like this: "Teachers may leave the building at the dismissal bell on Friday—but please don't trample the pupils."

1654. Teach—five letters . . . its meaning? "To make to know how." Five words define it; five thousand won't perform its delicate task unless the teacher himself is taught, trained, made aware . . . .

1655. The teacher who does not love poetry does a rather poor job of arranging a love affair between words and the child.

—FRANK JENNINGS

1656. When the Germans marched into Paris in 1870, it was the German schoolmaster who marched down the street. It was the Jap schoolmaster who made pre-World War II Japan. It is the American schoolteacher who has made possible America as we know her today.

Paraphrasing H. G. Wells: The next 25 years will be a race between great teaching and the destruction of our civilization.

Leverett Wilson Springs: evaluating Hopkins. "His enthusiasm continued for threescore years with no abatement."

The responsibility for inspired teachers rests on college faculties.

NOTICE
Monday through Thursday, teachers must remain until a half hour after students are dismissed. On Friday teachers may leave at the 3 o'clock dismissal bell ... just don't trample the students.

MAZE

Teachers' lounge.

When Dr. Frank McMurray retired as President of Teachers College, Columbia, he said, "Here we find the greatest thing in teaching, helping the student to find himself." He added, "If I had my educational career to live over again, I would take a greater interest in the individual student."

1657. During the obsequies of a friend who had taught school for years, the parson had many fine things to say, ending on the theme that she is probably carrying on her work in heaven.

A teacher in the group leaned over to a colleague and groaned, "Good heavens, don't we ever get to quit!"

—Eugene P. Bertin, *Pennsylvania School Journal*

1658. She is a charming and thrifty Frenchwoman who teaches conversational French. The other day her television set did not function and she called the repairman. He spent 18 minutes checking the set and putting in a new tube, then presented her with a bill for $9.60—$6 service charge and $3.60 for a new tube. The volatile Frenchwoman was voluble.

"Do you know," she said, "how long I have to work teaching French to pay that $6 you charged for 18 minutes' work?"

"No," answered the repairman, "but do you guarantee that your students can speak French? I guarantee that this TV set will run.'

—Mrs. Arthur F. Shuey, Shreveport, Louisiana

1659. The only trouble with psychology in teaching is that it is so seldom used. When the chips are down and in the classroom that may be nearly all the time, the teacher reverts to his own basic emotional pattern, which frequently includes impatience, irritation, and meeting hostility with hostility. He does not respond with the psychological pattern he has heard described as desirable in education lectures, for you cannot overlay a brand new personality on anyone by a lecture course in educational psychology or mental health, or even by an exposure to "the ideal group experience."

—Don Robinson, *Phi Delta Kappan*

1660. Don't be so disturbed by the fact that nearly half of the men in teaching, if they had their lives to live over again, would choose another occupation. Psychologists tell us that four-fifths of Americans are "so sick of their jobs they could spit at them!"

1661. But the average graduating class of teachers, you tell me, should consist entirely of Christ-like characters who will ignore the needs of their families, labor twice as hard as anyone else to make a living, work in unfavorable circumstances, handicapped by an uncooperative public (indeed, in many cases, by an uncooperative administration as well), and remain idealistic. All this for the reward of having contributed to the enrichment and betterment of others.

—Excerpt of a letter by Thomas Schneider, Cody High School, Detroit, Michigan *Phi Delta Kappan*

1662. An 1872 list of rules for teachers, posted by a New York City principal, included: Each teacher will bring a bucket of water and scuttle of coal for the day's sessions. Men teachers may take one evening each week for courting purposes, or two evenings a week if they go to church regularly. Aften ten hours in school, the teachers should spend the remaining time reading the Bible or other good books. Any teacher who smokes, uses liquor in any form, frequents pool or public halls, or gets shaved in a barbershop will give good reason to suspect his worth, intentions, integrity and honesty.

—From Esso Manhattan

1663. The saddest of all obituaries might well be: "His hidden talents were never discovered." The intense concern of some parents for their "gifted" children probably stems from a feeling of their own latent but underdeveloped talents. And in this, the wealthiest of all lands, some children and youth will rarely if ever be nurtured in the rich and provocative presence of a gifted teacher. Many teachers, too, will remain mediocre, their potential but hidden talents undiscovered or underdeveloped.

—EDGAR DALE, *The News Letter*

1664. He often deliberately posed a problem backwards—as if holding out a pair of scissors with the points toward you; you had to learn to grasp it from every angle. He squeezed knowledge from every experiment like juice from a grapefruit.

—"A Teacher Who Turned Learning Into Adventure," *NEA Journal*

1665. There is much more to good teaching than merely "keeping school." The attitudes, feelings, concepts, and practices that distinguish the fine teacher have been learned, and can, to a substantial degree, be taught.

—STEPHEN COREY, *Education Digest*

1666. Teaching is leaving a vestige of oneself in the development of another, and surely the child is a bank where you can deposit your most precious treasures.

—EUGENE P. BERTIN, *Pennsylvania School Journal*

1667. Before 1900 about one-fourth of all the teachers in the United States had not finished even a high school course; one-fourth more had not more than a high school education; one-fourth more had only two years beyond the high school; the remaining one-fourth were college graduates, most of them with no professional training.

—FREDERICK E. BOLTON, Dean Emeritus, College of Education, University of Washington, Reprinted from *U.S. News and World Report*, June 7, 1957, published at Washington

1668. Probably the best teachers in American colleges are the athletic coaches. It might seem to be undignified to employ teachers as we do coaches: "Win the games or seek another position." But it works. Even our colleges should realize that it is as important to teach a boy his mathematics as his football.

—GEORGE B. CUTTEN, President Emeritus,
Colgate University, *School and Society*

1669. The colonial schoolmaster is unclassifiable. He was a God-fearing clergyman, he was an unintegrated rogue; he was amply paid, he was accorded a bare pittance; he made teaching a life career, he used it merely as a stepping stone; he was a classical scholar, he was all but illiterate; he was licensed by bishop or colonial governor, he was certified only by his own pretensions; he was a cultured gentleman, he was a crude-mannered yokel; he ranked with the cream of society, he was regarded as a menial. In short he was neither a type nor a personality, but a statistical distribution represented by a skewed curve.

—*The American Teacher*

1670. Not one professor in 50 can understand that the process of learning can be, and should be, in Milton's words "so sweet, so green, so full of goodly prospects and melodious sounds, that the harp of Orpheus were not more charming."

—Reprinted by permission of Abelard-
Schuman, Ltd. from the book *Some of My
Best Friends are Professors* by George
Williams, copyright 1958

1671.   Since they are young, be watchful of the word;
For what today is spoken reappears
A rigid thing tomorrow to be heard
As even stronger truth by other ears.

Print carefully the message on these minds;
Grave deep the golden character of love;
Because of this you write tomorrow finds
A rusty sword or yet the trampled dove.

—EUGENE T. MALESKA, Former Associate Editor,
Intercom, Junior High School Ass'n., New York
City, now Coordinator of Teacher Recruitment,
New York City Schools

1672. Nobody knows all the answers. But I am sure—with a sureness that amounts to a passion—that along with our concern for refined, accelerated, toughened-up subject matter and raised standards of performance, we had better look to the fundamental prime-movers within our personality. In many a case the job is primarily to *release* and only then to *stimulate* the ability that is there.

—FRED T. WILHELMS, *Educational Leadership*

1673. A noted feminist once said that the best definition of education is that which remains in your mind after everything you have been taught has been forgotten. What remains in many a student's mind is something about the teacher—some trick of mind, some way of thought, some gesture, some view that he has towards life. Let us put it this way: some life style. And the life style of the teacher is something that can be communicated to the student.

—"The Training of a Teacher Elite," Max Lerner, daily columnist, *New York Post* and Professor of American Civilization, Brandeis University, 12th Yearbook, 1959, The American Association of Colleges for Teacher Education, page 24

1674. You cannot discover a youngster with fire in him unless the discovery is made by a teacher with fire in him. There are no ways of discovering promise and talent in youngsters simply by tests. Tests can tell you about achievement and tests might conceivably tell you about some kind of potential; but after you have taken the whole battery of diagnostic tests there remains, nevertheless, the indispensable element. Carlyle used to say: "The big question about any man is—have you a fire in your belly?" There remains the indispensable element that only someone with the fire in his belly will be able to discover a youngster with fire in his belly.

—"The Training of a Teacher Elite," Max Lerner, daily columnist, *New York Post* and Professor of American Civilization, Brandeis University, 12th Yearbook, 1959, The American Association of Colleges for Teacher Education, page 24

1675. A spark plug functioning properly gives the exact amount of spark to produce maximum performance. This proper gauging is an important function in school and one which the teacher must ever attempt to perfect.

—HOMER T. ROSENBERGER, Superintendent of Training, Federal Bureau of Prisons, Washington, D.C., Bulletin, NASSP

1676. A teacher's salary may not be everything, but to most, it has a strong lead on whatever is running second.

1677. Teaching and selling have some common ground. Both must arouse interest, maintain that interest and finally change the behavior of the target. However, the overlooked pupil often fares less well than the overlooked prospect, who is more likely to become a prospect again and again.

—M. Dale Baughman

1678. A teacher from abroad who had visited hundreds of classrooms in the United States said that there was one striking difference between their classrooms and ours. She said: "In our schools you can easily find the teacher. She is at the front of the room talking, a one-way transmission. Your teacher is not always at the front of the room. She may be working with an individual child or a small group."

1679. *Students describe their teachers*: It's hard to say what most impressed me about my new teacher. I suppose the first thing I noticed was her unique appearance. She was short, which is nothing really unusual, and she was plump. But it was her face that was distinguished. It lay in folds of soft wrinkles accented by many laugh lines; her mouth was little and always carried a slight smile; and her eyes were the biggest, brownest and roundest eyes I have ever seen. What's more, they were very bright and ever sparkling with mischief. Her hair was soft, requiring attention, and yet it was always full of expression. She looked like a little Pekinese ready to pounce on something new and wonderful—at least that's how she looked to me.

Just because there is laughter coming from a room, a teacher has not lost control of his class. This is something that just does not occur in his sessions. He is able to maintain discipline without a large show. With just a word of warning the students will become quiet again. This is mainly because they respect this teacher and want to please him, not because they will be sent to the office or have their grades lowered.

Take Mrs. Youth for instance; she really wasn't young, but her outlook on life was young. She must have been at least 35, but you felt as if she could understand your problems and feelings as if she were 17. She always had a humorous story to illustrate a point or break the monotony. I never worked quite so hard for a teacher as I did for her.

Every way I looked at him from his round so-called flat-top to his long, pointed brown shoes, I knew he was one of the teachers people talk about. His dress was real classy—striped suits and polka dot bow ties, along with loud shirts and red socks. His face looked so much like a bull dog, I kept wanting to say, "Here, boy, here." His face wasn't really that bad if he shaved more than once a week. It was just that silly smile and those big jaws.

His caption in the school's "Candyland" annual is "Lemon Drop." His attitude on the world is soured. There are only two things in all of God's creation which he reveres; Teddy Roosevelt and the Republican party. He dislikes teaching; he hates being required to help with extra-curricular activities; he despises crowds; he abhors church suppers; and he cannot tolerate people who disagree with him.

It was the firm conviction of everyone that he had to his name only one brown suit and a brown nylon shirt. He wore this suit and shirt every day. We were all greatly surprised one day when he wore a blue one, but we found out later he had to leave early that day to go to a funeral.

She reminds me of a walking mummy, because she never smiles, and looks like she is dead. She wears some of the weirdest dresses; they look like the ones my mother gave to our church to send to foreign countries.

Take Mrs. Gypsy, for instance, she was always dressed in a gaudy, glaring way. Not that I think a teacher should dress like a Puritan on Sunday, but who likes anyone to wear gaudy colors and tons of jewelry? Mrs. Gypsy wore chandeliers on her ears and bells on her toes.

Mr. H. reminded me of an extremely nervous cat. He would walk constantly back and forth across the room or around in a circle; it nearly drove a person crazy to watch him, especially if he sat in a front row. As he lectured, he had the habit of sticking his pencil into the large jowl of fat under his chin. Every time you asked him a question about English, he would look up at the ceiling, as if the answer was up there.

In the First World War, he was in the artillery, and the way he yelled and stomped around in class you would think the guns were still firing.

If you were in her classroom when she was writing on the board, you would have undoubtedly heard the jingle-jangle of her numerous bracelets. She had more armor on than the knights of old. After hearing this jingle-jangle constantly for an hour, you would adore the silence of the students shouting in the halls between classes.

Miss Stoneface is a serious lady who never cracks a smile and expects the same of her students. She believes that a little laughing spoils everything. There should be a lot of seriousness in the classroom, but just a little smile would make a serious matter much more interesting. Does she realize that life is not all work?

Mr. Business-Like never strayed off the subject. Mr. Business-Like was a great perfectionist and demanded everything his way. He never laughed or allowed us to laugh. If we did, we could be sure of getting an eraser or a piece of chalk thrown at us. From the moment we walked into the room until we left, the subject never strayed from English. This provided a dull hour and one to which few looked forward with anticipation.

His sense of humor smoothed over all the rough edges. When you went into his class, you had a good feeling about school, for he could keep his class in stitches and still teach the lesson and get his points across.

In my senior year at high school I entered my English course with a teacher who was a riot. He would begin and end every class with a sterling comment or clever joke. With these jokes he could control the moods and feelings of the class for a whole period.

Another teacher that I admire is Mr. J. From all indications, he seems to know his subject thoroughly and how to put it across. He has a wonderful sense of humor and knows how to mix it with the work to keep the attention of the class at all times. No matter what particular subject we are on, he knows how to make the joke that will put his point across to everyone.

Another outstanding feature about Miss O. was the delicate perfume she used. She used just the right amount, too, about half a bottle at a time.

Her hair has been dyed so often that it is all falling out, but what she does have is black—yes, just as black as coal. Anyone should know a teacher like her should have a few gray hairs—if not from age, at least from teaching.

I can see her in my mind's eye now; a short fattish little woman with tight, grayish, wispy curls framing her face. She reminded me of a top; it was as if the weight of her body would slowly topple her off her tiny feet. She was very proud of her feet. She tripped around in short, fast, little steps like an overweight ballet dancer.

The teacher I will never forget was my eighth grade teacher who taught English. He could never stick to a subject. He would be in the middle of a discussion on Rome which would remind him of Cairo, Illinois, and his boyhood. He was also the coach of our school, and half the period would be spent on the discussion of rules of baseball, basketball, and track, plus what we did wrong in yesterday's game. Since I played baseball reasonably well, I made an "A" in English all year.

—WILMER A. LAMAR, *Teachers as Students See Them*, Stephen Decatur High School, Decatur, Illinois

1680. There is an exaggerated notion at the moment, especially at the secondary school level, that curriculum reform is the be-all and end-all of our difficulties, with a seeming forgetfulness of the fact that the curriculum is but an educational instrument of small significance except as it derives integrity and strength and effect from the capacity of the teacher to instruct and inspire.

—J. L. MORRILL, Foreword to *The Two Ends of the Log*

1681. Someone said payola started when the first kid gave a teacher an apple.

—MARIE FRASER, *Indiana Teacher*

1682. A teacher who can arouse a feeling for one single good action, for one single good poem, accomplishes more than he who fills our memory with rows on rows of natural objects, classified with name and form.

—GOETHE

1683. Teaching school is like making love—it's not the technique but the enthusiasm and thoroughness that counts.

1684. When you think little of a fellow teacher, a parent, pupil, or administrator, then say as little as you think.

1685. Truly fine teachers of all times have the same characteristics. Indeed, today as in the past, the only reliable marks of great teaching personalities are the rich qualities of their interior selves.

—HOWARD K. HOLLAND, *Clearing House*

1686. What nobler employment, or more valuable to the state, than that of the man who instructs the rising generation.

—MARCUS TULLIUS CICERO, Roman Orator

1687. A good teacher has the ability to inject humorous remarks and illustrations when the classroom procedure becomes tedious, without becoming a clown and destroying an atmosphere of pur-

poseful learning; also avoids being overly reserved or becoming a
sour victim of pedagogical routine.

—HOMER T. ROSENBERGER, *Bulletin, NASSP*

1688. *Time* magazine once described Willie Mays in the following manner: "Willie plays baseball with a boy's glee, a pro's
sureness, and a champion's flair." Isn't this a colorful way of also
describing an inspirational teacher, one who teaches with a boy's
glee, a pro's sureness and a champion's flair?

—M. DALE BAUGHMAN

1689. Good teaching in all ages has been characterized by clear
vision, broad wisdom, judicious restraint, and a fine sense of balance.

—JAMES HAROLD FOX, *School and
Society*

1690. There is no final way to judge the worth of a teacher except
in terms of the lives of those he has taught.

—Editorial, *Peabody Journal of Education*

1691. The urge to learn is what counts. If you want to make
people hanker, you must develop skill in appealing to the emotions
through a convincing picture of what learning does for the learner.

—M. DALE BAUGHMAN

1692. The Research Institute of America lists these requirements
for those who train others: (1) Desire to teach (2) Knowledge of
the subject (3) Ability to communicate (4) Patience (5) Sense of
humor (6) Time to do a thorough job.

—DONALD KIRKPATRICK, *Supervisory
Management*

1693. Good teachers are like good parents. Their goodness is to
be judged by the extent to which they become increasingly unnecessary to the growth of the individual.

1694. Every instructional situation has an inherent emotional
component. The developmental appropriateness of the lesson, the
readiness of the individual students involved, motivation and the
orderly sequence of the presentation, the authenticity of the material covered, pace change and a variety of other rather observable
factors are those usually considered in our attempts to evaluate
the instructional effectiveness of a given lesson.

In short, the technology of applied mechanics of the teaching
effort are frequently identified by educators as indicative of the
degree of success or failure that attends a given learning experience.

If this recognition of mechanics is to the exclusion of the emotional component of learning then a state of imbalance evolves which leaves some of the real issues of education unattended.

Learning occurs not only at the level of reason but also at the level of feeling. Inspirational instruction has to feature a blend of both.

This blend is not easy to come by in a society where the display of honest emotion is often interpreted by others to be a symbol of frailty and an occasion for apology. But we must reckon with the fact that our basic human values which enable the discrimination between right and wrong, the perception of beauty, the interpretation of morality and the appreciation of life itself emerge from a "symbiotic" relationship of reason and feeling.

To learn and retain these things requires an investment, and the act of becoming invested is a feeling process. Educators must be emotionally involved in the significance of their offerings if the impact of this investment is to be communicated to students.

A deep appreciation of stirring literature is a felt thing, the satisfaction of a mathematical breakthrough is an exhilarating sensation, a true understanding of the magnificence of natural law is a stimulating, yet humbling, experience.

The beauty of dawning intellectual recognition can be achieved in no other way than through feeling and this feeling can be germinated in young people if the instructional program features an adult leader capable of skillfully fusing reason and emotion.

—JERRY SLOAN, *The Pointer*

1695. If you have a boy who just can't learn in your class, don't despair. He may be a late bloomer. It has now come out that Dr. Wernher von Braun, the missile and satellite expert, flunked math and physics in his early teens.

—*Mississippi Education Advance*

1696. A high school teacher who had an unruly class and also a sense of humor, came in one morning and found bedlam. He slapped his hand on the desk and lifted his voice, "I demand pandemonium," he said.

—*Wall Street Journal*

1697. Encouragement alone isn't enough; just as in gardening, water isn't everything, but you can't get flowers without it.

—M. DALE BAUGHMAN

1698. Director of Teacher Placement at the University of Illinois, J. Marlowe Slater sent a letter of commendation to a superintendent who had helped to organize a recognition program for retiring teachers in his system. The superintendent replied to the letter of commendation, in part, as follows:

"Thank you very much for your comments regarding our teacher retirement recognition and your excellent suggestion. The newspaper article carried only what happened that day. In addition to the gold watch which the teachers received, there will be *plagues* in the school buildings where each teacher taught. . . ."

—M. Dale Baughman

1699. Iam shocked to read the socialistic attitudes of so many people on the function of a teacher. According to George E. Sokolsky in *The Chicago American*, October 31, it is to "train the child to grow up into a man or woman, but most of all into a citizen with a sense of responsibility."

This is absurd! Rearing, training and educating is the job and responsibility of the parents. A teacher's job is to teach—not to train, motivate, understand, excuse. The job is to teach academic subjects which should be taught in classrooms.

Education is a lifelong process, but the teacher should be only concerned with a part of it—giving instructions in certain subjects.

Recreation, dental work and polio inoculations are clearly the job of parents, although many do appreciate that the schools have taken over these responsibilities. We are not underpaid; we are the most overpaid babysitters in the world.

—A public teacher

1700. Teachers ought to provoke curiosity, array experience and help people learn to perceive, to generalize, to practice and to judge.

1701. Teacher to colleague: "Not only is he the worst-behaved child in school, he has a perfect attendance record!"

—*Michigan Education Journal*

1702. Have you ever seen a plant with its leaves curled up? Have you watered it and watched the leaves spread out again, fresh and green? Almost as quick as that is the response of a child's mind to a teacher who knows how to nourish it.

—Frederic G. Cassidy, *Wisconsin Journal of Education*

1703. Teaching is mostly perspiration in putting a little inspiration to work.

1704. Some years ago a city educator on a cross-country tour stopped at a small rural township school. He asked the principal if it was difficult to get good teachers in that rather out-of-the-way section. The principal replied, "Oh, we have some very good teachers here. We have Plato and Shakespeare and Emerson and many others like them." To bring the best minds of the ages to enlighten the youth in small places—that is great teaching.

—RALPH W. SOCKMAN, "Big People in Small
Places," *Arkansas Methodist*

1705. A teacher, intent on impressing his pupils with an important point of grammar, stood on his desk and crowed like a rooster after he stated one of the best-known rules: "You will never forget this now," he told them. Years later he ran into one of the former students who said: "I'll never forget the day you stood on your desk and crowed like a rooster. But what was the rule we were supposed to remember?"

—JOHN G. FULLER, *Saturday Review*

1706. Teachers must have zeal, enthusiasm and a concern for the individual's place in society—just as much as knowledge of the subjects they're teaching and ability to transfer this knowledge to young minds.

Nothing is as important as inspired teaching; which means we must have inspired teachers.

1707.   Teachers can tell,
But never teach,
Unless they practice
What they preach.

1708. Summer is a good time for you to go fishing—for ideas with which to awaken the zest for learning in your lethargic pupils. Remember—an idea doesn't care who has it.

—M. DALE BAUGHMAN

1709. Let the cowards and the dullards find safety in the tenure trap! The true teacher joyfully accepts the call of strange tomorrows, finds security and immortality in the healthy, happy, and intelligent citizens he has helped to shape.

1710. No bubble is so iridescent or floats longer than that blown by the successful teacher.

—SIR WILLIAM OSLER

1711. When a man becomes content with what he already knows, he ceases to be a good teacher. He cannot communicate the excitement of learning because for him the excitement has ceased to exist. Research is the lifeblood of intellectual pursuits.

—LEONARD H. AXE, *Educational Leadership*

1712. In a way the great teacher—even the great mathematics teacher—does not teach anything quantitatively measurable. He performs certain actions, says certain things that create another teacher. This other teacher is the one hidden inside the student.

—CLIFTON FADIMAN, "Party of One," *Holiday*

1713. Those who educate children well are more to be honored than even their parents.

—ARISTOTLE

1714. One flower doesn't make a garden. Yet, with teachers as with flowers a pretty bloom and sweet aroma may have a lasting effect on the viewer.

—M. DALE BAUGHMAN

1715. Teaching is for many of us the most important profession of mankind. It is a creative one, requiring strength, experience, and imagination. If a beginning teacher has physical and emotional strength, experience will come. And only a person with imagination should teach.

—EVELYN ADLERBLUM, *Education Synopsis*

1716. I recognize three types of teaching: first, forced feeding, or "I know you hate it, but you've got to learn it"; second, spoon-feeding, or "Just remember what I told you"; third, invitation to learning, or "This is fine, let's share it." I believe that the most valuable and lasting results come from the third method.

—MARTIN STAPLES SHOCKLEY, *Journal of Higher Education*

1717. Many years ago when I was a young administrator, a wise superintendent said to me, with respect to selecting teachers, "Look for teachers who are green at the top." He went on to explain that anything "green at the top" was alive. He believed that a vital factor in the success of a teacher was to be alive. By that he meant love of people, curiosity in people and things, real interest in things people do. These are the things, he said, which cause people to sparkle and live.

This superintendent was not discounting the importance of knowledge and book learning. He was emphasizing that something more was necessary. How right he was. The vital factor in teaching success lies in the relation of teacher and pupils. Without vital interest in the lives of pupils, all his knowledge is largely useless. But with a strong interest in his pupils and their problems, his teaching can become a vital factor in their growth.

1718. My advice to pupils who thirst for knowledge: "Squeeze the teacher for her last drop of thought-provoking and curiosity-sharpening talents."

—M. Dale Baughman

1719. If you can't be the best teacher in your school, make the best one hustle to stay ahead of you.

1720. The good teacher is someone who can understand those not very good at explaining and explain it to those not very good at understanding.

—W. A. Palmer, Homorton College,
Scottish Education Journal

1721. A young teacher may choose his wife by moonlight, but it isn't very wise to select his teaching position with no more illumination that that.

—M. Dale Baughman

1722. In these days of teacher shortages getting a teaching position is good deal like going into a restaurant with friends. You get what you order and then when you see what the other fellow has, you wish you had his.

—M. Dale Baughman

1723. A mechanical teacher, which resembles a pinball machine, is developed in California. The other kids will be complaining that it never lights up the "Tilt" sign for teacher's pet.

1724. Even a profound knowledge of the subject is comparatively unimportant, except in advanced work; a brisk, idle man with a knack of exposition and the art of clear statement can be a scandalously effective teacher.

—Arthur Christopher Benson, *The Schoolmaster*

1725. We are frequently getting letters from parents praising their children's teacher—and one especially contained a most memorable statement. This mother wrote about two teachers. One, she said, had been intellectually stimulating to the point that her daughter became an honor student. The other teacher, because of her great patience and perceptive understanding, had helped her son to overcome extreme shyness to become a leader in the class. This thoughtful mother closed her letter with these words: "The power of a good teacher as an instructive force is almost awesome."

—Dr. CARL F. HANSEN, Editorial, *Journal of Teacher Education*

1726. Is there some fact or story you want your fifth-grade pupils to know without fail?

Then have the information printed on bubble gum wrappers.

—M. DALE BAUGHMAN

1727. I venture the assertion that teachers constitute the most unwisely utilized professional group in this country. The ablest and poorest of them are utilized in exactly the same fashion.

—HENRY DAVID, *Teachers College Record*

1728. I would rather have my students within 50 feet of a great teacher than within 5 feet of a nonentity.

—College President, *Seven Studies, National School Boards Association*

1729. The willingness to "stand by" just in case help is needed—stand by without interfering.

The ability to love and accept every child as he is, while you sense what he can be.

That saving bit of humor which adds a light touch.

The time to be an avid listener.

One eye that doesn't see quite everything and an ear that misses what you shouldn't hear.

Your consistency, with rare and happy lapses.

The fact that you are only human—and make mistakes, too.

The respect you show each individual—and the dignity with which you treat them.

Your resolve to work with each member of your class with faith, hope, and no little charity.

—Author Unknown

1730. The best teacher is . . . the one who kindles an inner fire, arouses moral enthusiasm, inspires the student with a vision of what he may become and reveals the worth and permanency of moral and spiritual and cultural values.

—HAROLD GARNET, *American School Board Journal*

1731. The faculty committee was organizing the order of examinations. It was decided that the harder subjects should be placed first in the list and that history should have the final place. The woman teacher of history protested stoutly:

"But," declared the chairman, "it most certainly is one of the easiest subjects."

With an air of resoluteness the young lady shook her head and announced firmly, "Not the way I teach it. Indeed, according to the methods I use, it is a most difficult study and extremely perplexing."

1732. Dear Lord! Help me to become the kind of teacher my principal would like me to be.

Give me that mysterious something which will enable me at all times to satisfactorily explain policies, rules, regulations and procedures to my students even though they never were explained to me!

Help me to teach, guide, and train the dim-witted, uninterested, stubborn, and reluctant without ever losing my patience or my temper!

Teach me to smile if it kills me!

Make me a better builder of men by helping me to develop larger and greater qualities of tolerance, understanding, sympathy, wisdom, perspective, mind-reading and equanimity!

And when, dear Lord, I shall have become the paragon of teaching virtue in this mortal world—Dear Lord, move over! Amen.

1733. I took a piece of human clay,
And gently formed it day by day,
And molded, with my skill and art,
A young child's soft and yielding heart.
I came again when days were gone—
It was a man I gazed upon.
The form I gave him still he bore,
But I could change him nevermore.
      —Author Unknown

1734. Teaching is an art, not a science; a duty, not a business; a personality, not a voice; an outright gift, not a calculated exchange.
    —CECIL CRAGG, *Queens Quarterly*

1735. Every child has a right to success—he also has a right to failure. It is the teacher's job to try to help him strive for the right right.
    —ROBIN L. HUNT, *Ozarkian Philosophy*

1736. All teachers who now deserve the name, recognize that self-control is the ultimate moral object in training youth—a self-control independent of temporary artificial restraints, exclusions, or pressures, as also of the physical presence of a dominating person. To cultivate in the young their self-control should be the steady objectives of parents and teachers.

—CHARLES W. ELIOT, educator, former
president Harvard University

1737. Teach the pupil not only to answer questions but also to question answers.

1738. Three candidates for a vocational agriculture teaching position were waiting to be interviewed. As they waited, the superintendent asked one of them, "And what do you think you're worth?" Somewhat on the spot, the candidate puzzled for a moment and then answered, $4,800. The superintendent's reply was an eye-opener to the hopeful teachers-to-be. Explained the chief administrative officer, "Our school board doesn't want to talk to any applicant who thinks he is worth less than $5,000 per year."

1739. No amount of pay ever made a good soldier, a good teacher, a good artist, or a good workman.

—JOHN RUSKIN

1740. A wise teacher sends this note to parents at the start of the school year: "If you promise not to believe everything your child says happens at school, I'll promise not to believe everything he says happens at home."

—IKE LONDON, quoted by Kays Gary in
Charlotte *Observer*

1741. Ace teachers don't like hobbles and can't stand fences.

—M. DALE BAUGHMAN

1742.　He is discerning, genuine, and kind,
In love with life, a seeker after truth,
Forever learning to delight the mind,
He leaves a priceless legacy to youth.

Not seeking to impress, nor yet to gain
The fleeting admiration of the snob,
He does not flaunt degrees as do the vain,
Intent on showing off before the mob.

His virtue lies in being what he seems,
A scholar and a gentleman at heart,
He never grows too old to share youth's dreams
And all the wistful longings they impart.

Possessed of gentle humor, wise and kind,
Aware of his responsibility,
He guards with patient care the growing mind
To nourish knowledge and integrity.

—MRS. VINEY WILDER

1743. Paying no attention to the red traffic light, the whizzing cars, or the policeman's outraged whistle, the little old lady marched across the street. Brakes squealed, horns blasted and the cop strode angrily up to her. "Say, lady," he growled, "didn't you see my hand raised? Don't you know what that means?"

"Well, I should hope I do," snapped the lady. "I've been teaching school for 25 years.

—*Texas Outlook*

1744. This is a moment I thought I had been waiting for ever since I was nine years old. Finally, I thought, I'm going to get a chance to tell a lot of teachers what I think of them. At about the age of nine that was my life's ambition. There was a slight difference of opinion between me and one of my teachers. We compromised, of course. That is to say, she had her way. She had her way, but I said to myself: "Just wait. Someday when I'm grown up, I'm going to tell teachers what I think of them." I would have added "and but good," except that the phrase had not then been invented.

So now I'm grown up, and now I'm here, and for the life of me I can't remember what it was I was going to scold about. All I can remember are the nice things teachers did for me. I'm willing to bet it's that way with most of us.

—ERIC A. JOHNSTON, Address at Chicago
Regional AASA Convention

1745. *Prestige of the Teacher.* Unfortunately, teachers are often made fun of by cruel cartoonists and thoughtless motion picture and TV experts. Teachers are subject often to unfavorable conversation in the home and in social groups. Young people are aware of all of this and when somebody suggests that they consider teaching as a career too many of them are likely to smile and say: "Who

wants to be a teacher?" But I repeat, prestige must first be established before an adequate supply of teachers will be available, and only the public can guarantee prestige.
—H. CLAUDE HARDY, *New York State Education*

1746. The makers of Burma Shave put up some signs not so long ago offering "a trip to Mars for 900 empty jars." A man in Appleton, Wisconsin, informed them he was busily collecting jars and would soon be ready to travel. Said the Burma Shave people: "A trip to Mars you may earn, but it does not include a return." When you teach you always get a return.

1747. *Need for Competent Teachers*: The importance of competence on the part of each teacher is emphasized by the fact that the average elementary teacher who retires this year will probably have taught approximately 1000 American citizens, and the average high school teacher about 5000 persons. Let us examine the educational ill effects of only 100 ineffectual high school teachers who retire. Fifty thousand American citizens would not have received adequate instruction in the high schools.
—WILLIAM ALEXANDER, president of ASCD, *ASCD News Exchange*

1748. Once there was a teacher and let it be said at once that by all ordinary criteria he was a poor teacher. His appearance was farmerlike, weatherbeaten, unpretentious. His tie frequently needed straightening.

He had none of the essentials that are supposed to make a good teacher. He had neither magnetic outgoing personality, nor evident enthusiasm for his subject, nor a clear speaking voice. He could hardly hold the interest of his students or enlist their active participation in classroom discussion or work.

While teaching, he remained seated throughout the hour. He seldom looked directly at his audience. While lecturing he would stare out the window. He seemed to be absorbed in private thoughts most of the time while in the classroom. Nor was he free of distracting mannerisms—ruffling his shock of hair or pulling his moustache on too many occasions. Questions from the students were not discouraged, but neither were they invited. Who was this teacher?—John Dewey.

1749. Wanted, then, a teacher! As Professor James H. Canfield stated nearly 60 years ago, "Not a recitation-post, not a wind vane, not a water gauge, not a martinet, not a pedant, nor a pedagog—the mere slave to the student, but, a teacher. One who is a combination of heart, and head, and artistic training, and favoring circumstances. One who has that enthusiasm which never calculates its sacrifices, and is willing to endure all things if only good may come. One who loves his work; who throws his whole soul into it; who makes it his constant and beloved companion by day and night, waking and sleeping; who can therefore see more in his work than can any other."

> —Dr. Lloyd N. Morrisett, Professor of
> Educational Administration, University
> of California, Los Angeles, California
> *NITPA Newsletter*

1750. John Steinbeck tells of a teacher who taught him in Salinas. "She aroused us," he says, "to shouting, book-waving discussions. We never could stick to . . . the chanted recitation of memorized phyla. Our speculation ranged the world. She breathed curiosity into us so that we brought in facts or truths shielded in our hands like captured butterflies . . . I have had many teachers who told me soon-forgotten facts, but only three created in me a new thing, a new attitude, a new hunger." He concludes by saying, "What deathless power lies in the hands of such a person."

1751. Good teaching is like throwing burrs at a blanket, and poor teaching like throwing beans.

> —R. L. Cooley, *Bulletin*, Wisconsin
> Association of Secondary School
> Principals

1752. A teacher affects eternity. He can never tell where his influence stops.

> —Henry Adams

1753. 'Tis noble to be good, 'tis nobler to teach others to be good —and easier.

> —Mark Twain

1754. Teachers pretend to know more than they do; they talk a great deal repeating the talk of the texts. The students repeat the talk of the talk of the text talkers.

> —Nathaniel Cantor, *Educational Forum*

1755. One teacher received the following note (as an excuse for tardiness):

"Dear Teacher. Please excuse John for being late. His uncle died last night and we had a hard time waking him up this morning."
—RALPH O. RAMSTAD, *Minneapolis Federation of Men Teachers News Bulletin*

1756. There are only two classes of teachers, so far as compensation is concerned—those who are underpaid, and those who have no business in the classroom. It is impossible to place a cash value on the influence of a good teacher. By good teacher we do not necessarily mean those of high academic training, desirable as the training may be. The good teacher is a pleasant, understanding person who not only is skilled in the art of presenting subject-matter but one who just as skillfully, by precept and example, leads children into desirable habits and attitudes.
—ROBERT E. McKINNEY, Speech to Southern Division, Illinois Education Association

Teacher Education

1757. Teacher's College—a place where the ignorant are incited to impart their knowledge to the indifferent.
—SHELDON ZITNER, *College English*

1758. There's no reason to educate teachers in upper schools, advanced studies and then to teach peasant's children for 35 years that B-A spells "BA"—what a waste! A man who has been shaped by advanced studies couldn't be satisfied with such a modest post. I've therefore decreed that, in the normal school for teachers, instruction is not to be carried too far . . . I'll go a step further. It will be a great problem to find jobs for the re-enlisted sergeants. A great part of them could be made teachers at village schools. It's easier to make a teacher of an old soldier than to make an officer of a teacher.
—H. R. TREVOR-ROPER, *Education, Hitler's Secret Conversations,* permission for use granted by Farrar, Strauss and Cudahy, Inc., New York, copyright holder

1759. An undertaker's apprentice decided to enroll in a teacher's college. One question on the entrance forms was "What did you like most about your former job?" He wrote, "Working with people."

1760. A beginning teacher just fresh out of college encountered some difficulties in his enthusiasm to make good with some new and imaginative teaching techniques. He sought the counsel of his father, an experienced teacher, who said to him, "Son, if a young man like you does not feel the urge to reform education overnight, he doesn't have professional zeal. But, if after ten years, he feels that education reform can be accomplished overnight, he doesn't have any sense."

Teacher Placement

1761. A low-paid teacher, father of three children, was getting desperate. When he wrote a personal statement for his placement papers, he included this statement: "I am a young married man, successful in my present position, but I want an interesting teaching job with less future and more present."

—M. Dale Baughman

1762. A teacher came into my office and asked for my help in locating him a new position. I soon learned in the interview that he had begun the school year on the staff of a small high school. I didn't press him for his reason for breaking the contract, and he didn't volunteer the information. Later in the week I called his former principal and asked for clarification of the situation. He remarked, "He worked for us one month and we were satisfied."

—M. Dale Baughman

Teacher Recruitment

1763. The superintendent of schools at Low Ridge was interviewing a prospective teacher. Having decided he wanted her, he was attempting to persuade her to sign a contract.

"We're not an extremely wealthy district and we don't have high salaries and unlimited funds like our neighbor Highwood, for instructional materials," he apologized, "but I just know you'll love our school family and our friendly community."

"I'm sure I would," answered the candidate, "but tell me more about Highwood."

—M. Dale Baughman, Teacher Placement
Consultant, University of Illinois

1764. A school recruitment official while interviewing a teacher applicant chanced to remark "You expect a high salary for one without experience."

"Don't forget," replied the candidate, "teaching is much harder when you dont know much about it."

1765. A school superintendent was checking on an applicant for a teaching position. He called his former employer and asked "How long did this teacher work in your school system?"

"About six months," was the answer.

The inquiring superintendent was astonished. "He told me he'd been in your system a long time."

"Oh, he has! He's been here six years," explained the applicant's former employer, "but he worked about one month a year."

Teacher Retirement

1766. A retired teacher carries a calling card which bears on one side his name and the legend: "Retired; no phone, no address, no pupils, no money," and on the other side: "Unworried, unhurried, unemployed, and unessential."

Television

1767. Television is an appliance which changes children from irresistible forces into immovable objects.

—*The Philadelphia Principal*

1768. Two serious teenagers were enthusing over the early morning TV course they were taking, when one said, "Gee, what would you do if your set went off during a lecture?" "I dunno," mused the other, then had a happy idea: "I guess you'd have to send in an excuse from your repairman."

—Jack Sterling Show, WCBS, New York

1769. In Falls Church, Virginia, PTA members kept eyes fixed on TV programs through the hours children would be viewing them. They observed 185 programs for 114½ hours, saw 281 assaults, 117 killings, 19 robberies, 16 kidnapings, 10 murder conspiracies, 3 arsons, 3 extortions, 3 jailbreaks, 1 lynching, 1 bombing, and 1 suicide.

Education, USA

1770. Television is educational. If it weren't for the old movies, today's kids might not know that there was a time when the Russians were the good guys and the German were the bad guys.

—BILL VAUGHAN, *VFW Magazine*

1771. We think of TV as new. So what's new? The picture has been a basic method for communication since the caveman scratched the first "Studio One" on his wall. There is an authenticated case of a cave mother who would not allow her children to even glance at the wall later than two hours after sundown, such was the violence and conflict depicted there. They went berserk and tried to choke the pet dinosaur.

—BILL LADD, TV Editor, *Louisville Courier-Journal*

Thought

1772. When you stop to think, don't forget to start again.

1773. There are men who can think no deeper than a fact.

—VOLTAIRE

1774. If you're a thinker, you're unique among your fellow men for it is estimated that 5% think, 10% think they think and 85% would rather die than think.

> Thou man a thinking being is defined,
> Few use the grand prerogative of mind.
> How few think justly of the thinking few,
> How many never think who think they do.

—JANE TAYLOR

1775. A child, asked how he happened to think of something, said, "I got a kick in the mind and it said itself."

—LINCOLN STEFFENS, *Education Digest*

1776. Did you ever have a brain throb when a man of greatness uttered a noble and creative thought? According to Genevieve Knudtson in *Farmer's Wife*, May, 1961, "Each of us has a touch of genius. Great thoughts and profound ideas wend across our minds like clouds across a summer sky."

Whereas most of us experience the flash of new and original thoughts without follow-up meditation, great minds nurture and polish these thought flashes.

Says Mrs. Knudtson, "Thank God for men like Frost, Aristotle,

Franklin and Thoreau who have redeemed our thoughts from mediocrity and made them immortal."

1777. According to a Pennsylvania State University researcher, the average person speaks at the rate of 125 to 160 words a minute, but thinks four times faster than he speaks. This department knows plenty of people who can speak that fast without thinking at all.

—Counselor

1778. No lions are ever caught in mouse traps. To catch lions you must think in terms of lions, not in terms of mice. Your mind is always creating traps of one kind or another and what you catch depends on the thinking you do. It is your thinking that attracts you to what you receive.

—Thomas Drier, industrial editor

1779. 'Tis much easier to learn and remember than it is to think and investigate.

—Thomas Gregory

1780. The natural tendency among the majority of people is to think by proxy; we lean upon others, or we follow in their footsteps.

—T. Sharper Knowlson

1781. All the great thinkers have been masters of metaphor because all vivid thinking must be in images and the philosopher whose metaphors are blurred and diluted is one whose thinking is blurred and diluted.

—T. Sharper Knowlson

1782. *Joe*: "Why does the average girl prefer beauty to brains?"
Flo: "Because the men who can see outnumber the men who can think."

1783. If you persisted in going to sea in a leaky boat, you'd know you had no excuse to offer when the boat sank under you. Yet you go about with leaks in your consciousness through which you allow negative thoughts to enter, warns Don Spencer in *Thought Starters*. Your consciousness must be sealed against such evil apparitions as selfishness, thoughtlessness, jealousy, pride, vindictiveness, anger, and the like, just as your boat must be sealed against the water on the outside. It is never the water in the ocean that sinks ships. It is the water that gets in where it has no business to be.

1784. The main reason that some of us get lost in thought is that it is such unfamiliar territory.

Time

1785. One of your greatest possessions is the 24 hours directly ahead of you.

—Grit

1786. E. W. Scripps, great publisher, once remarked of one of the men whom he had promoted: "He was obviously a good executive. He did not get excited and always seemed to have time on his hands." That's a fine ideal for others as well as executives: to organize and plan and concentrate on our work so that we always have time on our hands—time to think.

—Fred DeArmond, *Rotarian*

1787. Our days are like identical suitcases—all the same size, but some people can pack more into them than others.

—York Trade Compositor

Viewpoint

1788. In our junior high school science program we hope that our students can look at a star or any object from three points of view, that of a philosopher, a social scientist, and a scientist, as illustrated in the following poem:

> Twinkle, twinkle little star,
> Many light-years away you are.
> Your magnitude, distance, size we've measured,
> Your solacing light we've often treasured!
> Yet all our measures lend no clue
> To the biggest question: "Who made you?"

or

> Twinkle, twinkle little star,
> A beacon in the sky you are.
> At the zenith of the celestial plane,
> You wond'rously, yet indifferently reign.
> While serving us as goal and guide,
> To our humble zenith, without pride.

yet

> Twinkle, twinkle little star,
> I need not wonder what you are.

For viewed through spectroscopic lens,
You're heliums and hydrogens.

—The Greenwich Public Schools Bulletin

1789. Heard at the Lake of the Woods tournament: A low 70 shooter: "I didn't hit a good shot all day." A fellow who had 99: "Thank goodness, I finally had a good round for a change."

—T. O. WHITE, *Champaign-Urbana News Gazette*

1790. True contentment depends not upon what we have. A tub was large enough for Diogenes but a world was too small for Alexander.

—COLTON, *The Lion*

1791. If the grass looks greener on the other side of the fence, you can bet the water bill is higher.

—Laugh Book

1792. A little girl was trying to move a table which was in her way. Her mother called, "Mary, you can't move that table, it is as big as you are." And the little girl replied, "Yes, I can move it, for I am as big as it is."

—REVEREND FREDERICK W. HELFER, *Link*

1793. So he buckled right in, with a trace of a grin
On his face, if he worried he hid it.
And tackled the thing that couldn't be done,
It couldn't be done, but he did it.

—EDGAR A. GUEST

So he started the thing that couldn't be done,
With a grin and a will he set to it,
To tackle this thing that couldn't be done,
And by golly—he couldn't do it.

—BOYD J. HAGAN

1794. I spent a week there one night.

1795. As the Roman philosopher Epictetus remarked almost 2,000 years ago: "Men are disturbed not by things, but by the views which they take of them."

—EPICTETUS

1796. Grandpa was visiting Chicago and was frankly appalled by the heavy traffic choking every thoroughfare. "You gotta nice town here," opined Grandpa, "but it looks to me like you fellers let yourselves get a mite behind in your haulin'!"

—Santa Fe Magazine

1797. There was a little old lady munching a solitary dinner in a restaurant. Finally she summoned a waiter and said, "This is the stringiest spinach I ever ate."

"Madam," he said, "you're trying to eat it through your veil."

—OLLIE M. JAMES, *Cincinnati Enquirer*

1798. In a supermarket the other day, I heard a wife remark philosophically to her husband: "Look at it this way, dear—the more it costs the more green stamps we get!"

—IVERN BOYETT

1799. Nothing seems impossible to the person who doesn't have to do it himself.

—Nuggets

1800. The fact is, there are no big jobs; only small machines. The Panama Canal and the Suez were big because they were measured with teams of mules and a hand shovel.

—ROBERT G. LeTOURNEAU, *Mover of Men and Mountains*

1801. *Hostess*—I have a lonesome bachelor I'd like you girls to meet.

Athletic girl—What can he do?

Chorus girl—How much money does he have?

Society girl—Who is his family?

Religious girl—To what church does he belong?

Secretary—Where is he?

1802. When you are at the foot of the great Pyramid, you can only see the side which faces you. If I am on the opposite side, I only see the face opposite to you. We have no chance of viewing things with the same eye as long as we continue to remain on our positions. But if by chance we decide climbing to the top of the Pyramid, whatever be our start, we are sure to meet at the summit.

It is from the summit, by a higher view of things, that men of divergent trends of thought can find a ground of common understanding.

—ADLY ANARAOS, "The View from the Top of the Pyramid," *Rotarian*

1803. To a foot in the shoe all the world is like leather.

Vocabulary

1804. A teenage listener is said to have asked Dr. John Mackay why it is that theologians are forever inventing hard words like "ecumenical." ....

"My dear young woman," ran his reply, "the term 'ecumenical' is really no more difficult to pronounce than 'economical'; but more important, it is not only linguistically legitimate, but conceptually inevitable."

—JANET HARBISON, "John Mackay of Princeton," *Presbyterian Life*

1805. J. Hyde Sweet of the Nebraska City *News-Press* told of the recent church service where a rather deaf lady in town asked the usher to seat her up as far front as possible. "I've always had terrible trouble hearing," she said, "and some of these churches have terrible agnostics."

—*Laugh Book*

1806. John L. Lewis tells the story of the two coal miners who were inseparable buddies. One had gone to work in the mines as a boy and had received little or no formal education. The other, more fortunate, had received a college education.

One day they had a falling out and decided to settle the matter with their fists. "When either of us has had enough, he should say 'sufficient'," suggested the educated mine worker. "OK," said the other.

For two hours the two men pummeled each other with all their might. Finally the educated coal miner could stand no more. "Sufficient!" he cried.

His opponent stood up, dusted himself off, and said: "I've been trying to think of that word for an hour and a half."

—*Omaha World-Herald*

1807. A new word has been added to our American vocabulary. In describing a boy of his acquaintance, a youth said, "He's psycho-ceramic."

"What's that?" someone asked.

"Crackpot."

—*The Cab Stand*

1808. A man who had been waiting impatiently in the post office could not attract the attention of either of the girls behind the counter.

"The evening cloak," explained one of the girls to her companion, "was a redingote design in gorgeous lamé brocade with fox fur and wide pagoda sleeves."

At this point the long-suffering customer broke in with, "I wonder if you could provide me with a neat purple stamp with dinky perforated hem. The ensemble deliberately treated on the reverse side with mucilage. Something at about 4 cents."

—James J. Kelly, *Quote*

1809. Scott's *Ivanhoe* has a passage pointing out that in feudal days barnyard animals were called by their Anglo-Saxon names— cow, calf, sheep, pig. But when they were dressed for the table they were served as beef, veal, mutton and pork, all Norman designations.

By the same token, when educators are among themselves they speak of pupils, test, teacher or textbook. But when talking in public, they refer to them as student personnel, evaluative instrument, faculty members, and instructional material.

—*Southern Illinois Schools*

Wisdom

1810. Men of great wealth want to see more wise men. Notice their gifts to education. It is estimated that there are more than 10,000 foundations in the United States. Some of these are of great size. They have been set up by successful men who have a great desire to see their lifetime savings used wisely. They want to see wise men developed.

And yet we are not finding as great a wealth of wise men as we might like.

We are told "You can lead a horse to water, but you cannot make him drink. You can labor with your students, but you cannot make them think."

> And then answers a professor
> Who has handled many a colt
> You may make your horse get thirsty
> If you will just feed him salt.

—*Speaking to American Youth*

1811. If he is indeed wise he does not bid you enter the house of his wisdom but rather leads you to the threshhold of your own mind.

1812. Thomas Jefferson: "The wise know too well their own weakness to assume infallibility; and he who knows most, knows how little he knows."

Friendly Chat

1813. The difference between a "wise guy" and a wise man is plenty.

—Dr. GALEN STARR ROSS, president of Capitol College of Oratory & Music, Columbus, Ohio

1814. The wise man knows everything; the shrewd man everyone.

—*Round Table Talk,* Collegiate Cap & Gown Company

1815. The simple realization that there are other points of view is the beginning of wisdom. Understanding what they are is a great step. The final test is understanding why they are held.

—CHARLES M. CAMPBELL, quoted in *New Outlook*

1816. A college professor once said of a particularly poor student, "The trouble with him is that he does not know that he does not know." That is true ignorance. It is real wisdom to know when we do not know.

—REVEREND H. PLEUNE, *Christian Observer*

1817. Wise men are neither cast down in defeat nor exalted by success.

—PYTHAGORAS

1818. To be self-skeptical is the beginning of self-wisdom.

—H. A. OVERSTREET

1819. A man becomes wise by watching what happens to him when he isn't.

—*Dublin Opinion*

1820. A wise man will hear and increase learning; and a man of understanding shall attain unto wise counsels.

—*Song of Solomon*

1821. He is no fool who gives what he cannot keep to gain what he cannot lose.

—JIM ELIOT, *Defender*

1822. The older I grow, the more I distrust the familiar doctrine that age brings wisdom.

—H. L. MENCKEN, *Today's Health Wit & Wisdom,* by Noah D. Fabricant

1823. To profit from good advice requires more wisdom than to give it.

—C. COLLINS

1824. A gourd wound itself around the lofty palm and in a few weeks climbed to its very top. "How old may'st thou be?" asked the newcomer. "About 100 years." "About 100 years, and no taller! Only look, I have grown as tall as you in fewer days than you count years."

"I know that well," replied the palm. "Every summer of my life a gourd has climbed up around me as proud as thou art, and as short lived as thou wilt be."

—REVEREND A. PURNELL BAILEY, *Grit*

Words

1825. I'm careful of the words I say to keep them soft and sweet.
  I never know from day to day which ones I'll have to eat.
  —*Lay o' the Land*

1826. Learn this and you'll get along, no matter what your station: An ounce of keep-your-mouth-shut beats a ton of explanation.

1827. It is better either to be silent or to say things of more value than silence. Sooner throw a pearl at hazard than an idle or useless word; and do not say a little in many words, but a great deal in a few.

1828. Many wise words are spoken in jest, but they can't compare with the number of foolish words spoken in earnest.

1829. The next time you receive a letter that carries the word "Sincerely" above the signature of the writer, pause a moment and think of the origin of that word. As you may recall, it was first used as "sin cerely," meaning "without wax," by ancient sculptors to mark a flawless piece of work. Wax was then commonly employed to conceal defects, to patch a chipped nose, a poorly shaped finger, etc. Sincerely is too honest a word to be used loosely, but it is a good word when consciously employed.

1830. When you speak, speak clearly and naturally. Say what you mean and mean what you say; be brief and sensible. Words should drop from the lips as beautiful coins newly issued from the mint, deeply and accurately impressed, perfectly finished, neatly struck by the proper organs, distinct, sharp, in due succession and of due weight.

—ALFRED AUSTON, *Slips of Speech,*
Funk and Wagnalls Company

1831. The Army has had about 2,000 portable showers built for the use of missilemen who accidentally spill rocket fuel on themselves. They use ordinary water.

But the Army doesn't call them showers. They are "rocket propellant personnel neutralizers."

—*Laugh Book*

1832. Man lives by ideas, and words are the pieces of which ideas are built. Words can poison, words can heal. Words start and fight wars but words make peace. Words lead men to the pinnacles of good, and words plunge men to the depths of evil.

—MARGUERITE SCHUMANN, Director of
Publicity, Lawrence College, Appleton,
Wisconsin, *Secretary*

1833. A word fitly spoken is like apples of gold in pictures of silver.

—PROVERBS 25:11

1834. Here are some stumbling blocks in the way of the foreigner who is studying our language:

Bear is like bare, and pear is like pare, but tear is pronounced tier and tare. Then hear is like here, and sear is like sere, and dear, shear like deer and sheer. Beat's not like great, nor beak like break, and neither is freak like steak; while beam, strange to say, will rhyme with seam, as well as with cream and dream.

Feign, deign and reign rhyme with fain, Dane and rain, as well as with skein, rein, vein. Although sew is like so, still new is like gnu, and ewe we pronounce just you.

Though dough rhymes with toe, and rough with ruff; enough, tough, and sough with gruff. But cough rhymes with off, and bough is like bow, while plough is the same word as plow. With bow, too, like beau, we have dough like doe, and glow, grow, and owe like go. But growl is like owl, while grown, mown and own don't rhyme well with brown but with bone.

—Kalends, *Sunshine Magazine*

1835. Two men, members of a religious order, wanted to smoke while walking in the garden. They agreed that each would ask his superior for permission.

The first one returned to find the second one smoking and complained indignantly: "I was refused!"

"What did you ask?" inquired the second one.

"I asked if I could smoke while meditating."

"Oh," said the other, blowing his smoke reflectively, "I asked if I could meditate while smoking!"

1836. Use workhorse words that know how to sell. Scan the best sales jobs in print, and you will find them rich in short words that tease the taste, make glad the eye, tickle the nose, and please the ear. There are nip, twang, bite, and tang in short sales words. There is sweet, sour, tart, or dry, as need be. There are words that we can hear like the swish of silk; soft words with the feel of swan's down; words with a smell like musk, smoke, cheese, mint, and rose ... all of them good sales tools. With practice, words may be used like the notes of a musical scale, to create any mood you wish. To all of us in marketing, that is like money in the bank.

—T. H. TOMPSON, *Round Table Talk*

1837. Not only to say the right thing at the right place but far more difficult to leave unsaid the wrong thing at the tempting moment.

—GEORGE S. BENSON, *Friendly Chat*

Work

1838. A Georgia man was paid 50¢ an hour to tear down a chimney he had built 50 years ago for 37¢ a day.

—*Parts Pups*

1839. As a rule I do not rhyme.
My life is but a race with time,
When papers overflow the folder
A man must know he's getting older.

—M. DALE BAUGHMAN

1840. Soon after the great Edmund Burke had been making one of his powerful speeches in the British Parliament, his brother Richard was found sitting in silent reverie; and when asked by a friend what he was thinking about, he replied:

"I have been wondering how Ed has contrived to monopolize all the talent in our family. But then I remember that when the rest of us were doing nothing, or were at play, he was always at work."

And the force of this anecdote is increased by the fact that Richard always was considered, by those who knew him best, to be superior in natural talents to his brother; yet the one rose to greatness, whereas the other lived and died in obscurity.

1841. Can anything be sadder than work left unfinished? Yes—work never begun.

—CHRISTINA ROSSETTI, *Partners*

1842. Mankind is composed of those who work, those who pretend to work, and those who do neither.

—BATTISTA GRASSI in *Your Creative Power*

1843. Whether a job is large or small,
If I can't do it well I won't do it at all,
And I owe to such firm self-discipline
Job after job I refuse to begin!

—THOMAS USK, *Rotarian*

1844. It is the biggest mistake in the world to think you are working for someone else. Try to realize that someone is paying you for working for yourself.

1845. We know a lot of fellows who brag about being self-made men; but it's our considered opinion that most of them knocked off work too soon.

—*Minonk News Dispatch*

1846. Quite a few people are already working on a four-day week. Trouble is, it takes 'em five or six days to do it.

—EARL HALL, Hall Syndicate
—*P K Sideliner*

1847. Nothing stops work quicker than people who have nothing to do and spend their time with people who are busy.

1848. Tired businessman's observation: "It's simply fantastic the amount of work you can get done, if you don't do anything else."

—ELEANOR CLARAGE in Cleveland *Plain Dealer*

1849. Blessed is the man who has found his work. One monster there is in the world—the idle man.

—CARLYLE, *Friendly Chat*

1850. Working is more than a way of earning a livelihood. It is a way of keeping one's self-respect.

—*Friendly Chat*

1851. There is no better way to take the irk out of work than to put love into it.

1852. A farmer who was asked what time he went to work in the morning replied, "Son, I don't go to work. I'm surrounded with it all the time."

1853.   Work and Shirk are two little brothers;
   Work is always busy, doing things for others;
   Shirk is very lazy, and lies around the house,
   Stretching and yawning, as useless as a mouse.
   All through the day Work makes things hum,
   But Shirk sits around, and just looks glum.
   Which do you think is dearly loved by others—
   Work or Shirk, these well-known little brothers?
        —from *The Young Soldier*, Toronto
        Sunshine Magazine

Writing

1854. Reading maketh a full man; conference a ready man; and writing an exact man.
        —FRANCIS BACON, "Of Studies"

1855. Did you hear about the young spring poet who sent some verses to the editor of a magazine. The verses were entitled, "Why do I live?" It is reported the editor's reply was as follows: "You live just because you happened to send your poem by post instead of bringing it in person."

1856. "You waste too much paper," said the editor.
 "But how can I economize?"
 "'By writing on both sides."
 "But you won't accept stories written on both sides of the sheet."
 "I know, but you'd save paper just the same."
        —*Heywood Advertiser*

1857. How to write forceful prose: Mull over thoughts that are mullable, and cull every word that's cullable.
        —TOM PEASE, *Editor and Publisher*

1858. *Jensen:* "So your nephew has taken up writing. Has he sold anything yet?"
 Benson: "Yes—his overcoat, his radio, and his wrist watch."

1859. Unfortunately, a lot of people who have half a mind to write a book, do so.

1860. Webster has the words and I pick them up from where they be; here a word and there a word—it's so easy, 'tis absurd. I merely 'range them in a row; Webster's done the work, you know. Word follows word, 'til inch by inch, I have a column—what a cinch! I take the words that Webster penned and merely lay them end to end!

—Don Marquis

1861. After the young reporter had been repeatedly admonished to cut his stories to the bare essentials, he decided that the editor really meant it; so the next item he turned in read like this:

"J. Smith looked up the elevator shaft to see if the car was on its way down. It was. Age, forty-five."

1862. All authors know the sting of receiving rejection slips from publishers, but we have just read a rejection note from a superlatively elite Chinese publisher which would be almost a pleasure for any author to receive. Wrote the publisher to the author thus:

"Illustrious Brother of the Sun and Moon! Look upon the slave who rolls at thy feet, who kisses the earth before thee, and demands thy charity permission to speak and live. We have read thy manuscript with delight. By the bones of our ancestors, we swear that never before have we encountered such a masterpiece! Should we print it, his Majesty the Emperor would order us to take it as a criterion and never again print anything which was not equal to it. As that would not be possible before 10,000 years, all tremblingly we return the manuscript and beg thee 10,000 pardons. See—my head is at thy feet, and I am thy slave forever and ever!"

Youth

1863. Guidance has changed more in 40 years than children, says Francis S. Warner.

"In fact, kids basically have changed hardly at all," Warner says, and he should know—retiring after 40 years as school janitor and custodian.

The most valuable thing teachers can do in guidance, Warner says, is to manage the two or three mean kids found in every group, "so the other children will influence the mean ones instead of vice versa."

—Springfield, Massachusetts

1864. The belief that youth is the happiest time of life is a fallacy, declares Carl Holmes, the literary wizard of New York. Every age has its silver lining and its golden glow. When we are young in spirit, we cannot help but enjoy life, no matter how old we are. Youth lies not in years but in feeling. I was once told by a friend, "In the central place of your heart there is a wireless station. So long as it receives messages of beauty, cheer, courage, and strength from fellow men and from the Infinite, so long are we young."

—*Friendly Chat*

1865. Youth today demands the excitement of a quick realization of results from intriguing techniques.

—JAN DE SWART, quoted by Conrad Brown,
"The Pure Research of Jan De Swart,"
Craft Horizons

1866. A woman working in a greeting card shop asked a teenager who had been looking through the selection of cards if she needed help. The girl answered, "Yes. Do you have a sympathy card for a girl whose telephone is out of order?"

—*Chicago Tribune*

1867. Our young nephew, who lives on a ranch, was staying with us so that he could attend school in Denver. As he dressed for his first dance, I asked him if he was taking a date. "No," he said. "I'm just going stud."

—CHARLES CHRISTIANSON in *True*

1868. . . . It requires knowledge as well as imagination to translate a boy's aggression into a plea for help—as one approved school headmaster said when he heard a boy cursing at a housemaster; "He's not really swearing; he's crying for Mum."

—OSWALD BELL, *Girl Scout Leader*

1869. Youth is a world in miniature: bounded on the north by a thin substance called the skull bone, on the south by twin bits of shoe leather, and on the east and west by the outstretched finger-tips of expectation and hope.

—HENRY W. PRENTISS, *Journal of Education*

1870. Writing about children, an eminent physician recently affirmed he knew as much about boys and girls as any adult in the

world—which, he added, is absolutely nothing. This was his way of saying that the heart of a child is wrapped in mystery, as of course it is. But if the prayers written by the 12-year-olds in my (confirmation) classes are any indication, the soul of every child harbors the highest hopes as well as the deepest fears of mankind.
—WILLIAM S. HILL, *Christian Century*

1871. Youngsters aren't what they used to be. They never are. Each generation has its own outlook, its own problems, its own environment. Obvious as this may sound, parents tend to forget it. One expert who studied over 1,000 autobiographies of college students writes, "The youth of today has faced more moral alternatives by the time he is 20 years of age than his grandparents faced in a lifetime."
—"Teaching Children Right from Wrong." *Changing Times*

1872. Age and youth look upon life from the opposite ends of the telescope; to the one it is exceedingly long; to the other exceedingly short.
—*Defender*

1873. In the bright lexicon of youth there may be no such word as "fail," but he soon learns a lot of dandy synonyms.
—*Nuggets*

1874. The teenager sent his girl friend her first orchid with this note: "With all my love and most of my allowance."

1875. What America really needs is more young people who will carry to their jobs the same enthusiasm for getting ahead that they display in traffic.
—*Changing Times*

1876. The youth of a nation are the trustees of posterity.
—BENJAMIN DISRAELI

1877. If all you know about teenagers is what you read in the papers, you'd better get out and meet a few of them.
—BILL VAUGHAN, *VFW Magazine*

1878. After a ruthless process of rejection, five applicants for the post of errand boy remained to be interviewed.

The interviewer sought to amuse himself by asking the boys puzzling questions to test their real knowledge.

"How far away from the Earth is the North Star?" was the question fired at one shiny-faced youngster.

"I'm sorry I cannot give you the exact figure offhand, sir," was the reply. "But on a rough estimate I should say that it is far enough away not to interfere with my running errands."

He got the job.

1879. British Railways officials, appealing to the children of Bootle, England: "Stop putting your heads on the track in front of approaching trains. Locomotive drivers are getting so nervous over this practice that many refuse to operate trains going anywhere near Bootle."

1880. After a junior high school class toured the White House, the teacher asked each student to write impressions of the visit. One boy wrote: "I was especially glad to have the opportunity to visit my future home."

1881. There's little need to worry about what will become of today's young people. They'll get old and worry about what will become of young people.

—BILLY ARTHUR, *Quote*

1882. Today teenagers sometimes call their parents triangles. You know what a triangle is—that's a square with something missing. Perhaps the thing that is missing is consistency in adult thinking.

—JUNE PARKER GOLDMAN, Speech at Illinois
JHS Association Spring Conference, 1960

1883. In our civilization all is planned for youth and too little for age.

—ARTHUR BRISBANE, *The Kiplinger Magazine*

1884. Too many parents provide sanitary cups for their children's lips while letting their brains drink out of the dirtiest containers for words and thoughts.

1885. A man is as young as his faith, as old as his doubt; as young as his self-confidence, as old as his fear; as young as his hope, as old as his despair.

Nobody grows old merely by living a number of years; people grow old only by deserting their ideals. Years wrinkle the skin but giving up enthusiasm wrinkles the soul.

Fortunate are we mortals in discovering that each individual has a fountain of youth within himself—that to keep it ever flowing,

he need only be confident of the future and strong in the courage
of his convictions.

—Anonymous, (Courtesy of Sun Press, Inc.)

1886. Needed for today's youth: itching pills, not tranquilizers.

1887. I don't feel the least hostile to young people or bothered
about them. I don't understand them, but when I was young, people
didn't understand me. It's a perfectly natural process.

—E. M. FORSTER, quoted in *Forbes*

1888. There is a growing feeling that the juvenile is turning out
to be an incorrigible hoodlum threatening our standard of living.
... The teenager is weary of being brushed aside by a disinterested
parent. He is discouraged at being just another behavior study for
a child psychologist, too ... For every three juvenile delinquents,
America has 97 decent, honorable, law-abiding young citizens.
The sins of the three are visited upon the 97 and American youth
in the aggregate endures and suffers criticism for the unlawful
aggressions of the minority.

—EDWARD S. PIGGINS, Police Commissioner
of Detroit

1889. The biggest difference between men and boys is just the
cost of their toys.

1890. Teenagers who whistle at girls in the street are merely
going through a stage—which'll probably last 50 years.

—LEO FULD

1891. Youths who leave home to set the world on fire often come
back for more matches.

1892. Applying at the accounting department for his first job,
the recent high school graduate was momentarily stymied by a question on the application blank which read: "What machines can
you operate?"

Pausing briefly, he finally wrote: "Slot and pin ball."

—*Chicago Daily News Weekend*

1893. The girl who was invited on her first date called her pastor
to get some advice about it. He said, "If your boyfriend places
his hand on one shoulder, I'll not worry. If he places his hand on
the other shoulder, I'll not worry; if he places his head on your
shoulder, I'll do some conscientious worrying." She had her date
and came back to her pastor a couple of weeks later and he said,

"How did you get along?" "Well, pastor, my boyfriend placed his hand on one shoulder and then on the other shoulder and then, pastor, I decided to place my head on his shoulder and let his own preacher do the worrying about the situation."

—JUDGE LUTHER W. YOUNGDAHL, U. S. District Court
for the District of Columbia, *Indiana Freemason*

1894. A television producer recently planned to take his cameras to a large metropolitan high school in order to picture the confusion and drift of teenagers. A team of interviewers went into the high school beforehand to look for weird specimens of the shook generation, juvenile thugs, wild dressers, cool cats, and so on. The whole show eventually had to be called off because the interviewers could not find any wild people. The school was full of regular teenagers who do homework, drink Cokes, listen to records, cheer at football games, worry about their weight and acne, look at television, go to dances, and wonder about what they are one day going to do for a living. As far as American teenagers are concerned, these activities seem to be about par for the course—television and Hollywood notwithstanding.

—JOHN R. FRY, *Presbyterian Life*

SUBJECT INDEX

(Numbers in the index refer to selections in the text, not to page numbers.)